IN OUR HOUSE

Perception vs. Reality

MARALA SCOTT & TRÉ PARKER

Library of Congress Control Number: 2008907380

ISBN 13: 978-0-9820268-0-9

ISBN 10: 0-9820268-0-3

ATTENTION COLLEGES, UNIVERSITIES, CORPORATIONS, AND PROFESSIONAL ORGANIZATIONS:
Quantity discounts are available on bulk purchases of this book for educational, gift purposes, or as premiums for increasing magazine subscriptions or renewals. For information, please contact Seraph Books, LLC, Columbus, OH;

http://www.seraphbooks.net
http://www.inourhousebook.com

"Scripture quotations taken from the New American Standard Bible®, Copyright © 1960, 1962, 1963, 1968, 1971, 1972, 1973, 1975, 1977, 1995 by The Lockman Foundation Used by permission." (www.Lockman.org)

Cover design by George Foster.

DEDICATION

Thank you *Heavenly Father* for your strong arms carrying me when my strength was exhausted. Thank you for teaching me to respect your will. This book is a testimony of what faith in God will do!

This book is dedicated with love to my mother. It was written so that her life would not have been in vain.

Your Loving Daughter,
Marala

———————

This book is dedicated to my mother, for your love and guidance has given me the strength to succeed in life's journey. The reality of what happened to you in your house is different from what people perceived it to be.

Additionally, this book is dedicated to you, our readers. May this book inspire you to persevere through life's challenges and achieve the success and happiness *God* intended for you.

With Love and Respect,
Tré

Acknowledgments

Thank you to my wonderful son Aaron Lamont who has been my rock in so many ways. I love you son. I appreciate your unwavering faith in this memoir becoming a reality and your devotion. Thank you for making me laugh when I wanted to cry. Sonny, you know what your contribution was! Hi, Sir. My beautiful daughter Alyssa you believed in me and love me unconditionally in that special way you do. I love you, Pooh. And… I see you cry when I talk about Mom. Thank you to my brother Stan for encouraging me to tell our story. "Did you get the book out yet," is all you said for years! It's finally out! I love you always! Thank you to my brothers Colin, Clark, Jimmy and Selvin for the memories and love that got us through. My dear friend Charles, thank you for encouraging the strong spiritual message. That will cause this book to impact many lives! I love you for many reasons, you are awesome! Thank you Cole for years of encouraging me to walk away from those memories. Thank you to my friends and family that encouraged this book. You know who you are… (Kelly). A special thank you to Matthew Alexander Johnson, (Myles) for believing in this vision! Thank you for your faith, and all the sleepless nights! "Marala guess what …" Thank you to my wonderful husband for your unconditional love. This project consumed me and you helped me every step of the way from the time God put us together. I love that I wake up to you every morning and say, "Good morning gorgeous husband." Thank you Dad for the love you tried to give …And for helping Satan try to destroy me so God could show his power!

In Faith,
Marala Scott

FOREWORD

Having met Marala Scott, her father and brothers as adults, I was inspired by their success. Marala and I first met when she was coordinating a charity basketball game featuring the Dallas Cowboys versus local media personalities. I was a radio executive and she was doing marketing and consulting for various celebrities. Marala is sharp and passionate. Her intelligence, work ethic, and creative abilities have been instrumental in the success of her clients. Although Marala achieved great success in the business world, her passion is her children. She is an extremely loving mother with a fun and childish personality. That is why I was in complete shock when she eventually revealed her life's purpose to me. She was writing this memoir to give justice to her mother's life. A life that was filled with horror and pain induced by Marala's father and three women from a *church*. Marala's vivid recollections of the physical, emotional, and verbal abuse within their home will reveal terrors beyond your wildest imagination.

In Our House is a true story of a family caught in the snares of what evil can produce. Evil may attack you in various forms of abuse, but it does not have the power to defeat you. Your faith in God will determine your fate. There are men who are enemies of God, sons of disobedience who choose to inflict pain and suffering on their loved ones. Marala's father was such a man. The biblical references throughout the chapters indicate why events are occurring and how the Word of God can overcome Satan's attacks.

I have known Marala for over twelve years now. I am extremely proud that she is finally breaking her silence and telling her story, especially knowing how difficult these memories are to go back to. For so long she kept silent, holding the secret of abuse inside, afraid to speak out, remembering her father's threats and abusive behavior.

In completing this book, Marala has fulfilled her commitment to tell her story of survival and conquering of her family curse. Her message is very clear; your voice is a powerful tool. Don't assume that nothing can be done about your abusive situation – seek professional help and advice and trust in God!

I pray that those who are being abused or have lived in or know of an abusive situation will speak out and receive strength and healing as they read this book. Let Marala's story inspire you to do greatness in your life as she has. No matter how difficult your situation is, know that you are not alone, for God is with you.

Respectfully submitted:

Charles H. Richardson
Radio Executive

I had grown tolerant of whatever came next as part of my life's unbelievable script. I simply pondered how things would end. I'm sure we all did, but somehow it's not quite as I predicted it would be. The only thing that I've held on to all these years is that everyone accountable for what happened to my mother would have his or her day in judgment, and it won't be here on earth.

There are always a few unpleasant memories that one cannot endure. Unfortunately, for me it's my entire childhood. The recollections that should have been pleasant ones, calamity has eclipsed, so they no longer exist in my psyche. When I briefly observed the talk shows on television, Oprah, Montel, Maury, and the rest of that stuff, I couldn't fully empathize with whatever people were lamenting and complaining about. All I would say is, *They should have been in our house,* then I would abruptly change the channel with only a diminutive trace of empathy, because no one had it for us. As time passed, I came to realize that despite how I opted to analyze it, tragedy is tragedy with the degree to one person no less than the value that I had acquired in my life. I have learned to respect the pain others have had to endure in their lifetime and try to comprehend that they, too, had a significant purpose for their suffering. It's up to the individual to ascertain what the objective was. Nevertheless, I still say, *They should have been in our house!*

I never imagined that I would make it to this age. I used to think that if I hadn't committed suicide I would have lost my mind from the mental torture, but God shed his grace upon me and I turned thirty-seven at the time of this writing. He won't let it happen the way I projected it because *He* has a greater plan for me, which is the reason for this book. My purpose is to inform you of what existed, not in my mind, but in the reality and realm of this world. I hope that it will keep others from enduring what we did because of the lack of knowledge and understanding that we retained.

I began to compose this book years ago, but I sought justice or deliverance for Mom before completion. Therefore, I held off concluding the final chapters until I could have permanent closure. I believe that God has granted me deliverance from these events, but I haven't been able to accept it, not yet. Regardless, I comprehend that the justice that *I* was seeking is *His* and *His* alone. The only closure at this point is to continue to *pray*.

Jesus, I renounce the generational curse on my family. Please forgive any past, current, and future sins that have been or will be committed. I ask that you protect all of my family and future family members from any curses against us. Amen

Here is what happened in our house...

THE LEGAL

FUNERAL

For God so loved the world, that He gave His
only begotten Son, that whoever believes in Him
shall not perish, but have eternal life.

John 3:16
New American Standard

I knew I had an intrinsic resentment for Dad long before this day came. Nevertheless, when it did, my feelings were intensified. The irony of the situation was that Dad was the one to call and tell me about Mom's death. Long before the day she physically died, she had experienced a horrific death. October 13, 1991, was the day prior to my youngest brother's birthday, and the date of Mom's *legal* funeral.

The morning air was noticeably crisp with a wispy breeze flirting around me. I could hardly breathe inside my cousin's house, so I stepped onto the front porch so I could exhale and pull myself together. I had internalized the enigma and demons of my childhood, and no one could possibly know what that consisted of. I didn't engage in conversations with my cousin or her husband because I didn't want to allow anyone to intrude in our lives at this point. If I lost it now, I might not get it back, so all I could think to do was serenely breathe. I had already been through this once before with her. I deem it might have been arduous back then or I was trying to convince myself of that. To clear my head, I whispered part of a poem by Langston Hughes. Then the tears followed.

I was already dressed for the funeral, but I couldn't bring myself to wear black, so I selected a neatly tapered two-piece dark blue suit with gold buttons and a respectable neckline. As the afternoon approached, the temperature became more of a typical fall day. The crisp edge that began the day had relaxed and allowed the beauty in the brilliant multi-colored leaves to become the focus. Nonetheless, they didn't have the affect they typically did on me. Fall had always been my favorite season because of the beautiful changes it brought. Even with all of the beauty and fresh air, all I could smell was death.

Apprehensively, I walked into the small red brick Baptist church in Detroit. I noticed everything from the insignificant number of floral arrangements to people in quiet conversations of what happened. You could discern the eyes of strangers gazing at us in sheer speculation. Everyone there had an assumption. People have the tendency to concoct false theories about things they cannot grasp. Whatever anyone could have inferred would have been wrong anyway.

I quietly positioned my four-year-old son Aaron into the second row and gently instructed him to remain next to his Uncle Stan until I returned. He was sensitive to his surroundings and complied without opposition. I hesitantly began to approach the rose-colored casket with harrowing flashes of her existence in my mind. It felt as though at any moment someone would awaken me. Nevertheless, it didn't happen that way. Things never happened the way I wished they would.

When I reached the casket there laid Mom's shell, so still and more peaceful than I had ever seen her. Tears began streaming down my cheeks when I stroked my mother's hand one last time and placed a single pink rose in it. Although I realized she was gone and free from the confines of the tragedy her life had plagued her with, I remained consumed with the thought of where she was and who had her now. Who had *them*? Inside this frail, petite frame of the most beautiful woman I had ever seen resided the unimaginable. I stared at her in remembrance of how she arrived at this point. Her appearance no longer revealed any resemblance to the lucid visions of beauty or photos I kept of her. One could no longer see the mystification in her deep brown eyes or feel the anguish painted upon her weary soul. That reflection of Mom reminded me of her years of torment and abuse. Although I tried to conceal these recollections, they stayed carved into my very existence in the greatest of depth.

Although Dad physically and verbally abused Mom, the neglect of her family and society caused her rapid deterioration. Her affliction was unrelenting because she was never free from *them*. We didn't know of anyone on this earth powerful or knowledgeable enough to help our mother. This woman was insufferably besieged with an ordeal so horrific that it obliterated her and devastated us. I was certain the torment would carry her to a tragic death, and it did. None of us could have spared Mom from what happened to her because we didn't acknowledge the insanity, nor did we want to. We didn't know if we could save ourselves, let alone anyone else. I wanted to believe that I had tried, yet it didn't seem like it, especially from this view into her casket with *life* extracted out of her.

As the service was about to commence, I returned to my seat in the first pew, dazed. I was trying to evade questions from strangers or offerings of false sympathy. None of these people gave a damn about Mom. None of them knew her, or wanted to, especially after what happened. This was clearly a funeral for the curious, not the caring. I vigilantly glanced around the church and noticed my brothers adjusting to the uncomfortable atmosphere. I knew all of us would react differently, and each of us did. The relationship my brothers had shared with Mom over the past ten years was predominantly non-existent. Although Mom was with us for several years, she was mentally and emotionally absent from us. Such an irony that fate carries.

Mom had only seen Jimmy and Selvin once or twice in the past year. No one other than Cole and I chose to visit much after what happened. Looking around the room, I saw my four handsome and well-dressed brothers Stan, Clark, Jimmy, and Selvin, but not my father. I asked Selvin to help me find him. He looked outside, and I went downstairs. I discovered a room off to the immediate right with its door slightly open followed by a thin ray of light slipping inside. I opened the door and saw Dad sitting at a table in the dark. His heavy hand covered his face as he quietly wept. I watched him for a few moments, then without emotion sat next to him. I didn't console him, nor was I about to try. I would have been a hypocrite to do so. "Dad, the service is about to begin," was all that I was able to say. I grabbed his right arm and walked him upstairs. Guilt or repentance brought him here, and I was trying to fathom which one it was.

As we walked toward our seats, he stopped and sat several pews behind me. I went back to him and whispered, "Why don't you come sit with me? You were married to her." In a despondent manner he acknowledged and moved to sit beside me. His expression was completely that of self-reproach. He tried to hide it, but it was apparent. He knew he had played an award-winning and leading role in all of this. I wanted Dad to be in close proximity of her casket. I wanted him to reflect upon his significant contribution to this conclusion so he would remember it for the rest of his life. I already knew that he would.

As the pastor began to speak, I focused on her casket. I didn't want to hear anything anyone had to say. No one chose to converse with her while she was alive. In addition, I was quite sure the pastor had never laid eyes on her until now. No one knew *exactly* what happened except for her husband and children.

I couldn't help but recall how incomplete I felt throughout my life without Mom. Even though she was with me for the first eleven years, I never felt we connected as mother and daughter. I concede that time was stolen from us. Besides, there was always something irrepressible in our way, and now it was too late. As the pastor concluded the service, I felt a painful ache pull away from my soul and vanish into the confines of the casket with my mother. The pain I felt was the hope I carried, incessant tears, and prayers begging for her to be returned to us. My hands began to tremble while my legs were shaking uncontrollably and I cried out, "Mom, Mom, mommy… No," as if she were punishing me one last time. The service continued.

CHAPTER ONE

For the churning of milk produces butter, and
pressing the nose brings forth blood; so the
churning of anger produces strife.

Proverbs 30:33
New American Standard

Clark, Colin, and I were sitting on the large oval multi-colored rug in the small tenement living room. We were watching a late show on television while comfortably wrapped in old blankets. The bowl of popcorn in front of us was nearly empty. Our youngest brother, two-year-old Jimmy, was already asleep upstairs. The glare from the television and a slight trace of light coming from the small kitchen was all that illuminated the room. Stan sat placidly on the faded orange sofa sketching the beginning of a picture he would later paint. I never enjoyed scary movies, but I wanted to be like my big brothers, not like Jimmy. *The Creature Feature* was their favorite late night show, and we watched it on the black and white television, a big wooden 25-inch box.

"Man, this is what I call a movie," Colin Jr. shouted with excitement as he reached for the popcorn like a young film critic.

"It's empty, stupid."

Clark displayed the empty plastic green bowl with a silly grin. Then he held up the last fistful of popcorn and shoved it into his mouth.

"You greedy glutton," Colin joked, then flicked Clark playfully in the head. "My favorite part's when he gets into that teleportation thingamajig and that little fly—"

"And my favorite part is when you all get your little butts into bed," Mom called from the kitchen as she abruptly entered the room. She had one of Dad's wrinkled white shirts draped over her right shoulder and a can of spray starch in her hand.

"But it's not over yet," Colin and Clark cried out simultaneously as their faces displayed displeasure with her verdict.

"Maybe not. But it'll be over for *you all* when your father walks through that door. He'll be here any second, and I don't want to hear his mouth. Do you?"

We shook our heads no in full agreement.

"I didn't think so. Besides, it's after midnight," she scolded. "Stanley, how many times have I told you about drawing in the dark? Look at you over there squinting at the paper. I've told you over and over again…" she began as she put the starch on the end table and snatched the drawing tablet from him, "not to draw in the dark. It'll ruin your eyes." She reached to turn on the small ceramic green lamp next to the sofa. Her eyes widened, and her expression immediately changed to a pleasing one as the light hit the sketch. She studied the picture while Stan studied her striking features.

Mom was twenty-seven and a real knockout. She stood five feet five inches tall, and her body was thin and defined like a dancer. Prior to her marriage to Dad, she was planning to attend college to study dance and art in New York. Mom and Stan had a passion for art that only they shared. She was slightly bow-legged and had a feminine but athletic build. Her beautiful grade of jet-black hair was shoulder length. She kept the ends curled in a stylish upward flip. Mom's smile would light up any room, displaying her perfect white teeth. Her distinctive Indian heritage showed in the delicate structure of her sharp nose and high cheekbones that were dotted with chestnut-colored freckles resting on her perfect caramel skin. Her beautiful nut-brown eyes were softly traced with natural black eyeliner. Her ears hosted a pair of dainty pearl earrings. Such as the actresses Halle Berry or Jada Pinket-Smith, Mom had the same essence of beauty.

"You like it?" Stan asked shyly, with an inquisitive look on his face. He had features of both Mom and Dad. His medium chocolate complexion was a little darker than both parents. His coarse, curly thick brown hair didn't appear to come from either parent. It always gave the impression of being uncombed, even when it was. Stan was slender and shorter than most eight-year-olds, but there was a reason for that. Most people thought Colin was the eldest because Stan was born premature due to Dad's temper. His inquisitive brown eyes were always studying a person's expression and details. He seemed to examine everyone for a sketch. His smile displayed his little crooked white teeth and featured his high cheekbones. Overall, Stan looked more like Dad as a child, but when he smiled, his handsome face changed and became illuminating like Mom's.

With a notable wave of surprise in her voice, she began, "Stanley, this is beautiful baby. And the detail you put into the…"

Before she could finish, we heard the sound of a car door slam shut. Dad didn't have a car, so we knew it was him when he yelled "Thanks" to his friend. With swift movements, we sprang to our feet and raced up the stairs, grabbing the rod-iron rail on the way up.

"Go on! Get in your beds and don't make a sound. Hurry up now."

We could hear Mom rushing to straighten up the tiny living room, leaving no trace of our having been up that late. The front door slammed, and we did as she instructed. The four of us laid still and quiet in the two bunk beds. Clark and I shared the unlucky bottom bunk because Stan and Colin shared the top. One of them was always wetting the bed. Jimmy shared our parents' bed in the small second bedroom. When they wanted privacy, Clark made a pallet on the floor, and Jimmy slept with me.

We never knew what type of mood Dad was in late at night, and it wasn't worth the gamble to let him hear us awake because we'd definitely find out.

Dad made his way into the kitchen with movement that was heavy and intentional. He stood five feet eleven inches tall with a thin but solid muscular frame. His Irish ancestry showed in his silky-smooth yet wavy black hair parted and combed to the side. His handsome champagne face was clean-shaven. Dad's complexion was flawless. The thick black horn-rimmed glasses that framed his light hazel eyes gave more focus to the intensity he carried in them.

"What's for dinner?"

He pulled his dark blue v-neck sweater over his head leaving the heavily starched white shirt underneath. He laid the sweater on the back of the chair and glanced at the stove.

She cut her eyes at him, then pointed at the table and said, "It's right there."

"I didn't ask you where it was. I asked you what it was. Do I need to work more hours to buy you a hearing aid?"

"I suppose you need those thick glasses checked so you can find the table and the food on it, Colin. Or should I get you a guide dog? Please don't start your nonsense tonight. I'm not about to—"

"Look! Don't get smart with me! I've had a long and exhausting day, therefore, I'm not in the mood for your cynicism. Besides, I won't get much sleep tonight since I need to prepare for two exams. Speaking of which, why don't you make yourself useful and put on a pot of coffee. I'm going to need it."

Dad's enunciation was always proper and precise. His repertoire of communication was extensive. He made it a priority to let everyone know he wasn't one to be typecast as an uneducated black man back in the 1960s, let alone at any stage in his life. He corrected us if we didn't communicate properly or used fragments instead of complete sentences. He made it a practice to be the resident English professor for Mom. She hated his corrections and purposely didn't note them. We, on the other hand, had no choice, which wasn't necessarily a bad thing.

Alley finished putting the leftover food away. She reached in the refrigerator for the blue can of coffee and returned her attention to her husband.

"You know, Colin, every night you come home with the same grumpy attitude fussing and carrying on as if you're the only one who's had a long and exhausting day. Can't you come home for once and ask how my day was like you mean it? Do you always have to be a smart ass?"

He fixed his serious eyes on her and cast a patronizing stare, then he plopped down in the metal chair with green plastic seating and sighed.

"Alley, I call it like I see it. The reason I *don't* ask about your damn day is because you *don't* have one. You sit on your lazy ass, drinking coffee and playing with the fucking kids. Tell me, what aspect of your day could possibly be a challenge? I wish *I* could sit on my ass and do nothing all day. Boy, that would be a real treat," he said with a huff.

"You know, Colin—" she began as she pulled the sugar out of the cabinet, slamming it on the counter. When she began slamming things, he'd hit a nerve, and she was prepared to fight with him.

"Look, Alley, for the sake of an argument, how was your day?" he asked, shrewdly cutting her off and shifting the conversation. Dad always knew how to start and control an argument. He was all about control.

She took a deep breath and exhaled. Her annoyed expression relaxed, then disappeared.

"Fine, Colin," she said as she untied her pink and white flowered apron. She placed the apron on the back of the chair and calmly walked into the living room. When she returned to the kitchen she had Stan's sketch in her hand.

"How were the kids today? Any problems?"

"No. There weren't any problems. And the kids were good."

She stood behind him, placing the sketch in his view.

"What's this?" he asked, sounding disinterested.

"Now what does it look like? Stanley was working on this today, and I thought you should see it. That child has a natural talent for drawing, and I think we need to put him in an art class or something."

"Look," he said peering over his glasses, "I asked how the kids were, and you said *good*, so that's all I need to hear." He shoveled a spoonful of brown beans and white rice into his mouth as he reached for the newspaper.

She shook her head in aggravation and took the sketch back into the living room and laid it on the coffee table. She returned to her ironing while there was a long moment of much needed silence. When Colin finished the paper, he started again. His voice was stern and irritated.

"They convicted Cassius Clay today," he said shaking his head annoyingly. "He beat Terrell's ass, then Folley. Now they want to send him to prison for not taking the oath of induction into the Army," he sighed. "It says here he could receive five years and a $10,000 fine. Man, oh man, what's next?" he asked, folding the paper and dropping it on the floor beside him. Alley evenly sprayed his blue slacks with starch, then carefully slid the iron back and forth across them. "Out of sheer curiosity," he began, "why are you still ironing at this hour?" he asked skeptically. "Shit, Alley, you've had all damn day to do it. You see that's precisely my point. You sit on your ass all day long, then try to rush and get things done when I'm home. Need I say more?" he asked throwing his hands up.

Alley folded the ironing board, giving it a hard snap, and placed it into the small utility closet next to the refrigerator, then slammed its door. She was trying to ignore his comments. Composing herself, she pulled the milk from the refrigerator, added a small amount to the large brown cup, then poured the steaming coffee into it. She placed the cup in front of him and let her eyes meet his as he waited for a reply.

"It's hard to get everything done with five little children running around here. You seem to forget that I'm changing and washing diapers, cooking, cleaning, ironing, and handling everything else," she explained convincingly. "I'm held captive by the children all day. Colin, we go over this practically every day, and you constantly ask me the same annoying questions. Why don't I get this done? Why don't I get that done? All you do is fuss, fuss, fuss, and I'm sick to death of it!"

"Look dumbass, I asked if there were any problems and you said no. So enlighten me. What was the distraction that delayed your housework? As I stated earlier… sitting on your lazy ass, watching the soaps with your friend Dorothy and the rest of the neighbors, while drinking coffee. What is this, the fucking *Maxwell House* open from nine to five for lazy ass coffee drinkers? Shit, Alley. I work two jobs and go to school full-time, all in a day! You could never be me, that's for fucking sure," he added, displaying a clever smirk.

"Now, I really have to wonder… who in the hell would want to be your complaining ass? Tell me, who in God's name would want to be a miserable bastard like you?"

I'd grown used to their routine. They argued about anything and just about everything. It was usually over money, family, and us. Sometimes when they fought, I laid quietly in bed whimpering because I couldn't stop them or help Mom when their fighting got bad. I hated hearing our parents argue. There were occasions they were purely comical, of course unintentionally, so I enjoyed the entertainment and giggled quietly. Mom always had a witty retort to Dad's sarcasm. This time their voices escalated for a few more minutes before silence claimed the night as we drifted off to sleep. This was life at 319.

During the week Dad was usually gone from early morning to late in the evening. There were days that the only time we saw him was coming or going. Nevertheless, on a rare weekend if he wasn't working he spent time playing with us. Once in a while he came home with pizza, and we'd stay up late watching scary movies together. Regardless of whatever problems there were, for the most part we were happy. When Dad wasn't working, in school, or at home, he was with one of his friends. Mom always said it was a wonder he had any. Every now and then, three of our neighbors, Butchie, Kale, and Greg, watched us while she and Dad went out together.

Back then, we didn't relate to the invariable struggles Dad experienced. The impoverished way he grew up wasn't the way he intended to live the rest of his life. He didn't begin wisely because five children would definitely impede his growth. It was unquestionable that Dad encountered challenges we weren't cognizant of, which made him bitter, yet indomitable. It was discernable by his drive and extreme focus that he was trying to elude something.

He was born into *his* vicious generational cycle. His determination to attain a degree while working two and often three jobs to support a family of seven was challenging. He worked at Western Electric, a meat market and for a while, the city morgue. Today, people seem to quit if an opportunity isn't handed to them or the test is too trying. It has become common for a father to disappear and abandon his family to start a new life free of child rearing and financial responsibilities. Our father wasn't like that. He sculpted his own destiny and defied the stereotypes of African Americans. Dad worked to become an influential representation of our ethnic group. I don't recall that he ever quit anything he started despite how frustrated he became... except his job at the morgue. Late one night, Dad was working third shift at the morgue when he encountered the bodies lying on gurneys. He tried to stay clear of them, however, this time one of the bodies moved and so did Dad. He got out of there as fast as he could and never went back for his final paycheck.

Dad's vulnerability was his compulsive need to vent his provocations. His outlet was his wife and children when he considered it to have been provoked. His intention was to teach us respect for his efforts. A black man in a white world encompassed its own adversities. Dad's initial regret was not heeding to his mother's wishes and marrying Mom.

As far back as I can recall Dad never seemed to be partial to children, particularly his own. I always wondered why he had so many of us, and he maintained it was because, "Your mother wasn't smart enough to believe in abortions, therefore, I got stuck with the lot of you." Since we were here, he did his best to provide for us. I presume you could say at times he did it resentfully, but at least he did it. His realization of our existence, encumbering his efforts to reach his goals, was silently killing him.

Sadly, Dad held Stan with a tremendous degree of contempt since he was the eldest and first representation of Dad's mistake. The harder Dad worked to support us, the easier it was for him to show antipathy. The poignant aspect was that long before Dad verbally began proclaiming his increasing aversion for us, I'd already become conscious of it on my own.

Since Clark and I were younger, when we were disobedient or mischievous, Dad didn't deal with us by swinging his belt. He'd send us to bed for the rest of the day so we were out of his sight. Jimmy appeared immune to everything that transpired. Stan and Colin became terrified and exhausted from Dad's abuse, so their alternative was to run away. The first time I recall Stan running away, Clark and I were out back in the courtyard playing tag with our neighbors when we heard a heated discussion escaping from our apartment. We went inside and quietly sat on the sofa in the living room while Colin Jr. was closing the windows as Dad had instructed.

"I'm going to tear your little piss ass up! Do you hear me, mister?"

"Colin. Try and talk to him first."

"Who in the hell has time to talk?" he questioned, yanking a brown leather belt two inches wide from the belt hoops of his khaki slacks.

"Have you asked him what happened?" she said, standing sandwiched between Dad and Stan, trying to get his attention.

"I'm going to beat the shit out of that little pisser! Then maybe I'll feel like asking questions! Now get the hell out of my way!"

He shoved her against the wall and stormed into the other bedroom searching for Stan. He lifted the thin mattress off the bottom bunk, then tossed it aside. He heard the closet door creak so he yanked it open and began shoving the clothes aside. It was too late. Stan vacated the closet and was tearing down the stairs headed toward the kitchen door.

"I'm out of here," he mumbled, rushing past us. His brown pants had patches on the knees while his red and white-striped shirt was short and wrinkled. His eyes were bloodshot and his little face sweaty. At nearly nine years old, he was already terrified of Dad. With eyes as red as Stan's, Colin tried to prevent him from going out the door and put his arm up to block him.

"Stan, don't leave, just take it. Don't let him run you away from us," Colin begged.

Clark and I made our way over to him with the echoing fury of Dad stomping around upstairs yelling obscenities to Mom. Jimmy was sitting on a pale green blanket in the living room calmly stacking his building blocks.

"I have to get out of this place, he's crazy! You know what he's going to do to me," he said, choking on his words.

"But, Stan, then it's over," Colin explained, trying to convince him to stay.

"It'll never be over with him," he said in a hushed whisper. He ducked underneath Colin's arm and disappeared through the tattered screened door.

While Mom was upstairs arguing with Dad, Stan was long gone from 319. Mom didn't realize she had stalled Dad so Stan could run away. If she had, she never would have let him leave. But Dad's punishment never fit the crime, and Stan wasn't going to take the whipping up and down his little body if he had a chance to escape it. Often, he was gone overnight or for a few days before the police or someone brought him home. Ultimately, he received his punishment. Colin would stay and take his.

Stan and Colin continually got into trouble for minor things. Their teasing us, not responding to Dad's call, which was a loud whistle, cleaning improperly, or fighting with one another were generally the causes. Colin hit his growth spurt before Stan, so Dad used him as his punching bag and beat him harder. There were countless scenarios when Dad deliberately singled out Colin to solicit a fight.

Although Colin was abused, he didn't let it affect his relationship with us. But when Dad was home, Colin became introverted. Any random thing he said or did to any of us could upset Dad. He rarely walked past him without raising his hands to shield his face. He frequently tried to protect himself from an unexpected slap.

Stan and Colin were only ten months apart. He and Colin shared the same medium chocolate complexion and coarse black hair. Colin had a different look. He was the one who resembled Dad the most, right down to his soft hazel eyes with the same intensity. He had Mom's cheekbones, sharp nose and perfect teeth, but he mirrored Dad's smile and expressions. His forehead and fine black eyebrows were also Dad's. His frame seemed sketched by an artist who defined his lean, muscular physique at an early age. Colin desperately tried not to upset Dad, but he couldn't manage it for anything. Clark did a better job of avoiding his rage.

Clark was a year and a half younger than Colin and a year older than I. If Dad were biased toward any of us, it would have been Clark. Perhaps it was because his complexion was extremely fair. Mom's mother didn't look black. She could pass for white even up close. You never knew she was black until she spoke with her Southern accent. Most of her family was from Virginia, but ultimately ended up in Detroit. Clark favored her. She had a beautiful grade of long black and gray hair that she kept braided in two ponytails, then pinned up in coils. Grandma's smile was warm and gentle. She had an even softer color of chestnut freckles than Mom did on her heart-shaped face. Clark had them, too.

Clark looked as if he were Grandma's son instead of Mom's. He had most of her features. His grade of radiant, jet-black hair wasn't coarse like Stan and Colin's. His curls were soft and loose. Clark was a beautiful child who always received compliments. His eyes smiled when he looked at you. His teeth were straight and pearly white, and the tails of his button up shirts always appeared half-tucked.

Colin always alleged that Clark was retarded because he almost suffocated when he was a baby. He crawled underneath the thick plastic covering on the sofa and became entangled. Mom was outside hanging laundry in the courtyard with the neighbor Dorothy, and by the time she found him, he had turned blue and wasn't breathing. Fortunately, Mom resuscitated him, then rushed him to the hospital. Since Dad was protective of us, it left permanent ammunition for him to use against Mom.

Clark was the type of child who studied Dad's personality and adjusted his own to avoid getting whipped whenever possible. Most of the time it worked. If Dad asked a question, Clark was smart enough to answer in a way that was acceptable to Dad. He was mischievous; he just wasn't caught all the time. When Colin got into trouble, Clark would ask, "Now who's the retard around here?"

Dad's personality was unique. He'd proven to be highly intelligent and assertive. Everything he did was premeditated. He viewed everything from a business or psychological perspective and his recreation stemmed from his ability to manipulate the emotions of others. I am certain that Dad would make any psychologist an exceptionally interesting subject to analyze; much like Hannibal Lecter.

When Dad graduated from the University, the local newspaper heard about his achievement. They featured the story and captured a photo of him in receipt of his degree with his wife and children commemorating the occasion. Raising five children and graduating college, in that particular era, was a true accomplishment.

Shortly after Dad's graduation we moved from our small apartment and the bitter cold winters of Buffalo to brave the brisk winter chills of Poughkeepsie, New York. The only thing Dad would miss was the Bills stadium. He and Mom were among their most loyal fans. They watched the Bills win two successive AFL titles in 1964 and 1965 with running back Cookie Gilchrist and their star quarterback, Jack Kemp. Although they didn't have money to attend many of the games, they managed a few here and there. They would certainly remain fans. As for the countless days we spent trapped inside our apartment by six-foot snowdrifts feasting on Campbell's tomato soup and saltines, they were now over. Finally, 319 was history.

The move to Poughkeepsie presented us with a better standard of living. Dad had taken a job with IBM although the CIA heavily recruited him. At that time, the salary offered by IBM was better and consequently the deciding factor for Dad.

He purchased our first house, which was always my favorite. There was a well-manicured baseball field and playground directly across the street. The neighborhood was impressive and extremely inviting. This house, previously owned by a doctor, was as big as it was beautiful. This three-story white house sat on a grassy hill near the end of the street. Verdant, tall pines shaded the front porch and the remainder of the property. When it rained, the strong fragrant scent of pines filled the house.

Although there were other sizable and charming homes on this street, ours was the biggest. As soon as you walked through the front door, a beautiful wood staircase with a winding banister met you. The wood always glistened as though it were recently polished. There were four sizable bedrooms upstairs. Dad and Mom had their room. Jimmy and Clark shared the second bedroom. Stan and Colin occupied the third, and I had my own pink bedroom with a trundle bed and built-in shelving. A stairway led from my room to a large attic, which we utilized as a play area. The living room was spacious and had an enormous red brick fireplace trimmed with a white mantel. The superbly waxed hardwood floors flowed throughout most of the house. Imposing white French doors connected the living and dining rooms while impressive bay windows framed the exterior walls in both rooms.

Mom loved the bright airy eat-in kitchen because it had the counter space she needed for cooking. She sought a kitchen that comfortably fit all of us at one time, and this one could. There was a medium-sized window over the kitchen sink that offered a view to the neighbor's house. The door off the kitchen led to a small-enclosed porch. Downstairs, the family room had a built-in bar for entertaining, which extended half the length of the room. The floors had tan carpeting. Framing the room were benches made into the walls that doubled as storage chests. They had black leather cushions for comfortable seating. The russet wood paneling gave the room a nice cozy feel. Off the family room near the furnace area was a laundry room. One feature we all loved was that the first three floors each had a bathroom.

The backyard had impressive features of its own with a plush blanket of even, dark green grass. We had our own private picturesque commons. At the end of the yard sat the white garage adjacent to the alleyway. Awaiting discovery was a little white tool shed, with a small window that would become my playhouse.

This house was an enormous leap from the humble beginnings we had. Dad's hard work was beginning to pay off. For his first house, he went all out. You could have fit the entire apartment inside this house at least four times. There was plenty of room for us to play. This was 16.

The neighbors were nice. A few were nosey, but we adapted. My favorite was our next-door neighbor, Bernie. Bernie was quiet and strange. He had thick black hair hanging off the bottom half of his balding head. His eyebrows were bushy and his nose prominent. Dad said it was because he was Jewish. He stood about five feet nine inches and was soft-spoken. Bernie was nothing like his talkative and nosey mother who always asked us personal questions about Dad. Clark was the dummy who told her everything he knew.

Bernie tirelessly picked up trash with his long black poker stick because he had a compulsive disorder. He brought us candy from time to time, but Dad warned us not to eat it since Bernie found it while picking up the trash. He walked all over the neighborhood during the week, and sometimes we'd see Bernie on the highway in his black pants, black t-shirt, and poker stick. I always thought Bernie was one of the nicest retards I'd ever met, but I couldn't understand why a black stretch limo picked him up every weekend. One day, Dad explained that he was a brilliant classical pianist who played in New York City on the weekends. That clarified why I constantly heard the mesmerizing music. I thought it was a record.

We went to a Catholic school by Mom's preference. Dad never approved of the choice, but he couldn't win that argument because she was unyielding about her religious conviction. Once she made up her mind about that *no one could change it*. I had to wear the little plaid green-and-blue jumper with a starched white shirt. I thought it was pretty stylish. Stan and Colin attended an innovative educational program at Vassar's College during the summer months. My three older brothers became altar boys in the church, and Stan became a nuisance to the nuns in school. Like some children, he elected to amuse himself without entertaining the thought of his consequences with Dad. His list of pranks kept escalating. One of his favorite things to do was hide in the girls' locker room to watch them change for gym. When Stan wasn't around Dad, much like Colin, he was funny. The nuns at school made regular visits to our home due to both Stan and Colin's behavior. Stan always fled from his punishments if he had the opportunity.

Our first summer in Poughkeepsie Stan ran away and caught a train to Detroit where he ended up with Dad's mother. Three days went by before anyone knew where he was. The peculiar thing was that Dad couldn't call the police and draw attention to himself. Besides, he knew Stan had become resourceful from prior experiences. Just when Stan thought he was safe he overheard Grandma on the phone with Dad making arrangements to send him back home, so he tried to catch a freight train to Canada. He almost succeeded, but Grandma paid a couple teenagers to catch Stan. Fortunately, they did as he jumped for the train. For some odd reason, perhaps instinct, Grandma decided it might be a good idea to keep Stan for the rest of the summer.

By the time Stan was nearly ten years old, drawing was about the only thing that kept him occupied, calm, and out of trouble. He escaped to a better place when he had a pencil, chalk, or paintbrush in his hand. He wasn't as inspired to get into things like Colin and Clark, but he had his moments where he'd completely dismantle things, then put them back together. Stan was inquisitive and had an innate desire to understand how things functioned, but they never worked quite the same again.

Economically we were doing considerably better, but the pressure was on for Dad to maintain it. He worked lengthy hours, joined the country club, and associated himself with affluent people. Dad did everything he thought was vital to succeed and alienated himself from people who weren't in his echelon.

Despite everything Dad acquired, there was a major dilemma brewing with Mom. She wasn't emerging into the social or intellectual wife whom Dad was longing for. Involvement in social activities that could elevate their social standing wasn't on her "to-do" list. He made it into the corporate arena, and Mom remained a homemaker, which was equal to *nothing* in his assessment. Her arena was a playpen with children. According to Dad, she was impeding his progress.

With their sixth child now here, Mom was going to be at home for some time, if not indefinitely. Our baby brother Selvin received the rest of her time. Dad out grew his relationship with Mom at an alarming pace. Whatever initially brought them together had diminished. His stress and intolerance quickly escalated. The material surroundings were the advantages of Dad's achievements, and we were about to experience the disadvantages even more.

Mom's transformation was beginning to manifest, and Dad detected it immediately. She was beginning to withdraw from him, and their tension grew. Now, Mom had more children, a bigger home, and an abusive warden for a husband to take care of. Dad's family, their friends, and his co-workers always said that Dad was a good, intelligent, hard-working family man. The more people built up his ego, the more his condemnation of Mom increased. According to Dad, she was lazy, stupid, and a woman, which gave her all types of negatives that he despised having to contend with.

Although Dad saw the changes in Mom, he remained blinded by his own ugly transformation. His solution to getting Mom help was having *his* mother come for a week here and there. She didn't help Mom; Grandma made Mom miserable. They appeared to hate one another.

There was a great deal of conflict between Grandma and Mom. Grandma always made it known that Mom wasn't good enough for Dad, and she never hid her feelings. Her visits added nitro to the already burning fire. She invaded Mom's territory like a colorless, odorless, almost inert diatomic gas. She instigated many fights between the two of them and was a major irritant.

In a crackled annoying voice, she'd say, "Hi, baby, come to Grandma," while curling her pointed finger at me. "How's your mean old mommy treating you? Is Mommy feeding Daddy's baby right? Is she taking good care of Daddy's baby? Does your mommy play with you and make Daddy's baby girl have fun? You can tell Grandma, and Grandma will tell Daddy. We'll get mean old Mommy into trouble so she treats Daddy's baby girl right," she said with a big cunning smile.

"Would you like that?"

Of course not, you crazy old bat, is what I was thinking. Nevertheless, out of respect for Dad, I simply stared at her with a controlled expression of indifference. I didn't take to her because she didn't like my mom, *ever.*

Dad said she didn't go to their wedding because she was angry with him for marrying Mom. I never understood why she came around. She would spend a week at a time to give unfavorable reports to Dad with hope that he'd leave Mom. A week with Grandma felt like seven years. The only time Grandma appeared to be civil to Mom was when she had a nice tall glass of orange juice and vodka. Mom wasn't much of a drinker, but she had an occasional beer or two. In retrospect, this was probably a good thing. Most of the time she smoked her Kool Filter Kings, ate a Milky Way candy bar, had a Pepsi, and listened to her soulful music. She loved music, and she loved to dance.

I recall things being normal around our house when it was filled with the melodic sounds of the Supremes, Martha Reeves and the Vandellas, the Four Tops, Al Green, Marvin Gaye, and of course Johnny Mathis. Usually when Dad wasn't home Mom sang and danced while she cooked and cleaned. However, there were times when he put his evil twin away and danced with her.

Dad loved music almost as much as Mom. That one thing was capable of pulling the two of them together. They looked like a couple of teenagers flirting with one another when they danced. When he passionately wrapped his arms around her, she seemed genuinely happy. Music was the key to unlock Mom's soul, make her smile, and lighten the atmosphere in our house. Her preferred method of relaxation was through music, dance, and her cigarettes. I detested the disgusting odor of smoke that continuously surrounded her.

Mom was set in her ways and complacent with the basic things life offered. This conflicted with what Dad expressed that he wanted. He expected her to evolve with him, but she wasn't willing to change. The only growth she had was raising six children. This was a full-time job to everyone but Dad. I believed whomever he married, that person would never have been sufficient in any way either. It wasn't a personal thing with Mom, simply more of a personality trait for Dad. He was his own worst enemy, and he chose to make everyone around him feel inadequate to his superiority. Dad had a family that loved him and wanted to feel loved by him, but that too was beginning to fade.

It didn't take long before their arguments became frequent and turned into physical confrontations once again. Mom wasn't exactly passive. She was easily incensed by his accosting and more adamant about defending herself. If Dad was wrong about anything, she'd let him know. The thing was, even if he were wrong, by the time he finished with his rationalization, he'd make her doubt herself. Occasionally, the reasons for their fights remained unknown.

Whenever Dad knocked Mom down, she'd stagger back on her feet and keep fighting with him. The fights were brutal and lasted longer, causing her to have large contusions on her face and body. She didn't want us to realize what kind of pain she was in, so she tried to minimize the damage with makeup and by taking aspirin. However, Dad often had bruises, bite marks, and scratches, as well.

Even with a house full of children to take care of, Mom attempted to show a sincere interest in Dad's career. Although she'd ask questions about his day, Dad's demeaning response was that she wouldn't understand, and he didn't expect her to. His insensitivity and arrogance flourished as he reminded Mom that she was lacking the intellect and capability to grasp the world of business in which he had positioned himself.

Irrespective of Dad and his career, Mom had enough to do at home. She made the most incredible meals. Every day there was something wonderful filling the air. Mixed greens, fresh green beans, buttery sweet cornbread, fried chicken, macaroni and cheese, potatoes, biscuits, chicken and dumplings, chicken noodle soup, tuna fish casserole, meatloaf, fried fish, liver and onions, mashed potatoes, pork chops, fried cabbage with pieces of bacon, and the list went on and on. Everything was homemade.

When it came to baking, Mom was even better, which seemed impossible. I don't know how she did it, but she did. As soon as we walked through the door from school or playing, she'd pull something out of the oven. We knew when she was baking something sweet because the delicious aroma hit us long before we reached the house.

"Wash your little hands. I made a peach cobbler," she'd say, while releasing a tender smile. Mom took a great deal of pride in her cooking. If it wasn't her cobbler, it was white cake, banana pudding, cookies, cinnamon rolls, blueberry cobbler, rice pudding, or her specialty, lemon meringue pie. If Mom wasn't baking, she made homemade ice cream or strawberry pie with fresh whipped cream on top. Mommy always made something she knew we'd love. She made everything from scratch. Although Mom cooked all time, she kept her long shaped fingernails looking perfectly manicured.

After living in Poughkeepsie for two years, IBM transferred Dad to Cleveland. He had flown back and forth to find our home. Our furniture was shipped to our new house, and Dad drove us to Ohio. On the way, we stopped at a motel that belonged to a white couple that were friends of his. Surprisingly, he decided to stay for the night. It was strange because we were only two hours away and the trip itself was only four.

We sat in the room and watched television until Selvin, Jimmy, and I became hungry. At that point, we decided to find Mom and ask if we could get a snack. We followed the cool breeze around the back, where the owners of the motel, Al, and Ida, were talking with Mom and Dad. A tree had been cut down leaving the wide stump for a chopping block with an ax wedged in the middle of it. There was a wire fence with pretty white chickens inside. We wanted to see them, but Dad calmly instructed us to go inside.

I took them back to the room and turned on the television. Instead of staying with them, I went to the side of the little motel and peeked around the corner to see what they were doing. This time, Stan and Colin were out back as well. Ida grabbed two chickens from the pen and handed the first one to Dad who viciously rung the chicken's neck until it stopped moving. Stan and Colin seemed disgusted. It didn't appear to bother Mom or Dad. Al and Ida seemed unaffected.

Dad shoved the second chicken into Stan's hand and ordered him to do the same. Stan backed away, refusing, so Dad gave it to Colin. Colin clenched his teeth as he began twisting its neck, but couldn't finish. He looked nauseated. Dad grew angry and told them to get inside. Instead, Stan came around the side of the motel and stood beside me, with Colin peering over his shoulders holding his stomach. Mom finished the job. She locked both hands around its neck and twisted it until it cracked. Al got two more chickens with which he and Ida did the same. Then, Dad took the ax and chopped the head off one instead of ringing its neck. Blood squirted out, and the headless chicken kept hopping and jerking all over the place. It should have been dead after he severed the head. I broke into a cold sweat and opened my mouth to scream, but Colin clasped his hand tightly over it before I made a sound! Al did the same with the other three chickens. Colin whispered in my ear to explain that's where fried chicken came from and the only way to get it was to kill the chicken. But it didn't look like they were planning on cooking them. Ida drained the blood from the chickens and put them into four jars without lids. I wanted to throw up.

Mom, Dad, and Al stayed out back talking around the stump while Ida went inside, only to return a few minutes later with a plastic tray full of objects. They stood next to the stump, but turned their backs away so I couldn't see what they were doing. It sounded as if they were praying over the blood. The beautiful blue colors in the sky changed like a shadowy canvas. The air turned blustery and cooler. The clouds began churning as though a storm was headed our way. Something wasn't right, and this didn't seem normal. I was scared. I had a knot in my stomach and had to get away from there. I left Stan and Colin to watch as I bolted inside, passing Clark as he left his room. My parents spent the evening in the front office of the motel talking with these strange people.

When we left the next day, Al and Ida seemed content. It was as if they had accomplished or gained something. My curiosity remained. Stan said what they did when I left was peculiar, only I didn't want to know what it was. The ride to our new home was chilling.

This time Dad purchased a newly built white split-level with red brick around the front half. White stones surrounded three tall trees in the front yard. It wasn't as big as our previous home, but was more expensive. There were three sizable bedrooms upstairs with a bathroom attached to the master bedroom. The second room off to the left was for Selvin and me to share. The third room next to mine belonged to Clark and Jimmy.

The living room was a comfortable size with two windows. The larger picture window illuminated the room. The blended green shag carpeting ran into the dining area that had a sliding glass door leading to the large plush backyard. The kitchen was modern and spacious with plenty of cabinets and a window overlooking the double sink. There was a side door leading to the driveway. Downstairs to the left there was a small laundry room and furnace area utilized for storage. Across the hall was a bathroom. The rest of the area downstairs was a large tiled family room with windows surrounding it. Dad sectioned it off and made an extra bedroom for Stan and Colin to share.

Given that Dad had a large family, he considered the recreational areas in the neighborhood as an incentive for purchasing this home. He wanted us to have parks nearby so we could venture off to play. Down the street was a recreation center, swimming pool, and a large playground area with a baseball field. The schools were right around the corner, and there were many children to play with. Mom appeared to be content with this move. Perhaps it was because she was closer to her family in Detroit. Maybe she was hoping for a fresh start; we were.

At first things were going the same as they had begun in Pough-keepsie. Dad spent most of his time at work learning his responsibilities and territory while Mom spent her spare time getting familiar with our new environment. She didn't make many friends or often associate with others. A cup of coffee with a neighbor was a big stretch for Mom. Cooking, cleaning, washing, ironing, and disciplining us when necessary occupied her days.

Mom was far more lenient toward us than Dad. Periodically, she'd flare up, but usually it was due to something that Colin or Clark had done. She didn't like to whip us, but she would, after several warnings. Either we got it from her, or she told Dad. Nothing compared to his beatings, so we took hers and whined about it later. Most of the things that happened during the day, Mom never told him about because she knew how he'd react. If we were noisy or began fighting, Mom sent us outside. She'd lock the door so we couldn't get back in until we had calmed down or Dad came home. She'd send us to play at the park or recreation center to stay out of trouble.

For the most part, Mom was at her best when she was alone. She was turning into somewhat of a recluse. She didn't get much rest because she was always up before anyone else and the last one in bed unless Dad was working on a presentation. Mom definitely loved to watch her soaps early in the afternoon. *General Hospital* and all the soaps on that particular channel were her favorites. If the stories were good, they interrupted her housework for at least three hours. When Mom's work was finished, she'd sit in the living room in her green recliner, smoke her cigarettes, and listen to music.

Her routine was consistent. Mom didn't have her driver's license, so she walked everywhere. It never seemed to bother her, and she never complained. Mom thought about us when she went to the store. It didn't matter how much money she had, she'd buy us things such as bubbles, a paddleball, or jacks. Mom enjoyed playing jacks with me, and I took pleasure in seeing the lightheartedness in her. By the time Dad was expected home, she was irritable and on edge, in anticipation of his mood. To make things a little easier my brothers and I regularly helped with chores. If the house wasn't completely cleaned before Dad came home, he became agitated. Dad was stringent with everything. Two of his obsessions were organization and cleanliness.

Once we settled into this home, the stress from Dad's job routinely kicked in. Everything we did was an annoyance to him. His temper was more violent and enraged, and the beatings became more severe. Almost anything ignited it. As time went on, Mom continually tried to keep us away from Dad's raging path, but it seldom worked. Often, he took the same route we were on regardless of her efforts. As his career became more challenging and his expenses increased, he worked harder. The problem was that he took out the anger and frustration on Mom. Stan and Colin felt his venting firsthand as well. Dad was deficient in toleration for them.

Late one evening Dad came in from work after we'd already gone to bed. Mom was lightly moving around the kitchen warming up the pork roast, boiled potatoes, and collard greens. She set the plate in front of him and began putting the food away. As he picked up his fork, he noticed a water spot or particle of something on it and began his irrational questioning.

"Alley, who washed the dishes tonight?" he asked raising his eyebrow while staring at her crossly.

"The kids did," she replied nervously. "As a matter of fact, they cleaned the family room, their bedrooms, and cut the grass. They were good today," she replied defensively.

"Apparently not good enough," he snapped with his eyes transfixed on the fork.

Her nut-brown eyes sank and her mouth fell open when he began summoning us as though he'd gone mad.

"Get your asses out of bed," he shouted impatiently, pounding his angry fist on the table.

As if we'd already calculated his performance, we scurried out of bed half-asleep, clumsily wiping the crust forming in the corners of our eyes. We were disoriented because we didn't have a clue as to why he was angry. My three older brothers and I stood at a sloppy military attention in front of him while Jimmy and Selvin stayed in their slumber. As he continued yelling, the fear was seeping in, along with the reality of this episode. All we could do was brace ourselves for the worst.

"Don't you little idiots know how to wash dishes properly?" he asked displaying the fork as if it were so contaminated it could have killed him.

He got up from the table and positioned himself in front of us.

"*What's this?*" he shouted while placing the fork in front of our sleepy faces, one at a time. "Look at it! Am I the only person who can do anything right around this damn place? Am I?" We were too afraid to respond and still shocked that he awakened us over something so insignificant. "I'm going to teach you little dumb asses a lesson! The next fucking time you wash the damn dishes, believe me, you'll know precisely what *I* expect!"

Trying to intervene, Mom yelled back in an unconvincing contemptuous voice, "Colin, that's enough of your crazy shit! These kids have school tomorrow, and it's too late for your damn nonsense tonight!" She pulled another fork from the kitchen drawer and slammed it on the table in front of him. "Just use another fork! You make a damn issue out of everything," she shouted, storming back into the kitchen.

"I suggest you mind your own damn business and shut the fuck up," he said, heatedly flinging the contaminated utensil at her.

"You're fucking crazy," she shouted, dodging the fork. "Let these kids go to sleep." She picked up the fork and dropped it into the sink. "They don't deserve this. It's damn near eleven-thirty so—"

"So if you'd taught them how to wash dishes correctly in the first damn place they wouldn't be here now, would they?" He bit down on his bottom lip, cocked his head to the right, then added arrogantly, "When I want your fucking little opinion I'll ask for it!"

"Stanley, you kids go back to bed. I'll handle your father," she warned with a shaky voice, tugging on Stan's arm.

Locking eyes with Dad, Stan resisted. We knew better than to move. She looked at Dad in disdain and he shrugged back as if he didn't know why we hadn't raced back to bed.

"Get in the damn bed! Do you hear me? Don't listen to this man." Lightly shoving each of us she insisted, "Go on, scoot."

Still we didn't budge. She looked at us in fear of what we were in store for.

He clenched his jaws, sneered disgustingly at her, then sighed, "Alley, don't you know by now who the law is around here?"

Without a display of emotion, he dismissed her with his hand. She snatched her pack of cigarettes from the counter and headed up-stairs, mumbling angrily under her breath. "You're one crazy son-of-a-bitch." She didn't want to leave, but we gave her no choice. What Mom didn't realize was that we had just spared her from a beating. A strong wave of fear swept across our faces.

"Keep running your mouth and I'll have your ass down here help-ing," he warned.

The door slammed shut and there was a heavy silence.

I was all too familiar with his expression. Dad's eyes gave way to him being in profound thought by the way he cocked his head to the left side, scrunched his eyebrows together, then sucked his lips inward. He slid his belt from around his waist and laid it on the back of the chair.

He flashed a weak grimace and said, "As for you little bastards, I want every bowl, plate, saucer, glass, cup, pot, pan, and utensil pulled out of the cabinets, washed, dried, and then put away. If I should find one… and I do mean one… water spot or particle of food on anything, you'll keep doing these dishes again and again until you get it right," he ordered while giving us the same icy stare he'd given Mom, then added, "Now damn it, hop to it!" He got up from the table and went upstairs mumbling inaudibly.

Without pause, we removed every item from the cabinets. We didn't talk because we already knew the routine. Meticulously we washed, rinsed, dried, inspected, and neatly stacked the dishes, then put everything away with as little clanking as possible. We took it upon ourselves to wash the silver coffee pot, blender, pea-green canisters, and house-shaped cookie jar, as well as the other items on the counter.

My sleepy eyes tightened as I yawned. I glanced at the apple clock on the wall above the counter; it was nearly one o'clock in the morning. We sat on the kitchen floor waiting for him to inspect our work. The four of us had our opinions of this episode but one was unanimous.

Colin broke the silence mumbling angrily, "This is insane."

We shook our heads in agreement because we were tired of Dad's tantrums and irrational punishments.

"He has us doing all this cleaning over nothing! I didn't see anything on that fork. Did you guys?" Colin asked, as if he were validating his own sanity.

Again, we shook our heads no. We wanted to go back to our slumber and forget this ever happened.

Colin got up and pulled a fork out of the drawer. He placed his left hand on his waist and held the fork against his right eye, pretending to examine it closely while pacing. In a condescending tone he asked, "*What's this?*" We covered our mouths and laughed hysterically.

We knew better than to disturb Dad from his sleep so we sat sluggishly on the cold floor and waited. Shortly after two o'clock in the morning, when the mood finally struck him, he strolled downstairs.

Stretching and yawning as if we'd awakened him from a sound sleep, he smiled stiffly as though he were positive he'd come across something unacceptable. We knew for certain that he couldn't. We had carefully examined every inch of every item we washed to make sure he would let us go back to bed. Still, we displayed no sign of confidence while he randomly pulled dishes from the cabinet and inspected them.

He turned around to face us and let out a long exaggerated sigh. Then asked, "*What's this?*" displaying a coffee cup hanging from his index finger. "I'm working every fucking day so I can raise a bunch of dumb ass, filthy mother-fucking children!" He threw the blue cup into the sink, hard enough to break it before any of us could inspect it again. He reached over and grabbed Colin's right ear, then yanked him closer. He snatched his black belt off the dining room chair and wrapped it around Colin's neck, tightening what looked like a noose.

"Do I need to beat your fucking asses until you do it my way or do I have to *kill* one of you fucking idiots first… to prove I mean business?"

Colin, sweating with tears racing down his terrified face, stood at his mercy quivering and begging.

"No, sir… no, sir… no, sir…" until his words were raspy and faded.

With one swift jolt of the belt, Colin could no longer speak. He stood on the tips of his toes frantically gasping for air with the blood vessels in his neck grossly protruding. We cried out for him to stop choking Colin, but Dad kept him hanging in that terrifying yet routine position, pulling leisurely but firmly at the belt. Colin fought to pull the strap from around his neck but was no match for Dad's strength. His face reddened with terror as his last breath escaped. His body relaxed and fell limp. Dad winced proudly and let go of the belt. Like a puppet on a string, Colin collided with the floor. We froze in panic watching him taking pleasure in what he had done. That wasn't enough, so he violently kicked him in the stomach and ordered him to get up. Colin's wheezing sounded desperate. He fought to catch his breath until he began coughing. With exhausted strength he struggled to curl himself into a tight fetal position.

Dad turned his eyes and feasted on Stan. Stan clumsily stepped back, but it was useless. With one quick move, Dad grabbed him by his throat, gripping his Adam's apple with his claws. Stan's distended eyes turned bloodshot. "You want some too?" he asked slamming Stan's body into the cabinet. He let go of his neck and stepped back as though he were finished. Stan couldn't do anything but gasp sluggishly. Dad broadened his shoulders and exhaled. He let his adrenaline allow him to react savagely as his surge of evil consumed him. He balled up his fist as tightly as he could and punched Stan dead center in his face. Blood sprayed everywhere. Dad rendered a ruthless and intensely brutal blow to his stomach, clipping his rib. After a loud grunt, Stan collapsed into the same fetal position as Colin.

Dad shook the pain off his fist. We knew he wasn't finished. He grabbed Clark and me by our necks, deciding what to do with us. Then, using one hand, he gave me a powerful shove, and I flew out the kitchen and hit the floor.

He glared at me and said, "Get your ass up and take it to bed before you make me beat it." I rolled over, jumped to my feet, then ran up the stairs. Clark knew he was next. As the piercing screams and crying grew fainter, I heard him yelling in his insolent tone for them to begin again, with every plate, cup, and fork.

The break of dawn carried in the bright sunlight representing another day. I wanted to forget what happened, but it was unlikely. I opened my door and walked across the hall to the bathroom and turned the doorknob, but it was locked, so I headed downstairs. Stan, Colin, and Clark were jadedly placing the last few items into the cabinets. They had been up washing dishes the entire night.

The bruises on Stan and Colin were sickening and undoubtedly painful. Colin had a noticeable dark purple ring and scratches around his neck. His lips were split and swollen, with blood resting in the cracks. His left eye was swollen shut. Both had bruises on their face and arms as if they had been in a brutal fight with the devil. Belt welts layered their exposed arms, and some of the welts exposed raw skin. Clark's bruises weren't as severe but his pain and anger was visible. I kissed Stan on the cheek, but pitiably he moved away. His nose was swollen and the slightest touch caused more pain.

"You guys," I said, assessing Dad's imprint on each of them, "I'm sorry."

"Yeah, well, I'm sorry he's our father," Clark responded crossly. *"What's this?* is all he ever says."

Stan placed the last teaspoon in the drawer, and we quietly crept downstairs. Colin walked past the mirror as he entered the bathroom. He backed up and leaned over the white porcelain sink, seething as he examined his beaten reflection in the mirror with his right eye.

"Look at me! Look what he did to us. I don't want to go to school looking like this. He's so doggone arrogant that he's not worried about consequences. He knows no one will say jack! He's sick," Colin muttered under his breath. "That's what he is. Last night was unnecessary." We were silent because there was nothing to say. Colin said it all. "He didn't have to do this. There's absolutely no reason for it! What... Tell me what we did to deserve this? Tell me," Colin demanded, waiting for any excuse. His eyes overflowed with hatred, hurt, and then familiar tears. I felt every ounce of his hatred for Dad, and my own hostility as well.

After that psychotic episode, we knew things would only get worse, and they did. Our parents had become enemies living in the same household. They didn't make an effort to speak to one another, except for scathing insults and arguments. Dad habitually came home looking for anything wrong so he could relieve his frustrations from work. He communicated in an irate manner until he found a pretext to justify his anger and detonate. His mindset was locked in attack mode waiting for an opportunity to strike and feed his raging emotions. Stan, Colin, and Mom remained his victims. Was Dad like that at work? Were they afraid of him, too?

After living in our house for a year, we'd become used to a customary path of unstable emotions running rampant. It wasn't viable to adjust permanently because we never knew *what* was going to happen or when. We celebrated birthdays, went to the movies, played at the park, and had cookouts and family events like normal. Viewing our family from outside our walls, we appeared normal, but we weren't.

My brothers maintained the same routine and went to school with bruises that apparently no one else could see, including the large knots on their heads from Dad slamming them into the floor or wall. I recall a teacher calling home about it once or twice, and Dad's response was that the boys were competitive and often fought. Nothing else came of it. Mom stayed inside when her eyes were black and swollen or wore dark sunglasses if she went out for any reason. She had become withdrawn from anyone outside of the house. She didn't know if the neighbors heard what was going on and whom they may have told.

Dad was good at breaking down what little self-esteem we had. He did it blow-by-blow and word-by-word. He was the inventor of malicious verbal assaults and constant intimidation.

———————

Following work one evening, Dad came home soliciting a detailed report of what Mom accomplished throughout the day. In actuality, he wanted to know what she hadn't done so he could start his predictable performance. He took off his dark blue suit jacket, hung it on the back of the kitchen chair, then removed his red and blue striped tie. He took a quick look around, searching for something to erupt over. He walked into the living room and returned to unbuttoning his white dress shirt. He took it off and laid it on top of his jacket, then said, "It looks the same around here as it did this morning, Alley. What did you do all day, walk around in a tizzy?" He picked up the stack of bills she was supposed to mail.

"What in the hell do you think I did? Don't expect me to answer to you like one of the kids, Colin." After nervously adjusting her blouse with her left hand, she lifted the lit cigarette from the ashtray with her trembling right hand.

"Damn it, Alley, I asked you a simple question, so answer it! I asked you to send this shit out so they don't cut off the damn phone and lights. Mama's birthday card is still sitting here along with the Blue Cross claim. So need I rephrase the question so your simple mind can grasp it? And get rid of that damn cigarette for a change!" He snatched it from her mouth and threw it in the sink. "This place smells like a damn ashtray!"

He tossed the stack of mail back on the counter and shook his head disapprovingly. He grabbed his clothes, went upstairs and changed into a pair of jeans and a white v-neck t-shirt. When he returned fifteen minutes later, Mom lit another cigarette to calm her nerves. She paced the room and he began again.

"I left so your ass had time to fabricate a fucking excuse! The bedroom is a mess, I'm out of clean shirts, all my socks are dirty, but the ashtray is full! To top it off, there's a pile of dirty dishes in the damn sink and—"

"And what, Colin! What else is wrong? Go ahead, tell me what else I haven't done because you sure as hell don't see what I have done around here." She picked up the white basket full of neatly folded laundry and dropped it back to the floor.

"So you're telling me it took you all fucking day to do *one* basket of laundry?" he asked, positioning himself two feet from her, with his confrontational military stance.

"Get your ignorant ass out of my face! I don't have time for another one of your damn mood swings," she yelled angrily.

He didn't move, so she blew her cigarette smoke in his direction. He snatched the cigarette from between her lips and smashed it in the glass astray that rested on the end table.

"What do you have time for? Did you go to work today? Did you pay any bills? Why don't you get your damn driver's license so you can be of some fucking use to me?" he suggested pushing his glasses up on his nose. "So answer the damn question. What did your ass do today?" She tried to leave the room, but he firmly clutched her arm forcing her to remain where she was. "I asked you a damn question."

"Let go of me, Colin," she demanded squirming to get away.

"Let go of you? Are you telling me what to do?" he asked tightening his grip.

"Just let go!"

"Answer the fucking question. What did you have time for—*The Guiding Light*? It looks like your ass didn't do shit except drink coffee, smoke cigarettes, and watch the soaps. You need to *guide* your lazy ass around this house and do some housework for a change." He picked up the empty cup and half-empty pack of cigarettes on the coffee table and inquired sternly, "What's this?" then slammed them back down.

"Damn it, Colin! There you go looking for things to fuss about! Is that all you have to say, *What's this?* That's your standard line to start shit! You look and look and look until you find something to make you angry! That's what makes you happy! You beat me, you beat those boys, and one day you're going to kill little Colin or Stanley! Why can't you leave us alone? Just leave us, Colin! We'd be better off without you," she insisted trying to pull away from him.

"Alley, if I left your sorry ass, you couldn't make it! You can't drive, you don't work, and you can hardly clean a house properly. Who in the hell would hire you to work for them? You're a useless bitch," he shouted, pushing her. He turned to walk away and added, "There's one more thing, Alley. This is my damn house. If you want to leave, then leave, and take those bastards with you!"

"Go to hell. You're nothing but a fucking bully. Don't you think I get tired of your shit? Stop calling our kids bastards. They're not bastards! Your mother raised a bastard herself! You! I'm sick to death of your put-downs!"

She did it. She stepped right into his trap. Quicksand. He instigated an argument, and it worked. Now he had his motive to release his weekly frustrations. In a split second, with one swift, brutal blow, her head hit the wall like a bat hitting a baseball. The loud crash spread through the house. She slid down the wall, then dropped to the floor like a flimsy rag doll and laid there completely discombobulated. Stan and Colin dashed upstairs to the living room as Clark and I darted downstairs. We froze once we were within his reach. With blood dripping from her nose, staining her powder blue nylon shirt, she struggled to her feet using the wall and sofa as a crutch.

"Leave her alone. You already hurt her," I said timidly. That's all I ever seemed to do, plea for Dad to leave her alone.

My body grew stiff when I saw him grip his waist. He turned around and with one powerful wave of his hand slapped me so hard I went flying against the wall. Tears quickly formed. As I lay holding my stinging face, shivering with fear, Mom staggered to her feet using what little strength she had and lunged at him as hard as she could. She jumped on his back and dug her long nails into him screaming insanely. She clawed ferociously at his face while biting him wherever her teeth landed.

His iron fist tightened and he threw a concentrated blow to her stomach. Her feet flew off the ground and she crashed to the floor landing on her back. He leaned over and delivered an excruciating blow to her face, with his right fist clipping her left eye. Her screams were intolerable. Her eye swelled like a balloon. With no sign of remorse, he drew his leg back and kicked her in the stomach. As if that weren't enough, he made sure his foot smashed into her rib cage. A deafening cry escaped from her throat.

"Had enough, Alley?"

Her muffled voice, making its way past her swollen bloody lips, started again. "I hate you," she muttered, then tried to lick the blood off her lips. Her head rolled from side to side as if she were heavily intoxicated. Her bloodstained eyes fluttered uncontrollably.

Lifting her head by a fistful of hair, he replied, "I hate you, too! Look at yourself; as I said before, you're pathetic." He released his grip by thrusting her head forward. With an air of disgust, he brushed the hair he ripped from her head off his hand. "Go clean yourself up before I throw you in the damn trash where you belong," he threatened. He turned to face us. "So, which one of you little bastards is next?" he asked, waiting impatiently for an answer. We were silent. "Exactly what I thought. None of you! Get out of my sight!" As Colin turned to walk away, Dad jabbed him in the back of his head. He locked both hands around his head and ran down the stairs. "Hold on, not so fast," he added, while grabbing me by the back of my scrawny neck. "Don't ever beg for that bitch or I'll knock your ugly ass out the same way I did her," he cautioned, forcing my head in Mom's direction. "Do you want that to happen to you?" he asked, thumping his index finger into my forehead. "Your ugly ass can't help her!" He tightened his grip, swung me backward and thrust me forward causing me to stumble across the room. "I can't stand the sight of you. Go drop dead or something!" My frenzied eyes emptied as a queasy feeling traveled into my stomach. My face turned crimson with humiliation as the moisture from fear induced perspiration dripped down my slender body. I scurried away like a poisoned mouse.

The echoing sounds escaping from our house were torturous. The crying and screaming was loud enough to have brought the police to our door, but it never happened that way. The neighbors either grew used to our routine or thought we incessantly watched a lot of horror movies on a blaring television.

The next few hours continued with Mom moving stiffly between the living room and kitchen, cleaning the mess made from their fight. The six of us remained in Clark and Jimmy's room anticipating what was going to happen next. Clark and I sat on the double bed with Jimmy and Selvin sitting in silence next to me in their matching red footy pajamas. Stan paced back and forth with a troubled expression. Finally, Colin broke the silence, fatigued from the physical cruelty.

"I don't know about you guys, but I can't take this anymore. One day he'll really snap and *kill* one of us," he said convincingly.

Clark stopped gnawing his nails and looked at Colin with surprise, "No kidding, you think? Of course he's trying to kill us. It's recreation for him!"

Colin threw his hands up and continued, "Since you know that, are we supposed to sit here scared to death and wait for it to happen? Huh? This crap's ridiculous. I'm getting the heck out of here. Who wants to come with me?" he asked bravely.

Colin was always clear-cut and dry. He rarely hid his emotions from us, but he reserved them when it came to Dad.

"He's nuts. I wish someone would beat him the way he does us and Mom," Clark added.

"Geez, you guys, just chill out a minute and listen. I've been running away for years, and they keep bringing me back." Stan walked over and put his hand on Colin's shoulder. He clenched his jaws, carefully selecting his words. "Think about it. I was asking *you* to run away with *me*, and you wouldn't go. All of a sudden, everything's changed because it's about you. It's been the same since we were little. Haven't you learned from *my* experiences that we'd end up right back here? It's much worse when he catches you and I have the scars to prove it. If we did run, where would we go? Tell me, where?" None of us responded. "Okay then, all we can do is deal with it, for now. Besides, what about them?" he said, pointing at Jimmy, Selvin, and me.

Selvin turned his little head toward Stan, then looked up at me. He was studying my expression. I didn't want him to worry, so I rubbed his hair and gave him a slight smile, but that didn't suffice.

Selvin sat upright and asked, "What does he mean, what about them? Who are them?"

"Nobody's going anywhere, spider monkey," I said, kissing him on the cheek. I gradually forced him to lie down.

Jimmy sat with his face half buried in the green bedspread. His face carried an obstinate expression. He didn't comment. Jimmy simply internalized everything and thought we never noticed, but I did.

A frustrated Colin pushed Stan's hand off his shoulder. "Man, anywhere is better than here. Anywhere," he said, slightly raising his voice. He pulled the gray muscle shirt over his head and threw it on the bed. "I'm tired of being his whipping board and beaten to a pulp because he's pissed off," he said displaying unsightly marks covering his chest and back. "I'm sick of seeing our mother like that! Aren't you? We hear that crap every other night. I can barely sleep around here," he said letting out a wide yawn. "I have belt and extension cord welts all over my body."

Colin plopped down on the floor and sat with his knees bent. He clasped his hands together, then rested his chin on them. The pulsation of the veins in his temples grew more visible as his jaws tightened, and the muscles around them pounded in and out.

"I know exactly how you feel. That's why I've tried to get out of here because, like he says, we're a bunch of useless you know whats. Technically, he's right. Who cares about helping us? Man, we've gone to school black and blue, obvious bruises, knots on our heads, black eyes, swollen lips, and belt marks. Think about it, has anyone shown concern? Remember last month when we went to school beaten to smithereens? Who said anything about it? The only person who ever questioned us was Mr. Barnes and still nothing happened. What about the neighbors? Tell me they don't hear this screaming. This is nuts and you know it. Grandma knows what he's like, but it's her son so she doesn't say anything. When I told her what happened the last time I ran away she called and told him where I was. People don't care, man, so there's nothing or nobody out there who can protect us. If I thought there was, I'd keep trying to find it. It's a bummer but this is it," he said looking around the room. "All we have is each other and nothing else."

"That's an understatement," Clark mumbled. "I hate his guts."

"Stan, we're always pissing him off for one reason or another. And Mom... He's never going to stop beating her. He brags about how much he hates us. Why are we even here? He doesn't want us," Colin announced, pounding his fists on the side of the dresser.

"Sshhh," I whispered. "He'll hear us and then—"

"Who cares about him?" he asked dismissing my warning. "Think about all the stuff he's done to us, then look what he did to our mother. Go ahead. Look at her. What'd she do to deserve that? Black eyes, teeth knocked out, bruises all over her. How many times have we seen her with swollen, bloody lips, and a swollen jaw? What about the time I picked on Marala for wearing dresses? Do you remember what he did to me? That was plain sick! You don't think that stuff affects me. It does. It stays right here," he said, pointing at his temple. "Right here! I'll remember this crap for the rest of my life... if I live long enough!"

I lowered my head as embarrassment swept across my face since I was the one who asked Dad to make Colin stop teasing me. I should have known better. I did know better.

Colin didn't look at me. He continued. "He put me in one of her dresses and tied ribbons in my hair... ribbons! Then he made me sit in the front yard so people would see me! Do you know how I felt? Do you know how many people saw me like that, because I teased my kid sister?" His eyes welled with tears. "He beats the crap out of us and sends us to bed without eating. One meal is no big deal, but for three days... that's insane! What kind of punishment is that? Marala and Mommy have to try to sneak food down to us by rolling it up in their shirts. And we all know what happens when they're caught."

"I know exactly what you're saying about the teachers," Clark admitted. "If little Johnny or Susie went to school like that, the police would be at their door tomorrow. But because we're black, we have no value to anybody. They think since our ancestors were slaves, we're used to being beaten! We're prisoners in this house," he said wiping his sweaty palms on his pants.

"Look you guys; like I said before, running away isn't the solution," Stan acknowledged.

Clark stood and faced Stan. "Then what's the solution? Like Colin said, are we supposed to sit here until he kills one of us? I'd rather take the risk and get out of here! We're older now. Let's jump a freight train and ride it the heck away from here."

"You know that's not the solution," Stan explained.

"Then what is? What's the solution?" Colin questioned. "What do you think we should do, let him kill our mother or continue beating her to a pulp? We're afraid to help her. Think about it. He's got us so terrified that we don't help her. This is a sick way to live."

"That's right it is. I agree with that," Stan admitted. "You know it's not that I don't feel the way you guys do but—"

"But what? You want us to stay and take it? I'm sick of taking it. You don't know what it's like for me. You have no idea!" He got up and walked over to the window with his temples flaring from his clenching teeth. He pushed the curtains aside and stared out the window so we couldn't see his tears.

Stan walked up behind Colin and stood quietly for a moment beginning to choke up. With his voice cracking, he confessed, "I'm not siding with him. All I'm saying is it's not worth running anymore because we're running to nowhere. Don't you get that?" Stan's eyes were glassy. "You forget, I'm right there with you. I get it, too, dork," he said patting Colin's back. "Don't you think I hurt as much as you do? What about the rest of us? How would you feel if Mom ran away? Think about it, every time we run away, it only makes it worse for everyone. Remember I used to ask you to go with me. What'd you say then?" he asked with a light chuckle, trying to hide his uneasiness. "*It only makes it worse*. And, man, don't ever say that *I*, of all people, don't know what it's like, especially after the beatings he gives me. Screw that," he said.

"Yeah, Colin, I have to agree with Stan on that one. It's not just you, it's all of us. That's kind of selfish for you to think you're the only target when Mom's downstairs like that," Clark stated angrily rolling his eyes.

"No... No... No! You don't understand either! He hates me more; that's why he beats me harder! You've seen how he hits me! Every blow... it's like he's trying to kill me," he said overflowing with raw emotion pounding his fist on the window ledge. "That's why I have to get out of here. Then I won't have to worry about him coming home. It'll be like he doesn't exist. One day he won't be able to find me, and I'll stay as far away from him as possible, you'll see! That's if he doesn't kill me first." He took a deep breath and asked, "Why does he hate me so much? What'd I ever do to him?"

The door swung open, banging against the wall. Dad stood with his hands on his waist and his belt hanging from his right hand. Stan and Clark jumped to an attention position as they backed away from him. Colin didn't move. I slid to the corner of the bed and wrapped my arms around Jimmy and Selvin.

"What did you do to me? Let me help you with that answer," he said with a lackadaisical attitude. "You were born, sorry ass," he replied, staring at Colin. "So… if I understand correctly, I have a bunch of bastards who want to run away. Be my guest! You're all useless! Who would like to be the first?"

None of us said a word as he examined our faces.

"I'm not the one who wanted you ugly ass motherfuckers in the first damn place," he insisted, looking over his glasses. "Had it been up to me, I wouldn't have any of you now." He shifted his eyes toward me. "All of you are nothing but a fucking inconvenience. Do you get that? I'd like nothing more than to pack every one of you up and ship you off somewhere to get rid of you for good. The fact remains that I'm the one who's stuck with you and that pathetic bitch downstairs."

I dropped my head so he couldn't gain the satisfaction of seeing the devastation he filled me with. My head ached. I sat biting my lip as my body absorbed his hefty dose of hatred. I knew he felt that way, but hearing it so often slashed through me like a razor blade.

"If any of you motherfuckers don't like it here… we can always arrange something else!" He grabbed the other end of his folded belt and snapped it. "Now, back to my initial question, who wants to be the first to run?"

Stan was nearest to Dad, and already trembling with fear when Dad reached over and grabbed his arm. He viciously swung the belt buckle with as much strength as possible letting it rip through Stan. The painful hollering reverberated off the walls. Stan's thin body savagely jumped and jerked any way possible to avoid the pain from the skin being carved off his body. Jimmy watched out of the corner of his eyes as Selvin shoved his head into the narrow of my back weeping quietly.

Almost instantly, Mom staggered into the room, having forgotten her own beating twenty minutes prior.

"Colin, that's enough! Enough, I said! Enough… enough… enough… enough… enough!" Passionately, she yanked her son from Dad's evil grip, wrapped her badly bruised arms around him, and dropped to the floor with her back shielding his body.

"Look who's back for more." He bent down and whispered invitingly in her ear, "I thought you'd had enough."

She glanced at him from the corner of her eye and admitted apologetically, "I did."

He stood and suggested adamantly, "I suggest you take your simple ass back down those stairs before I throw you down them."

"Throw me down the damn stairs. If that's going to make you feel better, then come on, throw me down the stairs. Beat me… Beat me, Colin! But damn it, leave *my* kids alone! Leave them alone! They never did anything to you," she said yelling in a frenzy. "Never!"

"You're right. You did. You had them. Let's get one thing clear… these little bastards are my fucking financial responsibility and I'll beat their asses whenever and however I want!" He leaned down and thumped his finger into her swollen forehead, causing her to draw back.

"Colin, that's enough! Look at Stanley. Look what you've done to this boy." Mom rose to her feet and shoved Stanley behind her back, then ushered the rest of us out of the room before he noticed what she was doing. With a swift movement, she blocked the doorway and waited for him to confront her with more of his brutality.

A heavy silence flowed throughout the house for several minutes as we sat clustered in Stan and Colin's room with the door shut. Breaking the silence was the sound of the side door slamming, followed by the car speeding away from the house. Clark peeked out of the window, sighing with relief as he announced, "He's gone!" We rushed back upstairs to find Mom sitting on the edge of her bed with her back to us. Her blouse was torn and hanging off her left shoulder. She was staring blankly out the window into the backyard, trying impatiently to light a cigarette. We stood quietly behind her, not knowing what to say.

"Why don't you kids get in bed before your father gets back? We've had enough of his mess tonight."

"Mom, can we sit with you for a little while... please?" I asked warily.

"No, Marala. I need you kids to get in bed," she said breathing with great difficulty. "You know he's never gone long, so you'd better do as I say. He'll start up again if you all are up when he gets back," she explained, holding her side as she spoke.

"At least, let me put some ice on your eye before it—" Colin began.

"No. No! Now go on, I mean it... Get in bed. Get out of here."

"Thanks, Mom," Stan said softly. He left the room, gently shutting the door behind him.

The next few days were quiet due to the choking tension that filled the air. Dad went to work and by the time he came home, the house was spotless, dinner was cooked, and we were fed and in bed. She helped us avoid him whenever he was around so we were less of a target. We spoke in soft whispers so he wouldn't detect our conversations. The apprehension lived within us.

At this point, terror reigned. Mom's confidence was gone, and she became reticent. She wasn't the same person she used to be. The mother I had always known threw her body in front of Dad to protect us. Nowadays she'd leave the room and come back when and *if* she gathered enough vigor to deal with him. Until now, she returned the hostility and fought back. Now, she shields her body and accepts the abuse while begging for mercy he doesn't have.

CHAPTER TWO

He who neglects discipline despises himself,
but he who listens to reproof acquires
understanding.

Proverbs 15:32
New American Standard

It was a blistering ninety-two degrees outside with the sun's rays burning the cement beneath our bare feet. I raced into the house with Stan, Colin, and Clark trailing behind me with their hands full of firecrackers wrapped in red and blue paper. As Stan yelled for Jimmy and me to come outside and watch them go off, he caught Mom's attention.

"Hold on just one minute there," she said, stopping them in their tracks. "Where'd you all get those things? And don't tell me you bought them or you'll be taking them right back to the store, and I mean *right back*," she said disapprovingly.

She lifted the lid on a large silver pot of collard and turnip greens with two large ham hocks beginning to boil allowing the delicious aroma to escape.

"Robbie gave them to us," Colin lied. Colin loved to blame Robbie for things, and most of the time it worked.

Robbie was an unmanageable redheaded eleven-year-old flunky who lived next door to us. He hung out with my brothers and always claimed to be black although he was white. He would have been black… and blue if he lived in our house! My brothers loved playing with him because Robbie was daring, fun, foolish, and as Colin said retarded. Mom said he wasn't retarded; he just acted that way.

Whenever Robbie came across something that he shouldn't have, he brought it directly to my brothers because he was certain that they would know what to do with it, which they always did. When Robbie's mother went grocery shopping, he snuck boxes of the good cereal over to us. "Good cereal" was anything other than oatmeal, cornflakes, or a plastic bag of puffed wheat. His father was always looking for the snacks that Robbie gave to my brothers before his mother had a chance to put them away. Whenever Robbie said that he couldn't get something they wanted, Clark threatened to tell his father. The threat usually worked. Generally they got whatever they asked for.

"I don't know if I like the idea of you all playing with firecrackers. Before you go burning down the neighborhood, I want you to wait until your father gets home so he can supervise you all. I have work to do. Go back outside and play. Now go on … get." She pointed for us to go out the side door, then turned the greens down to a low flame. She went into the living room and began wiping the last bit of Pledge wax off the record player with a white cloth.

"You know Dad won't let us light these. He thinks we're idiots," Stan said following behind her.

"No, he thinks you're an idiot," Colin said chiming in with a long raspy laugh.

"We'll be careful. I promise. You have *my* word." Stan begged with his most believable face. Colin and Clark supported Stan's plea, but it was completely unconvincing.

"I don't know… you all *always* seem to find trouble no matter what you're doing. It doesn't take much," she said shaking her head distrustfully.

"*Always*, Mom? Don't you think *always* is a little extreme? Sometimes trouble happens to find us," Stan said with a playful chuckle as he gave her a big hug. "I'll be the one who lights them. How's that sound? Will that work?" He locked eyes with her and she studied his face with a loving expression. "Mom, look, this is it. This is all we have. This can't hurt anyone." Stan pulled his front pockets inside out and opened his fist, displaying what was in his hand. He turned to face Colin and said, "Show her what you have."

"Naw, man," Colin said defiantly.

"Don't make a big deal out of it. Just show her," he insisted.

Colin opened his fist with a sly crooked smirk. "This is it. This is all *Robbie* gave us, right here. See?"

"Boy, you'd better empty those damn pockets! All you ever do is get into things you're not supposed to. If you want to know the truth, you'd be the one blowing up the damn neighborhood." She slammed the furniture polish down and squinted her eyes at Colin. "Now let me see your pockets… Or you know the damn answer," she scolded impatiently.

"Come on, Mom, don't you trust me? I'm not going to blow up anything." Colin's eyes widened as he caught sight of Clark standing behind Mom covering his mouth laughing hysterically.

"Hell no, I don't trust you. Colin, let me see your pockets! This is the last time I'm asking."

"Geez," he said, pulling his pockets inside out. He turned around and patted his butt. "See, I don't have anything in my front or back pockets. I just have these." Once more, he showed her the few firecrackers he had in his hand. "Are you happy?"

"Am I happy? Boy, you'd better be the one happy that I'm not whipping your ass for getting smart with me. Watch your damn mouth," she said threatening Colin with the back of her hand. "I already get that shit from your father and I'm not about to take it from a child! You wouldn't talk to him that way, now would you?" Colin dropped his head. She stared at him disappointedly. "*If* I let you light those things and I do mean *if...* you'd better be damn careful because they can really hurt someone."

Mom walked over and stood directly behind me, then began braiding my ponytail as she deliberated for a few moments. I knew she was trying to determine what the odds were that something would go wrong.

"Okay. I'm sorry, Mom," Colin conceded without conviction. "Can we get back to the original question? Can we ... I mean, can little Stanley light the firecrackers?"

Stan frowned.

Even while doing housework, Mom was absolutely beautiful. She had on black knee-length shorts, and a blue and red sleeveless blouse with black trim around the neckline. The tone muscles in her arms and legs were defined. Her hair had soft curls held off her face by black bobby pins. Tiny beads of sweat were beginning to form on her nose and on her soft freckles.

Mom saw us standing there with our most pathetic yet persuasive faces. She picked up her half full glass of Pepsi and took a long drink. Still considering our request, she leaned over and picked up the cigarette in the ashtray on the table, then took a drag and held it. After blowing the smoke out of her nose, she looked at us one at a time then agreed.

"I have to wax the kitchen floor, and you all need to stay off it until it's dry, so... *fine*. But *you* light those firecrackers, Stanley," she demanded, pointing her cigarette at him. "And Colin, you'd better make sure the rest of them stay far back and watch... And I mean just watch! It's your responsibility to keep the kids away from those things. What you two have in your hands better be all you plan on lighting. I'm not playing with you all! That better be it. And I don't want to find out that little Robbie boy got blown up, so keep his little behind back. Do you hear me?"

We shook our heads and anxiously darted out the side door, leaving it to slam before Mom had a chance to add anything else. She could have given us any rules she wanted, and all we would have heard was "*fine.*"

Stan, Colin, and Clark went into the middle of the street to set things up. Stan laid his firecrackers on the ground when Colin pushed him aside and said; "Thanks, buddy, but we've got it from here. Go sit with the kids, twerp."

Clark pulled about ten more firecrackers from his pockets, which were double what Stan and Colin had shown Mom. Carefully they arranged them, then Colin pulled a bag of rocket powder from his left sock and added it to the pile. Angrily, Stan protested.

"Mom said we could light *firecrackers.* She didn't say anything about that stuff. And where'd you get those?" His eyes scrunched together and he pointed at Clark's full hand. "Where'd that rocket powder come from?"

"Man, shut up. You sound like a little girl," Clark said haughtily.

Stan circled them in the street as he wiped his sweaty forehead with his shirt.

"We can't use that stuff. Let's do what she said for a change," Stan continued. "*I* promised we'd be careful."

"You're right. *You* promised," Colin joked.

"Come on, man. We told Mom all we were lighting was what we showed her—"

"Wrong," Colin exclaimed, interrupting him, "*You* told her that. You didn't say anything about what I have in my sock or what Clark has." His raspy laugh seemed to ricochet off the houses.

Clark stepped in front of Colin and said, "Don't worry about it. Firecrackers are like snap n' pops. But this stuff here..." He shook the bag of powder in front of Stan. "Will really set them off."

"Why do you have to act like an ignoramus all the time? You're nothing but Colin's flunky. Mom's right, we need to start listening before something happens. If anyone gets hurt, it's on me, not you," Stan said, grabbing Jimmy and Selvin around their shoulders and walking them to our plush green yard. I followed as Robbie impatiently jumped around like a monkey, yelling for them to light the firecrackers as if he'd lost his mind. "Guys, are you sure about this?" Stan asked with a great deal of concern controlling his voice, one last time. "Because I'm not!"

"Are *we* sure?" Colin pulled the lighter out of his sock and lit them. "What do you think?"

"Yeah, punk, we're sure," Clark said, slowly backing away from the firecrackers.

"You guys are out of control," Stan added, giving a dirty look to Clark.

"So what," Clark replied.

"Here they go, buttheads," Colin announced. "This one's for you, *Manley Stanley*."

Colin and Clark raced across the street toward the neighbor's lawn.

Robbie clapped with an impish smile on his face and repeated, "Here they go. Here they go, buttheads!"

Eagerly we watched but nothing happened. Gradually, smoke began to spread, but still no blast.

"Man, it didn't light. Something's wrong with them."

"Instead of being Curious George the monkey, you're Curious Clark the idiot. Don't be impatient. Just wait. It takes a few seconds for everything to catch," Colin explained.

"Look idiot, it's not lit. I'm going to check it out." Without hesitation, Clark ran to the pile of firecrackers and got down on his hands and knees to see what the problem was. Audaciously, he tinkered with the fireworks as the flames continued to travel up their fuses.

"No, dummy, get back! Get back, you little maggot," Stan yelled, running toward Clark.

"Leave them alone," Colin insisted. "Don't be a fool. They'll go off any second!" He sprung to his feet and sprinted toward Clark.

Disregarding the warnings of Stan and Colin, Clark remained in a kneeling position trying to determine why there wasn't an explosion. However, Stan and Colin couldn't reach him before the most thunderous blast filled the air with the acrid smell of sulfur, followed by a loud discharge of random pops like a machine gun. Billowing smoke encased us as the explosions continued to erupt. Stan and Colin jumped back while covering their faces as the blast propelled Clark. Hysterical screams filled the air. The blast was only a foot away from Clark's face, leaving him in a terrible state of shock.

"Brother," I screamed, running toward him. "Are you all right? Are you okay?"

Robbie, Selvin, and Jimmy were speechless as our panic took over. His peeling hands covered his face as he laid there screaming as loud as he could, "Help me! Help me! It hurts!" Colin quickly removed his white t-shirt and covered Clark's face shielding him from the powerful rays of the sun. He tried to sneak a quick look at his face to assess the damage, but Clark kept screaming while refusing to reveal it. Colin grabbed his legs, and Stan lifted his shoulders as they carried him into the house while trying to calm him. Clark jerked back and forth as the earsplitting screams grew more intense.

"I can't see! I can't see," Clark hollered.

I instructed Robbie to go home, then rushed into the house, dragging Jimmy and Selvin by their hands. The door slammed behind Stan and Colin as they placed Clark on the living room carpet.

"Mom! Mom," I shouted, leaping down the stairs, searching for her. "Clark's hurt! The firecrackers blew up in his face! They blew him up!"

She dropped her laundry and followed the hysterical screams upstairs. She saw Clark lying on the floor shuddering. His skin was peeling away from his trembling hands and face.

"Clark! Oh, my God, Clark! What happened to him? How did this happen? Stanley, answer me," she demanded dropping to her knees.

"It was the firecrackers. We told him to get back, but he didn't listen," Stan explained.

"Firecrackers didn't do this!" she said, trying to pry Clark's trembling hands from his face.

Stan dug his toes into the carpet, lowered his head, and said in a hushed tone, "They added rocket powder, M80s, and lady fingers."

In complete disbelief, she paused long enough to glance at Stan, then Colin. Her caramel complexion had a sweltering wave of crimson pass underneath it. Her eyes narrowed and became furious.

"Damn you kids! Damn you!" she shouted angrily. "Stanley, get a bowl of cold water, washrags, and a towel. Hurry! The rest of you… get out of here. Get out!"

"For the record, we told him—"

"Colin, enough! I don't want to hear a word from you. Not one word," she said shaking her finger at him. "I know this was your doing! I know it!"

"Mom, you don't understand. I didn't know he was going to—"

"Brother, just leave before you upset her even more," Stan advised, pushing Colin away from Mom.

"Stanley, help me get him upstairs. Lift his legs."

She grabbed his shoulders and lifted him. As soon as they moved him, he started screaming even louder, "Don't touch me! Please don't touch me!"

Once they laid him on Mom's bed, she began nursing Clark as if she were a doctor trying to relieve the pain and calm him down. She knew exactly what to do, but it didn't include a trip to the hospital. Stan was the only one she let in and out of the room.

A half hour later, the screaming ceased, but neither Stan nor Mom came out of the room. We sat quietly in the family room and waited. Two hours afterward Stan came down to see if we were all right. He kept his eyes fixed firmly on the television and walked past Colin without a word. Stan fell back onto the yellow beanbag and let out a long wispy sigh.

With a guilt-ridden expression, Colin sat slouched in his chair looking at the floor. After a few minutes he broke the silence. "I warned him. I told him to get back! He didn't listen so what was I supposed to do?" he asked throwing his hands up. "I ran after him but he's hard-headed. You know how he is," he said observing the rest of our expressions.

Selvin and Jimmy looked at Colin shamefully.

Stan explained, "Listen, brother, now's not the time to start blaming anybody. You're right, Clark didn't listen, and neither did we, but it doesn't matter at this point."

"How is he?" Colin asked, moving to the edge of his seat with his hands clutched together.

"He's not in the best of shape. I mean, he's pretty messed up is all I'm saying. I thought he needed to go to the hospital, but Mom doesn't drive; she's afraid of Dad finding out and whatever else. His skin is peeling and he doesn't look the same, at least not now," Stan said.

"What's she going to do?" I asked.

"I don't know; just keep taking care of him, I guess. She said she wants to make sure he doesn't run a fever since that's a sign of infection."

"Did he blow off his hands or anything?" Selvin asked twisting in his seat.

Stan reached over and rubbed Selvin's hair and replied, "Naw, he didn't blow anything off, thank God."

Colin looked up and surveyed the room examining everything except Stan. "Is Mom pissed at me?" he asked worriedly.

"You'll have to ask her. She didn't want to talk about what happened. She was busy taking care of Clark."

Jimmy reached for the television and changed the channel to *Speed Racer.* He folded his arms tightly across his chest and sat without saying a word.

"Do you want to know anything, Jimmy?" Stan asked as he leaned over to kiss him. Jimmy pulled away, trying to avoid his kiss, but it was too late. Annoyed, he wiped it off his forehead and folded his arms tightly again. He focused on the television and nothing else.

Twenty minutes passed before Mom called us upstairs so she could inform us about Clark's condition. With the door closed behind her, she stood in the hallway explaining that he'd eventually heal, but with some scarring since most of his burns were to his face and hands. His facial hair, including his eyebrows and eyelashes, were completely singed off. His pink skin was peeling and blistering. He had some contusions and lacerations that would eventually heal. He could have lost his sight but didn't. He was spared only through the grace of God. She put some type of cream on him, gave him aspirin for the pain, and closed the curtains so the sun's heat wouldn't aggravate the burns.

"Why didn't we take him to the hospital?" I asked.

"So your father would find out and beat you all for it?"

Again, the wrath of Dad influenced Mom's actions, even in the event of a crisis. The trepidation of what would happen to us caused Mom not to provide Clark with proper medical attention. Dad had full Blue Cross and Blue Shield insurance, but it didn't matter. Clark had the risk of infection, scarring, and whatever else, but the threat of Dad finding out was more daunting.

We were grateful that she knew what to do because in reality, Mom was keeping all of us from a beating. We entered Mom's room to find Clark serenely lying across the queen-sized bed with cool washcloths covering his face, arms, and hands. There was a plastic bowl lying on the floor filled with water and a bottle of aspirin on the nightstand. Selvin, Jimmy, and I sat on the floor next to Colin and Stan, waiting for Mom to begin her animated lecture.

"You all just don't listen, do you? I've told you all repeatedly what to do, and you'd think by now you'd do it! Disaster follows you all like flies on shit, and you never think about the consequences! Never! Oh, and you think you're out of the woods? Well, not yet. Trust me, it's not over either. You know what that man is like or have you all mysteriously forgotten? If your father finds out what happened today, you know what will happen. You can count on it! I don't think I need to tell you what he'd do over something like this, now do I?" She pulled a cigarette and book of matches from her purse. As she ripped a single match from the book, she glanced at Clark, then shoved them back into her purse. "I never understand why you all don't listen to me! Your father and I fight because of this kind of nonsense." Stan looked over at Colin. Colin looked away. "If you all want to do something for me, learn to listen. You all think you know what you're doing half the damn time and you don't. And you don't because you don't think! Your brother could have lost his damn sight over this mess! Stanley, I told you to light those things, and Colin, I told you to keep the kids back.

Now what didn't you understand about that? Clark wasn't supposed to be near those things. But again, you all don't listen!" She turned around, took a long look at Clark lying across the bed, and shook her head. Now she had to worry about Dad finding out.

Mom instructed us to go downstairs and let Clark rest for a while longer. We remained quiet because we didn't want to upset her any more than we already had. Sorely, Clark crept downstairs four hours later. When we saw his face, no one said a word for a few moments. We were sitting at the kitchen table in shock!

Finally, Selvin broke the uncomfortable silence. "Did the bomb do that?" he asked innocently.

"No, it wasn't a bomb that did this," Clark softly explained. "It was the firecrackers we lit."

Jimmy stared at Clark for a few minutes with a stern look on his face. His eyes were always serious, and they rarely smiled. He was a handsome little boy who was usually quiet and calm. Every so often, he turned into the same rambunctious child that Robbie was. His reddish brown hair had soft fluffy curls about two inches high. He had the best grade of hair of us all. His butterscotch complexion was smooth and unblemished except for the small chickenpox scar slightly above his left cheekbone. Like Mom, he, too, had freckles that matched his hair color. His frame was lean and his posture good. He didn't talk much, but he was vigilant. Jimmy was extremely intelligent and frequently made remarks that were pragmatic.

"Was it fun?" Jimmy asked with a shrewd look in his eyes. "You didn't listen to anyone, so you must have thought it would be fun. So was it?"

"Does it look like I had fun to you?" Clark asked growing louder.

"I thought it did, the way you fell back and started rolling around." He shoved his hands in his tight pockets and shrugged. "Stan told you to listen to Mommy but you didn't. You always think you're so funny, so I thought it must have been fun. Then we wonder why Dad beats Mommy up all the time." Jimmy didn't wait for a response; he opened the freezer and reached for a Popsicle. He gave Clark a restrained smile while shaking his head disapprovingly. He slid the patio door open and went out back.

"Can I have one, too?" Selvin asked tugging on my shirt.

I handed him a cherry Popsicle and sent him outside with Jimmy.

Everything was quiet for a few minutes. Clark slouched in the chair next to me. Colin sat directly across from him. It didn't take long for Colin's look of remorse to turn into a smile. His lips began to quiver as he tried to hold in the laughter.

The three of us began to examine Clark more closely... then we lost it.

"Wow," Colin started. "All I can say is don't go near a mirror, little buddy. You belong in a circus!"

"Piss off," Clark snapped angrily.

"Stop it right now! There's nothing funny about this, so cut it out!" Mom said turning the corner. She was trying to control her own smile. She reached inside her purse and pulled out a black eyeliner. "Boy, come here and let me work on your face." Delicately moving the pencil, she created the appearance of eyebrows while Clark flinched and grunted at each stroke.

"Stanley, you're the artist. What do you think?"

Stan laughed harder as he touched up Clark's eyebrows. Mom handed Clark a blue hat and said, "Wear this until you look normal again."

"Normal? That won't be for awhile." Colin chuckled.

"You're probably right about that, but let's hope not," Mom replied.

"Mom, what are you going to do about Clark's eyelashes and nose hairs?" Colin teased with us giggling in the background.

"That's enough! Leave your brother alone. Clark, stay out of your father's way and I don't want him to hear a word about this, do you hear me?" she asked glancing at the four of us.

We nodded in agreement, still laughing.

"Go in the backyard or find something to keep busy so you're not around your father when he comes in. And if you go outside, don't leave the yard because I don't want you all anywhere near that old biddy's damn house," she explained while opening a bottle of aspirin.

"Don't worry, we'll stay away from that old bat," Colin joked.

"You'd better, Colin. And you're damn lucky nothing happened to that little bad ass Robbie! You have the nerve to call him retarded. But he's smart enough to give the damn firecrackers to you all so you can let your brother practically blow off his damn face. Colin, the only reason I'm letting you go *back* outside is that if you keep walking past me, I'm going to beat your behind for not listening. So get out of my sight before you upset me even more." She paused and turned toward Clark. "You've had enough activity for today, so I want you to stay inside since the sunlight will only make the burns worse. You'll probably blister," she said closely inspecting his face. "Take this aspirin and go lie down."

She handed him two aspirin, then kissed him gently on top of his head. Clark headed into the kitchen to pour himself a glass of water. Mom returned to the living room with her purse and rested in her favorite chair. She crossed her legs, pulled the cigarettes out of her purse, and began nervously rocking back and forth.

"Mom, you want Clark to light that for you?" Colin joked, following her into the living room.

"Colin, take your ass outside or put it to bed. You got that?"

"You know, Mom, instead of playing outside, I'm going downstairs to play Battleship with Stan. We're going to *blow up* ships."

"Colin, shut up," Clark snapped. "This isn't funny. It could have been you."

"No way, firecracker boy. If I played you in checkers, you'd probably rub them together and catch the rest of your stupid butt on fire. At least you can bet your life on one thing, little buddy. And I do mean, little buddy. You're the only person dumb enough to pull a stunt like that, Gilligan!"

"Colin! Now that's enough. You and Stan were supposed to be watching your brother, so I don't want to hear anymore teasing out of you. I mean it! Keep running your mouth and I'll get out of this chair and whip your butt for not doing what you were told. Now go outside and play before I change my mind. You're getting on my last damn nerve."

"All right, I'm sorry, Mom. Come on, Stan. Marala, let's find Clark's eyebrows before it rains and they wash away." Colin's hysterical laughter continued.

Around nine-thirty that evening Dad strolled in from work as we were filing in from the yard. He went upstairs, changed from his gray suit into a pair of jeans and a blue short-sleeved shirt, then came down for dinner.

"Hi, Dad," I said.

"How was your day, sweetheart?" He kissed me on the forehead and sat down with the *Chronicle Telegram* in his hand.

"It was okay. How was your day?"

He opened the paper to the funnies and handed them to me.

"It's the same as always. Long, tiring, and busy."

"Alley, what went on here today?"

"Nothing out of the ordinary. Why?" Her eyes instructed me to go downstairs.

"I have a feeling something happened that I should know about, that's why. Don't you think it's unusually quiet?"

"Colin, you always have a feeling there's something you should know about because you're nosey."

"No, that's because I'm concerned," he said with a deep chuckle. "Did Mama call today?"

"No, Colin, your mother didn't call today, thank God. But if she had, she would have asked me the same damn question. *What went on there today?*"

"Don't start running your mouth about my mother. You have a family of nosey and lazy ass sisters calling to find out my business. Mama's not nosey, she's inquisitive," he added, throwing Mom a gentle smile.

"Oh, that's what you call it?" She released a big smile and set a large plate of her pot roast, potatoes, greens, and cornbread in front of him.

"Thank you, Alley," he said, then took a few seconds to bless his food. "I had a taste for this tonight. Is that your homemade peach cobbler I smell?"

"You know it is," she said pleasantly. "Would you like some later?"

"Of course, thank you. What a pleasant surprise for a change," he said.

"Well, I'm glad I can finally make you happy." She kissed him on the cheek and went back into the kitchen. She pulled the metal ice tray from the freezer, loaded a glass with ice, filled it with Pepsi, and took a sip.

"Can I get another piece of cornbread?"

"Is there anything else?"

"I'll have a beer. Thanks."

Mom cut the cornbread, placed it on a saucer, and set it on the table with a beer.

He opened the newspaper to the business section, then began eating. At that moment, Clark came downstairs and timidly turned the corner, heading into the family room. Dad caught him off guard.

"How are you, son?"

"Oh, I'm all right," he replied nervously.

"Then take that hat off in this house, and you'll continue to be," he added pulling a piece of tender meat away from the bone with his fork.

"Yes, sir."

He watched Clark as he removed his hat. Clark kept his head down low so he wouldn't focus on his face, but it was too late. He sat the paper on the chair next to him, and stared at Clark's face with confusion.

"You look fucking weird," he announced.

Quickly, Clark disappeared downstairs without bringing further notice to himself. Stan and Colin began to head toward the kitchen, but saw Dad sitting at the table and turned to go back downstairs.

"Hold up," he said snapping his fingers two times. "Where are you clowns going in such a hurry?" They shrugged. "Tell me something. What went on here today?"

"Today?" Stan repeated.

"No. Tomorrow, idiot. Of course I mean today." Stan and Colin caught Mom in the corner of the kitchen leaning against the counter, shaking her head for him not to say anything. He hesitated for a moment before answering.

"Nothing, sir," Stan said, answering quickly.

"Nothing. Then what's with the hesitation?"

"Sir, all I'm saying is that nothing major went on besides the usual."

He turned his attention to Colin and said, "Well, then, let me ask you and see what kind of answer you give me. I find it amusing that your brother there said nothing went on because that's not what your mother told me. I've already heard her version, so now I want to hear it from you. I'm going to ask you one time and one time only. What went on here today?"

With clear apprehension they looked at Mom. Again, she shook her head for them not to say anything. When Dad was suspicious of something, this was the way he obtained the facts. Most of the time it actually worked.

"Sir, nothing went on, sir," he said, fumbling over his words. "The only thing was that Mrs. Kelly accused us of throwing tomatoes in her yard and we were playing out front at the time. Mom knew we didn't do it because she was in the backyard with Selvin."

"Is that right, Alley?"

"Colin, the boys didn't do anything. That woman's just mean."

"Did she say something to you or the boys?"

"Yeah, she came over here wanting them to clean it up. That woman claims there were rotten apples and tomatoes flying over the damn fence from our yard this morning. Now I know that's not possible since I was out back with Selvin at the time. I told her crazy behind that. That's like accusing me of doing it since the boys weren't around."

"Well, did you?" he asked with a light-hearted smirk.

"What do you think, Colin?"

"You all stay away from that woman's yard and her. Let me deal with the neighbors around here. She's always had a problem with us. I'll talk to Bob about it. Maybe she's seeing things or having an early menopause."

"Let the boys go take their showers so they can get ready for bed."

"You're both dismissed."

The funny thing about Colin was he could throw a ball, and he definitely threw the rotten tomatoes and apples all the way from Robbie's backyard over Mom's head into Mrs. Kelly's yard. We didn't have a garden, but Robbie's Mom kept tomatoes, squash, and all types of fruits in baskets on her patio table until they ripened. The ones that rotted, Robbie turned over to Colin for ammunition.

Dad still had a difficult time accepting that nothing else had happened. He finished reading the paper and used his last piece of cornbread to soak up the gravy from the pot roast and ate it.

"Do you want anything else before I take a bath?" she asked.

"No, thanks. Dinner was delicious. I'll have some of that cobbler a little later."

"Just tell me when you want it."

Mom began putting leftovers in the refrigerator when Dad's inquisitive mind ignited again.

"Alley, you know I can always tell when you're keeping something from me, and I don't like it," he said sternly.

"You're still on that nonsense. Drop it, Colin."

"Didn't you notice something strange?"

"Strange? What's strange now, Colin?"

"Clark."

"Nothing's the matter with that boy."

"Well, call him up here, and you take a look at him. I swear, all you do is piddle around all day. Can't you tell when something's wrong with the kids?"

"Colin, if you *were* here all day long and something *did* happen, you wouldn't be able to figure out what it was, even though you're the one with the degree."

"That's it," Dad exclaimed.

"What's it?"

"What the hell's the matter with Clark? He didn't look that damn weird yesterday."

"Colin, leave him alone, he's fine. You're going to give the boy a complex. Who says their son looks weird? He's fine."

"Like hell he is. Look at his damn face, then tell me he's fine. He looks weird as hell. It's as if he has a fucking disease or something."

"Colin, does there always have to be something wrong with your children? Can't you leave them alone? He's a little sunburned from being out all day."

"Funny, I've been in the sun all day, too, and I don't look like his fucking weird ass."

"Tell me, what do you think is wrong with Clark? Since you know so damn much, what's wrong with that boy?" Mom put a piece of aluminum foil over the cobbler and placed it in the refrigerator.

"Let's find out. Clark, get up here," he shouted.

"Is this really necessary?" she asked.

Clark slowly climbed the stairs holding his head down. He stood several feet away from Dad. "Yes, sir?"

"Yes, sir, my ass."

"What in the hell's wrong with you?"

"Nothing, sir," he said shrugging.

"I want to be perfectly clear on this. I don't know what it is about you, but *you* stay the hell away from me. Far away! Whatever it is you have, I sure as hell don't want. You look repulsive!"

Clark agreed.

"You look like you've got some kind of fucking disease," he said without concealing his brewing air of disgust. "What the hell is wrong with your damn face? Have you seen it lately? Shit, get away from me!"

He motioned for him to leave and Clark disappeared without uttering a word. He knew Dad was right this time. He did look repulsive and weird.

Dad was in tune with almost everything that occurred at home. If there was something he wanted to know, he'd keep pushing the issue until he got his answer. Somehow, this particular time Mom actually tricked Dad. We were lucky he didn't find out. The funny thing was that Mom had her moments when she outsmarted Dad and enjoyed doing it. She would jokingly ask, "Can you believe the CIA wanted him?"

Had we followed Mom's instructions, none of this would have occurred. It took some time for Clark to recover from his little mishap and of course, he had more than enough teasing from all of us. I doubt he'll go anywhere near anything flammable from now on. Naturally, Colin taunted Clark more than anyone else, especially around the Fourth of July. Occasionally, Colin swore he saw one of Clark's eyebrows blowing around in the wind, but he could have been mistaken; it may very well have been an eyelash.

CHAPTER THREE

When I am afraid, I will put my trust in You. In
God, whose word I praise, In God I have put my
trust; I shall not be afraid. What can mere man
do to me?
You have taken account of my wanderings; Put
my tears in Your bottle. Are they not in Your
book?
Then my enemies will turn back in the day
when I call; This I know, that God is for me.

Psalms 56: 3-4, 8-9
New American Standard

I have never seen anyone thrive on the reactions or emotions of others the way my father did. We were nothing more than characters in a humiliating and heartless scene he staged. Inadvertently, we had fallen prey to his script, allowing him the intellectual and stimulating psychological studies that were vital to him. Conclusively, he displayed no sympathy for the way things transpired. Instead, he feasted on our fear of his reaction, which provided nothing more than gratification to him.

He had an insatiable appetite for fear. It was analogous to a twisted game of cat and mouse. He calculated our reactions in every situation and was primed for his own retort. Facial expressions, eye and hand movements, along with body language were critical in his psychoanalysis. We were his field experiment. In my observation of Dad, the perplexing note was his mood swings, which came without notice from deep inside of him. For an individual who was excessively controlling in an unprecedented way, when it came to his family, he lost his self-control.

My brothers and I were out playing at the recreation center. It didn't matter that it was another blazing hot, summer afternoon. Kickball and football were our own release from tension. The day was enjoyable because it was Stan, Colin, Clark, and me against several kids in the neighborhood. As usual, we won every game. The other team had more players who were bigger than we were, but it didn't matter. My brothers made sure we scored. I was good in kickball because I kept making it to base before anyone tagged me. When we played football, I was lousy, but they told the other team if anyone hurt their little sister, they were going to pay for it. They warned everyone that whatever happened to me was going to happen to them, but worse. I scored a few times because no one would tackle me when I had the ball. I loved playing with them because they played competitively and passionately. Each time Colin scored, he yelled, *What's this? Another touchdown?* He'd laugh hysterically in the end zone. Only we knew what that meant. By the end of the game, we were soaked in sweat and our stomachs were growling.

While away from the house, laughter was in abundance and we were completely at ease. After the game, we hung around listening to Colin and Clark boast about their skills to the other kids. They were warriors in our neighborhood. Everyone wanted to defeat my brothers because they were unbeatable in everything, and they stayed that way. They were legends!

As we approached the house the mouth-watering smell of Mom's buttermilk fried chicken drifted toward us. It was late, but we didn't have a designated time to eat on weekends. Mom knew where we were and the streetlights weren't on yet. Nevertheless, for whatever reason, Dad chose to make this occasion an issue as well. We were dirty, smelly, and hungry and I looked like my brothers.

My complexion was a smooth walnut color and my shoulder-length russet hair was pulled back into two sloppy pigtails with thick pink ribbons tied at the ends. Mom usually braided them using Royal Crown and a sprinkle of water to keep them looking silky. This time she didn't braid them since I was going to play ball, and she knew I'd get sweaty. My medium brown eyes were shaped like Dad's. I had his nose, eyes, and smile. My teeth were straight and pearly white. A tiny black mole rested on the left side of my lower lip. I was slender and shapeless for a girl, but had notable muscle structure like an athletic boy. I've always heard that I was an even mixture of both parents. When someone said I looked like Mom, I always wondered where my beauty was.

Dad was leaning against the kitchen counter finishing the last sip of his beer. He put the can down as we raced through the door, excited from our victorious day. We removed our shoes and lined them against the wall. Mom was sitting at the table with a half full cup of coffee and an ashtray in front of her, nervously rocking her leg as usual. She appeared stressed, but that was typical when Dad was home.

"Hi, Dad," I said, giving him a big hug. He didn't say anything, nor did he hug me back, so I stepped aside as Clark greeted him. I kissed Mom on the cheek and she forced a weak smile as she rubbed her hand across my back.

"Hi, Dad," Clark added cheerfully.

"You kids get washed up for dinner," she instructed timidly.

"You want them to get washed up for dinner at this hour, Alley?" he asked raising his eyebrow as he looked at his watch. He flashed Mom a cold confused stare. "Since you kids couldn't make it home on time for dinner, let's just say you've missed yours. It's way past eight and I think that's long past your dinnertime, don't you?"

"Sir, Mom told us to play outside until dinner was ready. That's what we did," Clark explained.

"Yeah, well common sense should have dictated it was getting late, and you needed to bring your little asses home because dinner *was* ready... An hour ago!"

"But, we stayed out of your way so you could concentrate. Mommy said you had a show-and-tell to work on, and she didn't want us to bother you," I added naively.

"Colin, she's right. Remember, you said you had that presentation to prepare for tomorrow. That's why I told the kids to—"

He threw his finger up warning Mom not to say another word. She didn't.

"Marala, you should have been home on time. Let's just hope this will teach all of you a lesson on punctuality," he scolded, eyeing each of us. "Clean up this kitchen, then get showered and ready for bed. Now snap to it!" He motioned for Mom to go upstairs, grabbed another beer, and followed her. The door slammed, and there was silence for a few moments.

Although none of this was conceivable, we knew this development was premeditated, and it was useless to try and defend ourselves. We went downstairs and washed up before we started cleaning the kitchen. We regrouped in the kitchen and Stan instructed us on what to do.

"Colin, I'll wash, you dry. Clark, you put them away and Marala, you can wipe down the counters and sweep. We'll mop afterwards. But first let's put our dinner away," Stan said jokingly.

"It's not funny. How can you joke about this?" Colin asked.

"Man, that's how Dad is," Stan began as he put the stopper in the drain. "If he's going to be pissed, what can we really do about it? Nothing. We can't let him keep getting to us over dumb stuff. Let's clean up, get our showers, and go to bed, like he said. We already know how he is. We need to do exactly what he told us to, and he won't have any reason to beat us. Now will he?" He rolled up the sleeves on his plaid shirt, squeezed dish liquid into the sink, then started running the water while agitating it with his hand.

"Stan, you don't know when to be serious. Besides, why do we even listen to him? He's nuts. I mean, here he goes again with his phony rules starting crap. He should have been a magician because he can fart a rule out his butt without warning," Colin complained. "We didn't have anything but a bowl of slimy oatmeal this morning and I'm starving," Colin added angrily.

"We're all starving, moron. So shut up and let it go already," Clark added dismissively. "Stan's right this time. Let's clean up and call it a day. If you keep acting like a doggone crybaby you're going to make it worse for all of us. You know he puts his ears to the vents. I'm tired anyway. So we don't get dinner; what's new? This isn't the first time and it won't be the last. Deal with it."

Colin began scooping the well-seasoned green beans with pieces of meaty ham hocks into a plastic bowl. Stan began washing dishes, and I put the seasonings away so I could wipe down the counters. Inquisitively, Colin lifted the lid on a medium-sized silver pot on the white stove and, before you knew it, using his fingers as a spoon, he took a big scoop of fluffy, buttery mashed potatoes and shoved them into his watering mouth. He sighed with relief as if that one taste would alleviate his hunger.

Catching him off guard was a powerful blow upside his head that knocked him into the cabinets before he hit the floor. A stunned Colin looked up, and there he stood, sliding his black glasses back upon the bridge of his nose with a perplexed look on his face. He leaned over and snatched him from the floor, hoisting him by his neck. He took his right fist and continually jabbed vigorously into Colin's tightened stomach, demanding that he spit it out. Colin began to take each blow as if he had mentally become immune to them until the pain overcame his body. We cried for Colin to spit it out but he couldn't. He had already swallowed it. The incessant blows increased in intensity, but Colin continued to take it. Trying to anticipate where the next blow would land he blocked his abdominal area, but Dad threw two quick jabs to his head, and Colin plunged to the floor again.

"So you want to play Mr. Tough Guy tonight? Well, I have something just for you," he said generously.

Colin rolled over onto his side and tried to curl his body into a protective fetal position, but Dad yanked him from the floor by his short afro. Once more, he wrapped his heavy hands around Colin's neck and began to strangle him causing saliva to ooze from his mouth. He looked as if he were trying desperately to squeeze the life out of him. Colin struggled to pull Dad's hands from around his neck, but the more he struggled the harder Dad strangled.

"Spit it out! Spit it all out," he demanded like a crazed lunatic. "So you want to eat? You don't want to listen to me?" He tightened his grip, forcing every vein in Colin's upper body to swell like it was about to explode. Colin's face was soaked in perspiration. The vacant look appearing in his eyes was terrifying. He coughed and gagged until Dad raised him off the floor by his neck, choking tighter and tighter restricting the air to his larynx. His feet wiggled and stretched to find the floor, but didn't. His last gasp for air ended the sounds as his face began to turn blue. Dad's hands reddened from his grip as the veins in his own face swelled. Heavy sweat soaked his face and his white t-shirt. His work was coldhearted and vile.

Colin stopped struggling after his body made a hefty jerk, before it wilted. The struggle ended. With a loud thump, Colin collapsed flaccidly to the tiled floor when Dad released his grip.

My mouth fell open and I was stiff with fear. This was another hellish nightmare. I tried to turn away, but my eyes kept returning to Dad's evil. My insides burned and my head pounded out of control.

"When I tell you not to do something, then damn it... don't do it! So again you've placed me in the position to teach your ass a lesson. Look what you made me do," he shouted while pounding his fists on the countertop. "Look what you made me do! Why must I deal with your constant disobedience?" He leaned on the counter and began breathing deeply staring straight ahead at the wall. Suddenly, he closed his eyes. It appeared that he was trying to compose himself.

Colin wasn't moving. Dad's brief moment of what I thought was self-composure turned into rage. He started aimlessly kicking and stomping on him repeatedly while demanding that he get up for more. The only movement from Colin was the blood trickling from his nose. Dad's foot collided against his left eye, but Colin remained unresponsive. The swelling to his eye and face was instantaneous. "Get up, damn it. You want to challenge me? Show me what you're made of! Get up! Get your ass up!"

Colin lay motionless.

"What's going on down here?" Mom yelled, racing down the steps with her hair soaking wet from the shower.

She was wearing her yellow robe and her face was covered in Ponds skin cream. Once her eyes locked onto Colin's lifeless body sprawled out on the floor, she panicked. He mimicked playing the violin gracefully and smiled. He appeared to be savoring her fear as though it were feeding his fury.

"Take your ass upstairs, Alley. I'll handle this," he said calmly.

"What did you do to him? What did you do?" she asked forcing her way past him.

Mom dropped to the floor, scooped her son onto her lap, and began searching for his pulse. Guardedly, Clark and Stan tried to inch toward her by creeping around a chair. Dad tossed the chair aside with one hand and stepped between them.

"Oh, I see. You want me to knock your asses out, too? You little bastards want some?" he asked balling up his fist and shaking it in their faces.

"Damn it, Colin! Not now! He needs help," she shouted trying to rouse her son.

"Then help him. I'm not doing shit for his sorry disobedient ass."

"Stanley, please?"

With slow timid movements, Stan tried to navigate around Dad to help Mom with Colin, but Dad was too angry and quick. He grabbed Stan by his throat with his left hand, digging his thumb into the side of it, followed by a series of punches with his right fist. Stan's head swung back and forth. His slender body jolted heavily with every blow.

"Do you want me to do the same thing to you? Do you?"

Blood dropped from his nose and ran down his clammy neck, as he repeatedly blurted out of control, "No, sir. No, sir."

Holding Colin's head in her lap Mom continued begging for help.

"He's barely breathing, Colin! He's barely breathing! You have to do something! Look what you've done," she cried.

"Shut up! He's playing for sympathy and you're too damn gullible to realize it. Offer his ass some more potatoes and watch him get up."

"Colin, we have to take him to the emergency room! We have to do something," she begged trying to prop Colin up. Again, Colin was flaccid and didn't respond.

"Shut up!"

He slammed Stan against the counter then shoved Colin with his foot to stir him. A heavy stream of blood drained from the corner of his mouth.

"Colin!" This time Dad's voice was ill at ease. "Get up, Colin."

"I'm calling the paramedics," Mom shouted.

"No. I'll handle it."

"You'll handle it? You? You're crazy! Look at him! I think you've done enough! Stay the hell away from him! Get away from my son," she yelled uncontrollably, pushing him away.

Mom's hysterical screaming frightened me even more. The chill in my spine and stabbing pain in my abdomen wasn't helping matters. I tightly gripped my stomach, trying to stop the spreading pain. It didn't help and I didn't know what else to do. I kept shaking my head to clear my fatal thoughts. I was praying this was just a dream and it didn't happen. But it had. When I looked down, Colin was still lying there, in Mom's lap. Dad went too far this time, just as Colin alleged. My thoughts were still fatal.

After several minutes of Colin's unresponsiveness, Dad began shifting his body uncomfortably. His alarm was becoming noticeable. He ordered us downstairs as he lifted Colin's limp body and rushed him up to his room. Within a minute, we heard the bath water running and Dad yelling for Colin to wake up as he dropped his body into the bathtub. Mom ran up and down the stairs with bowls of ice and towels from the laundry room. She didn't say one word, but her eyes spoke volumes. We knew it wasn't good.

Hours later, Jimmy and Selvin were already in bed asleep. Stan and Clark were downstairs waiting impatiently. My room was dark and quiet. I sat on the edge of my bed with my legs trembling out of control. My whole body was trembling. I tried to hear what was going on, but since Mom closed my door, and theirs, it was hard to tell. I was certain Colin was dead.

Mom's broken voice faded and Dad's anger had deteriorated into something more contrite. Clouded tears covered my aching eyes at the thought of Colin. How could such an enjoyable day end up like this? There was always some random evil waiting in our house to desecrate the day. No wonder Colin opted to run away. He was right; we didn't know what it was like for him. We really didn't. He was always Dad's target.

I didn't want to think about anything. I wanted to see my brother. I needed to see him. He couldn't die like this. Not like this. I glanced across the room at Selvin. He was in a deep sleep and unaware of what took place. He and Jimmy didn't know how bad it became when the hours of darkness fell in our house. I was still sick with fear and the painful stabbing in my stomach wouldn't go away. I buried my face into my pillow and cried harder than I ever had. It didn't help, so I began to pray, "Our father, which art in heaven..."

———

The small lamp on my nightstand was turned on. I rolled over and wiped the sleep trying to form in my eyes. I wasn't asleep. I was talking to God. The forty-watt bulb cast enough light for me to see Mom sitting on the edge of my bed. She ran her fingers through my hair, then gently massaged my scalp. I looked at my black clock radio; it was two twenty-three and a hint of the moon's glow made its way in from the window.

She cleared her throat, then whispered as not to awaken Selvin. She explained that Colin would eventually be all right. That's all she could manage to say. She choked on her own heartache, then looked away to hide her puffy, red eyes. She folded back my bedspread and whispered for me to go to sleep, then she removed my pink robe and laid it across the bottom of my bed. I knew better than to riddle her with questions.

Dad was downstairs talking to Stan and Clark, but his low and heavy voice could barely be discerned. Within minutes, they came into the room with us while Dad got into his car and sped off.

"He's gone," Clark stated.

"I know," Mom replied.

"Can we see our brother now?" he asked agitatedly.

"No, Clark, your brother needs to rest."

"He needs to rest? We thought he was permanently resting, as in *dead*! That's it! That cocksucker tries to kill—"

"Watch your mouth, Clark! Just watch it! You know better than to use that language."

"What I try to watch out for is *Dad*. What are you going to do about him, huh? He beat the heck out of my brother because he ate a small scoop of potatoes. He almost killed him over that! I thought he was dead! Who does he think he is, God? Even if it's an accident, he's going to kill one of us soon if you don't do something. In case you haven't noticed, he gets closer to it each time."

"I know, baby. I know," she said grabbing the gold cross hanging around her neck. She held it tightly and stared at the ceiling.

"What are you going to do about that, that monster?" Clark asked coldly.

She didn't look at him.

"I just need to figure something out. Let me think about this mess. I'll figure something out, I will. It's not that easy having six kids and no job." Mom got up and headed across the hall to her room. She heard Clark's stomach growl and remembered we hadn't eaten. "Clark, since your father's gone, go downstairs and make yourselves a peanut butter sandwich or something."

Clark turned around angrily and snapped, "No, thanks. Eating holds a near-death experience for penalty around here. It almost killed my brother, and you couldn't help him. It's not worth it." He stormed out of the room mumbling, "And you wonder why we steal."

"Stanley, come with me," she said grabbing his hand. "Marala, get some rest and say a prayer for your brother."

"I already did but I'll say another one. Will you tell Colin I love him, and I'm glad he's all right?"

Her sad eyes dropped to the floor, she paused, then said, "He's not all right, yet. None of us are."

Soon after that incident, Colin ran away. He knew he couldn't escape Dad's next episode. He needed to have some peace of mind, even if it was for a little while. He needed time to heal. He went to the local shopping store, picked out a yellow ten-speed bike, some camping gear, threw everything into a blue knapsack, then put it on his back. He jumped on the bike as if he were test riding it, and rode it right out of the store.

Colin stayed away for a few weeks. He camped out wherever he found a good site until he met a white woman who took him in. He explained to her what Dad had done and showed her proof, the welts, bruises, and knots. He begged her not to call the police because they'd only take him home. For the first time, Colin was in safe hands. Every few days he rode his bike, stopping in front of the house if the car was gone. Often it was around the time the mail came because he knew I got it to put in Dad's top drawer. He'd let me see him, then ride away after mouthing the words *I love you.*

My brothers and I had our own share of worries. It was irrefutable that there was never a comfort level in our house. The air stayed laced with a heavy dose of tension and poison. Life always has challenges and our family had an abundance of them. I prayed that Dad would eventually grow out of his hostility toward us, but it didn't happen. I hoped that one day we could become a normal family. Maybe this was normal and I didn't know it?

I wasn't aware that prior to Dad amending his ways to produce a healthier environment for his family, he had to learn a great deal about himself. It was vital for Dad to become conscious of the reasons he preferred abuse as his method of releasing his emotional distress. The fact that he devastated his family in such a contemptible way didn't seem to trouble him. If he discovered what triggered his antagonistic tactics, maybe it would allow him to liberate us from enduring the cycle he inherited.

Although Mom withstood the abuse throughout the years, she managed to hold onto her religious beliefs. For the most part, as long as things were peaceful, you could find a forced smile on her face and hear her nervous laughter when Dad was in a joking mood. When the radiance that once came from Mom's eyes began to wane giving way to the stare of doom, I too, lost hope. With every incident in our house, Mom still had a great deal to offer us, but didn't seem to realize it.

I recall the point that Mom reached her limit on the emotional roller coaster Dad subjected her to. I remember the day that she lost faith that the abuse would end. *I remember that day when things changed for all of us... forever.*

Chapter Four

For many deceivers have gone out into the world, those who do not acknowledge Jesus Christ as coming in the flesh. This is the deceiver and antichrist.

Anyone who goes too far and does not abide in the teaching of Christ, does not have God; The one who abides in the teaching, he has both the Father and the Son. If anyone comes to you and does not bring this teaching, do not receive him into your house, and do not give him a greeting; for the one who gives him a greeting participates in his evil deeds.

II John 1:7, 9-11
New American Standard

It was calm on this late Monday afternoon. The sky was a bit darker and more ominous than it had been all fall. A light jacket was needed, but that was about it. I was upstairs reading in my room when I heard loud knocking on the front door. Mom was placidly resting in her favorite recliner and wasn't too anxious to answer it because it was usually a neighbor kid asking for my brothers. The loud knocking continued, so I headed downstairs to answer the door. By that time, Mom had already answered it with a stream of irritation flowing from her voice. I stopped on the second step from the bottom to see who it was. There stood three noticeably strange white women. Two of them were asking for a few minutes of her time.

Reluctant to let them in, she began to make excuses why she couldn't take the time to listen to whatever they had to say. The heaviest of the three women, with her dark brown hair pinned up into an unattractive beehive, no makeup, and a plain blue and white-checkered dress, moved forward to speak. The other two women stepped back and grew silent.

"Good afternoon, sister. I understand that this may be inconvenient but we were in the neighborhood and thought it was time we stopped by."

"Why?" she asked sounding scarcely interested.

"I can see you're troubled. We know you're in need of some spiritual counsel. We're here because *he* has sent us to help you."

"You're saying somebody sent you here? Who is *he*?"

"Let us in, Alley, and we'll tell you about our mission," she said, placing her hand on the doorknob, ready to open it.

"Now, how did you know my name? And who are you all anyway?" she asked with a raised eyebrow.

"We see the agony in your face, child. The reason we're here is to help you end your pain. We mean you no harm, dear. At least let us in for a few minutes to explain who we are and exactly why we're here. It's a little uncomfortable talking through this glass door."

"I was just about to start dinner," she explained, smoothing out her apron. She put her hand on the black latch to unlock the door but paused for a moment and took a step back. "Perhaps another time. I ... I don't think this is such a good idea—"

"Dear, we won't take much of your time. And if you're not interested in what we can do for *you*, we'll leave and you'll never see us again. We're only here for you."

Alley lifted the latch and let them inside our house.

"Well, come on in, but you can't stay too long because my husband will be home soon. He doesn't like strangers in his house."

"Dear, you won't have to fear him any longer."

The three of them looked around and smiled covetously.

"Oh, well then, you don't know my husband," Alley mumbled under her breath while leading them into the living room.

I went back up to the top step and sat quietly.

***

The woman with the large beehive reached into her large black bag to remove what looked like a Bible. They fell into light conversation engaging Alley. She began quoting verses from it while Alley listened attentively. The other two women studied Alley's expression while agreeing to what their sister was communicating. It didn't take long for them to obtain her full attention. She quickly forgot that she had told them her husband would be home at any time.

"Would you all like some coffee? I'm sorry; I didn't get your names," she quizzed.

The woman doing most of the talking reached over and eagerly extended her hand to shake Alley's.

"Forgive me; you can call me Sister... Sister Cyprus. This is Sister *Lewis*, and that's Sister *Sypher*. And yes, we'd love some coffee, but if you don't mind, the sisters can get it since we're talking. Once you've been in one kitchen, you tend to know your way around. Now, where were we?" she asked before Alley had a chance to respond.

Sister Cyprus continued talking and handed Alley several pamphlets to read. The other two women took their purses into the kitchen where they made coffee. Mom appeared extremely captivated by every word Sister Cyprus had to say. She sat on the edge of her chair as if she were a young child being shown something fascinating.

"Alley, we all have gifts that we were born with. Some of us have gifts that are much greater than others are. You also have gifts that you must learn how to use. Ultimately, you will be able to call on these gifts, or powers, to help end your suffering," Sister Cyprus explained.

Alley's response had a sad overtone, "The Lord knows that my children and I have already been through so much. I don't think there's too much anyone can do except *God* at this point. And as far as gifts or any kind of power is concerned, I don't believe in all that nonsense." She leaned back and crossed her legs and began rocking in her chair.

"Dear, in time you will. We know all about the difficulties you and your children are faced with. Alley, we know the cause," she said convincingly.

"No, you don't. No one knows what's wrong with my husband because I don't even know. Colin's never been a heavy drinker or had any problems with nonsense like drugs," she said dismissively. She stopped rocking in her chair and put her hand under her chin and asked, "Have you been talking to Clark?"

"That's the third son from your eldest, right?"

"Right."

"No, we haven't spoken to him," she said with a clever smile.

"That boy sure runs his mouth too much. He'll tell anybody's business if you listen to him long enough."

"Alley, I haven't spoken to any of your children. And I'm aware that Colin's problem isn't because of any substance," Sister Cyprus said. "It's simply because he's the enemy. You know what they say about enemies. Get rid of them, before they get rid of you. Once you do that, Alley, you'll find your place in this world."

Alley removed her blue and white apron and laid it across the back of the stool next to the kitchen counter. She turned to see what the two women huddled together were doing. Sister Cyprus walked up behind Alley, gently took her hand, and led her back into the living room.

"We can help you, dear. We only want what's best," Sister Lewis insisted while making herself comfortable on the sofa. She carefully nodded, trying not to disturb her gargantuan hairdo, also an unsightly beehive. Sister Sypher placed two blue and white coffee cups on the marble coffee table, then sat back down on the sofa and smoothed out her plain black dress.

"Alley, dear, you must unite with us to save yourself," Sister Cyprus continued. "Your children will also be freed from the enemy."

Alley took a sip of the steaming coffee as the three women eyed her closely. She set her cup down and leaned back. Sister Cyprus continued preaching in an aggressive and alarming way. Alley kept looking at her coffee cup while Sister Cyprus was talking. With a bewildering look she lifted her cup and stood.

"What's wrong, dear?" Sister Sypher questioned nervously.

She paused for a second, and let her forehead scrunch together. Then she replied, "I prefer a little more pet milk in my coffee. This tastes a little bitter," she said licking her lips. "Maybe I need to clean the pot out again."

Before Alley walked into the kitchen, Sister Sypher stood and stepped in front of her, then said, "Oh, I washed the pot, dear. You must need a little more pet milk. I'll get it for you."

"You're probably right. But, how did you know I take pet milk in my coffee?"

"Like she explained, Alley, we know everything about you." Sister Cyprus gave her a lengthy stare, observing her reaction.

"What I'd like to know is who's *he*? You mentioned him, so who is this person? Do you mean God or the pastor of your church? Who?"

Alley sounded concerned with the direction their conversation was heading.

"We'll get to that, but first we must explain other things to you."

Sister Cyprus was vastly evasive and controlling of the conversation. They continued to talk for about an hour before the conversation reached its closing stages.

"It's time for us to leave since your husband is on his way. We'd like to come back tomorrow. That's good for you, isn't it?" Sister Cyprus insisted.

"Well, I suppose… Sure, that'll be fine. It was nice meeting you all. You may be exactly the encouragement I need in my life."

"We know. We'll talk more tomorrow."

They held Alley's hand and recited a prayer of some sort. They left as quickly and mysteriously as they came. Within minutes, Dad pulled up in his blue Buick LaSabre.

For the duration of the evening, Mom picked up her Bible and read a few pages as though she were trying to make sense of what these women discussed during their visit. She cooked dinner quickly so she could resume her reading. Although the women were peculiar, they were intriguing to Mom.

After Dad finished his dinner, he relaxed with the newspaper on the living room sofa across from Mom. He began telling her about his day, but noticed her preoccupation.

"Did you hear what I said? Honey, Ted had me up in Sandusky all morning meeting with clients. After lunch, I rushed back to the office for a major presentation and found out that it's tomorrow. My boss was certain the client rescheduled the meeting with my secretary yesterday, but her ass neglected to mention it to me. At any rate, as always, I was prepared," he said boastfully. "I wasn't wearing my favorite blue suit since it was in the cleaners, but I was sharp. Didn't you think so?" he asked, grinning. "IBM is no joke, especially for blacks. You have to stay on top of your business at all times. They're all about quotas and image. If you're not achieving either mark, they'll get rid of you. It's that simple. You see *The Thinker* sitting on the stereo cabinet… Well, it's there for a reason. It reminds me of," he said, pausing for a moment mimicking the pose, hand to chin, left elbow to right knee, then completed his thought with a clever smile, "*me.*"

"So you're giving your presentation tomorrow?" she asked joining the conversation from a trancelike state.

"That's what I said." He got up and walked over to her. He went to place his heavy hand on her neck and then cheek, causing her to jump both times. "Hold still," he said with a slight grin. "I'm not going to hit you. I'm simply checking your temperature." She wasn't warm so he felt her forehead. "You're not running a fever but are you sick or something?"

"No, Colin, I'm fine. I have a lot of things on my mind, that's all," she replied, rocking comfortably in her chair.

"What kind of things? Which soap opera you're going to watch tomorrow? It's a good thing you don't have to think about the shit I do. It's quiet around here. Where are the kids?" he asked looking around.

"They've already had dinner and taken showers. Marala and Selvin are watching television upstairs with Clark and Jimmy. Stanley's drawing, and little Colin is reading or something."

"Did anything go on here today?"

"Like what, Colin?"

"Such as any problems with the kids, visitors, phone calls, or don't you even remember?" He snapped his fingers in front of her face. "You seem out of it tonight."

"No, the kids were fine, and the calls that came in were for me."

"Anything I should know about?"

"One of the calls was my sister. In a roundabout way, she implied they were coming down this weekend."

"Who are they?"

"My sisters. But Danielle said Momma might come this time."

"Boy, three more of you and your mother. I don't know if I can handle that this weekend, honey." He hesitated, then said, "It's your call. They're your family. Was there anything else besides that bad news?"

"I'll tell them to come next weekend if it's going to be a problem," she replied with annoyance. "Some women from a church came by. Is that all right with you?"

"A church? Which one? What denomination are they?"

"I don't remember the name of their church, Colin."

"Don't you pay attention to what people tell you? What did they want? Did you let them in the house?"

"They came around here knocking on the door like those Jehovah Witness people do. They do the same thing, I guess, trying to increase their membership and spreading the word was all it was. They were talking about their church and their religion."

"Both of which you don't know the answer to. Interesting, go on," he said motioning with his hands.

"Does it really matter?"

"Yes, it does matter. I want to know exactly who's hanging around my house with my wife and kids when I'm not here. Sometimes you never know about those religious freaks. They come bearing all types of superficial gifts and smiles to get your attention. You need to discern how to form an opinion of people. They aren't always who they seem to be."

"Yeah, and neither are you."

"What was that?" he asked sharply, cutting his eyes at her.

"You know what it was. It was a smart remark like you taught me to give."

"And that had better be your last one. That's for damn sure," he warned eyeing her from head to toe.

"Now there you go again," she huffed.

"As for those religious freaks knocking on *my* door... I don't want them around here. As I stated before, you never know what motivations people have for that sort of enthusiasm. You don't let strangers wander up to your door and start teaching you things just because. Don't let people get into your fickled little head with all that religious mumbo jumbo unless you know them and agree with what they represent."

"And how will I get to know these people if you don't want them around, Colin?"

"Alley, don't be condescending with me. Besides, your ass is an easy target. The fact that you *do not* recall the name of their church, or religious conviction, tells me that they were, in all probability, vague for a reason. It's essential that you be a prudent judge of character before you sit down and hold a conversation about religion with strangers. If you aren't cautious, that shit can mess up your stupid little head. You could be talking to members from an occult for all you know."

"Colin, let's not get carried away. These women were harmless."

"You said women. So that's plural. How many were there?"

"There were three of them."

"Okay. So your memory is finally coming back. You let *three* strangers into *my* house to talk about *some* religion?"

She was no longer paying attention, although he continued voicing his opinion. She pulled out a cigarette and book of matches from her purse, then picked up the pamphlets they left. Without saying a word she went out the sliding glass door into the backyard.

Early the next morning, he rushed downstairs dressed in a dark blue and white pinstriped suit with a crisp white shirt and a smart deep blue silk tie dotted with tan specks. His black polished wing-tipped shoes were his final touch.

"Don't you look nice?" she said, smiling flirtatiously. She handed him his second cup of steaming coffee and kissed him on his smooth cheek.

"Nice. Is that all?" he asked disappointedly.

She whispered softly, "You look magnificent, Colin. Absolutely magnificent. There's no one as attractive as my good-looking husband," she sighed, then poured a cup of coffee.

"Now, that's much better," he said with a wink, nodding approvingly.

"Oh it is?" she said fanning herself. She reached to open the window over the sink and let a cool breeze rush in. She pulled open the refrigerator door, grabbed the pet milk, and looked at the expiration date before dousing it in her coffee.

"Something wrong, Alley?" he asked frowning as he looked into his cup.

"No. I was checking the date. Yesterday, my coffee didn't taste the same. I wanted to make sure the milk isn't spoiled."

"Well is it?"

"If it were, obviously you wouldn't know the difference anyway," she teased. "It's fine," she said putting it away.

"At any rate," he said clearing his throat. "I don't intend to let those jokers catch me off guard again with this presentation. Debbie informed me that we have an internal meeting today with our branch manager. Of course, *my* secretary neglected to tell me about this too. I've had enough of her shit."

"How are you going to handle her? I know you're not going to let her get away with that," she said, turning to face him.

"You're damn right I won't. After the meeting, I'm sure as hell going to deal with her ass. I think she and Joe are up to something. You know how people stick together when it comes to office politics. Well, on the other hand, perhaps you don't."

"Colin, I understand what you're talking about just fine. You need to stop with your little remarks," she replied, then straightened his tie.

With a slight touch of sarcasm he added, "All I'm saying is that I don't see how you could, since you don't work in an office."

"Put it this way, smart ass, I understand the games you play better than you think." She flashed him a clever smile, then kissed him on his puckered lips.

"Make sure the kids are on top of their homework as soon as they get in from school. They need to be on a tighter schedule. Especially Jimmy and Selvin. They ought to be in bed by eight-thirty on a school night." He headed out the door, then caught himself and stopped. "I almost forgot," he said snapping his finger. "I need you to do me a favor and send out the light bill today. I won't have time to get to the post office so hand it to the mailman when he comes." He opened his tan leather briefcase, removed several pieces of mail, and set them on the kitchen counter. "Oh, and I left some money in my top drawer in case you need anything."

"Thank you, Colin," she said beginning to wipe down the counters.

"Don't forget that mail."

"I'll get it out," she said tossing the dishtowel on the counter.

"It's too bad you don't drive. It would be nice for you to have a car to get around in during the day. Why don't you try to get your license so you can go shopping and make some new friends." He smiled as he patted her on the butt.

"You know I don't like these damn people around here. They're nosey as hell. Besides, the minute you come home and catch them sitting around *your* house, you'd pitch a damn fit." She laughed.

"Well, it would depend upon who you had sitting around my house. Bring home Lena Horne, and I definitely won't have a problem," he joked slipping his arms around her waist.

"And if I brought her home, you wouldn't know what to do with her anyway," she teased.

"Oh, now you're a comedian. That's funny, Alley. Just think about getting your license and if you do, I'll buy you a little car. How's that sound?" he asked pulling his keys out of his pocket.

"We'll see, Colin. Is there anything else?"

"Alley, if I gave you anything else to do, you wouldn't remember anyways. Have a good day." He smirked, then kissed her silky-smooth cheek while brushing her hair off her face. He picked up his cup and drank the last sip of his coffee. He glanced at his watch, then added, "Oh, and remember to be wary of strangers. Don't let them tickle your ears. Shit. I'm late again," he announced, rushing out the side door.

Upon Dad's leaving, my brothers rushed to finish breakfast and get dressed for school. By the time Mom came back downstairs with Selvin neatly dressed for kindergarten, they left the house in single file, kissing Mom on the cheek one at a time. Mom followed a few minutes later to take Selvin to the bus stop. Upon returning home, she had a pleasant smile on her face as if she were enthusiastic about the visit from the women she'd met the day before. At this point, it was nice to see her happy about anything. The peculiar thing was that the three mysterious women appeared to know too much about Mom and how to appeal to her emotional needs. The knowledge these women possessed captivated Mom.

The house was finally quiet. Mom brought me breakfast in bed and a couple of aspirin. She checked my temperature and covered my chest and nose with Vicks, then pulled the covers up to my neck and gave me a warm hug, cheek to cheek. I couldn't smell the Ponds Skin Cream that Mom rubbed on her face, but I could feel the smoothness on her skin. Covering her face and neck in Ponds was part of her nightly routine. Most of the time, you could still smell it in the morning.

"Thanks for taking care of me," I said, sniffling.

"That's what mommies do," she smiled gently. "I want you to stay in bed and get plenty of rest. My baby has a bad cold, that's all," she said lightly touching my nose. "I made you a bowl of cream of wheat and a piece of toast in case you're hungry. Make sure you drink that orange juice." She nodded toward the nightstand. "And I already filled your water pitcher just in case you get thirsty."

"Do I have to eat now? I'm not hungry. Besides, I can't taste anything."

"Well, just eat what you can."

"Okay," I said, reaching for another tissue to blow my nose.

"When you're ready for lunch, just holler downstairs and I'll make you a nice hot bowl of chicken noodle soup. How does that sound?"

"That sounds good. Thank you," I said, pulling the blankets down a bit.

She pulled the blankets back up and tucked them around my neck.

"This Vicks makes me sweat a lot," I complained.

"That's what it's supposed to do," she replied, softly smoothing my hair off my forehead.

"Oh."

"I'm going to be right downstairs so if you need anything don't get out of bed, just call me."

"Okay. Thank you."

———————

Alley put on a fresh pot of coffee and began the housework. She ran the sweeper in the living room, polished the coffee and end tables with Pledge, and went downstairs to begin sorting the laundry before placing the white clothes in the washing machine. A few minutes later she heard loud knocking on the front door. She turned the washing machine on and ran upstairs to answer it.

"Good morning, Alley. You were expecting us, weren't you, dear?" Sister Cyprus boldly commented.

The trilogy of evil had returned.

"Yes. I was," Alley replied as she unlocked the screen door. "My husband's at work and the boys are in school. Come in and have a seat. Make yourselves comfortable. I just put on a fresh pot of coffee. Would anyone like a cup?"

"Why, that was thoughtful, dear, but we brought some tea. I think you'll love it. Tea is more relaxing."

The other two women agreed.

"Oh, no, thank you. I'm a coffee drinker. You can leave it here for Colin. He likes tea. I thought you said you knew everything about me?" she asked refreshing their memory.

Sister Cyprus reached into her purse, pulled out a small plastic baggie full of tea bags, and gently handed them to Alley.

"Yes, dear and that's why we brought this for you, not Colin. Once you try it, you'll love it. I assure you."

"What kind of tea is this?" she asked.

"It's an herbal blend. I find it good for the nerves, dear. Now you will try this, won't you? It's my own special blend. Whenever I'm in a quandary, why, I simply have a cup of this tea and it works like magic," she said suspiciously.

"Thank you. Maybe I'll try some later." Alley casually placed the baggie full of tea on the coffee table.

Sister Cyprus pointed her finger toward the turquoise curtains for the two sisters to draw. After they did so, she asked, "You don't mind if we close the curtains, do you? This way we'll have more privacy."

"Sure. I guess that's fine since you've already closed them. I can turn on some lights to brighten the room a little. Once you close those heavy drapes it sure gets dark in here."

"Oh, no, this is just fine. Now let's get back to where we left off," Sister Cyprus began.

The three women held hands, adding Alley to the link, and began praying. Alley guardedly looked around without closing her eyes. Instead, she carefully observed them. As the prayers grew intense and bizarre, the house filled with a strange sensation. The women continued praying with a nonsensical babbling. The reverberation was foreign and upsetting in every aspect. The more they babbled at a disturbing speed, the more uncomfortable the atmosphere became. Their prayers sounded as if they were summoning someone or *something,* and it appeared as though it had worked. The noises they made were simply chilling.

A few minutes later their voices began calming as they concluded their praying. Sister Cyprus animatedly plunged back onto the sofa and laid there for a minute with her hands stretched over her head. The other two sisters embraced Alley trying to alleviate her suspicions.

"I don't pray like that!" Alley said with a great degree of alarm in her voice.

None of the women commented. Instead, they stared at Alley cautiously and wiped sweat from their foreheads with their handkerchiefs. Sister Cyprus was trying to catch her breath.

"Does someone want to tell me what's going on here?" Alley demanded with her voice growing louder.

"Alley, dear, we—" Sister Cyprus began.

"I want to know who you all were praying to because I've never heard sounds like that before. I certainly don't pray that way. Not ever! What is it that you're trying to do here? What do you *really* want? Who sent you to pull this mess with me?" she asked backing away from them with her hands on her hips.

"Dear, calm down a minute. What we did is simply called speaking in tongues—" Sister Lewis tried to explain.

"No. No it's not! I know what speaking in tongues sounds like. They speak in tongues in my sister's church and that's not what you all are doing. I think you'd better leave now," she shouted pointing to the door.

With great authority, Sister Cyprus spoke up, "Now calm yourself and let me explain. It might appear that we pray slightly different than you may be used to, but our results are the focus here. The focus is *your* adversary, Alley. Don't lose sight of that! We must deal with the problem, which is your husband," she warned.

"Colin's everybody's enemy," interrupted Alley. "I already know that. But you haven't answered my questions. I don't want you coming around here causing more trouble. I don't need it! Now Colin's already warned me not to have you here to begin with. And if you're trying to pull some old witch or devil worshipping mess with me, you'd better get out of my house right now! I'm a Catholic woman, and I'm not about to get mixed up in your nonsense."

Sister Cyprus motioned for the other women to sit.

"Alley. If you want us to leave we'll do that, but not until you've heard us out. We came here to teach you things you don't know. All we want to show you is—"

"See, that's where you're dead wrong! You all don't need to teach or show me a doggone thing! I don't appreciate this mess! Not one bit! I was listening to you do your little thing! You don't know me like that to come up in here with some old foolishness!"

The two other women stood and began gathering their possessions. Sister Cyrus motioned for them to stop.

"Foolishness. We're not here for mere foolishness!"

"Wait one minute. If you have something to say, say it! But don't go raising your voice with me in *my* house."

"Don't you mean in *his* house?" she said, casually scanning the room.

Alley stared at all three women with confusion. She looked around the room and her face fell blank. These strangers struck a nerve. The cold reality of the situation hit her. This wasn't her house and she didn't have control over anything in it. She calmed down and made the decision to listen to whatever they had to say. Slowly, she sat back in her rocking chair; the only true thing she felt was hers.

"You have power, but must learn how to use it. We're here to enlighten you on how to defeat your enemy, child."

"What power? Don't you think if I had some sort of power I'd already know?"

"You see, Alley, women are preordained to preside over this world. We're chosen to be influential. You have the power, yet you allow yourself to be led unnecessarily. This must stop."

"Stop how? You all can't stop Colin from doing anything. He stops when he's ready to stop and not a minute sooner. My husband runs things around here and that's all there is to it."

"We'll teach you how to handle him. But first you must learn how to pray and summon the powers from within yourself."

"I don't understand something. Why are you all talking about *handling* Colin and *defeating my enemy*? If you're supposed to be church-going people, why are you talking about getting even with Colin? It sounds to me like you want to make mischief with my husband, and get back at him for some reason or another. Now why's that? What's he done to you? Since you all are some kind of religious people, why don't you just let it go? I know the Bible, too, now. I've already put it in God's hands; so let God deal with him. He made him!"

"We're not here to argue with you. We're here to give you wisdom."

"Women ruling the world, what world are you all from? Do you all believe in God or something else? Look, if it's something else, then there's the door. I suggest—"

"Alley, listen to me. Where does it say that a man is supposed to beat you unspeakably until your eyes are swollen shut, lips bloodied, or you're knocked unconscious? All of these things have happened to you and to your children because of Colin. God doesn't condone this type of behavior. It's not in the Bible that a man is to eradicate his family and the woman is to sit by and take it. You must trust us, Alley. We're your only hope at this point."

Complacently, Alley leaned back in her rocking chair as if they had persuaded her to join in their efforts. Her eyes displayed sheer confusion. She seemed afraid, but out of options.

"This is what we must do. We'll begin by teaching you how to translate this book." Sister Cyprus held a thick black book in her hand. "Once you fully understand its contents, you'll be ready."

"I'll be ready for what?"

"You'll be ready to understand your own inner powers. All of us here have them."

"Would you like some tea dear?" Sister Lewis asked.

"Sure, why not?"

Sister Lewis went into the kitchen as if it were now her own, once again taking her purse with her like the previous visit.

———

Mom headed upstairs to check on me, and I scurried back to bed.

"How are you feeling, baby?" she said placing her hand on my forehead.

"I have to go to the bathroom."

"Are you hungry?" she asked, noticing the empty bowl.

"No, I'm just sleepy."

"Well, go use the bathroom and climb back into bed. Call me if you need anything."

"I will."

"Marala," she said sadly.

"Yes."

"We won't have to worry about your father too much longer." She dropped her head and left the room, closing the door behind her.

———

Alley returned to her company to find Sister Lewis entering the room with a piping hot cup of tea. Carefully, she handed it to Alley and the women sat down.

"Now tell me if that's not the most relaxing cup of tea you've ever had," Sister Lewis said.

Without hesitation Alley softly blew into the cup, took a sip, and then leaned back in her rocking chair.

"This is different," she said looking into the cup as if she could see what was in it. "Aren't you all having any tea?" she asked noticing she was the only one with a cup.

"No, we're fine, dear." Sister Cyprus quickly dismissed Alley's observation. "As I was saying..."

The conversation continued for several hours without interruptions. By the time Mom finished one cup of tea, Sister Lewis handed her another. Things were quiet until Colin junior rushed through the side door and raced around the corner into the living room.

"Um. Excuse me, Mom," he said in his husky tone.

"Yes, son. What is it?" Sister Cyprus replied, looking up from her book.

"No, see, I was talking to my mother. Not you," he said without turning to face her.

"Well, son, we're in the middle of something. You children must go outside and play until your mother calls you," Sister Cyprus said more sternly.

Colin disregarded the woman and tapped Mom on the shoulder. Mom didn't respond so he tapped harder and faster.

"Mom... Mom... Mom, can I talk to you for a minute?"

She began looking at him as though she were trying to escape a deep meditation.

"What is it, Stanley? I mean... Colin?" she asked lethargically.

He went into the kitchen so she'd follow. By the time he had her attention, Clark and Jimmy darted through the door.

"Hi, Mom," Jimmy said excitedly, reaching for a hug. He glanced around the kitchen with his nose in the air. "I don't smell your cookies," he said with the grin fading from his face.

"I'm sorry, sweetheart. I forgot," she admitted. "How was school?"

"I guess it was good. I got an 'O' on my spelling test."

"Outstanding. I'm so proud of you. That's what I love hearing." He handed her the paper to review and watched her light up. "Keep up the good work for Mommy, okay?" She gave him another tight squeeze and placed the paper under a pear-shaped magnet on the refrigerator.

"Mom. I have to ask you something," Colin began.

"What is it, Colin?"

"Can we go to the basketball game at school tonight?"

"Who are *we*?"

"Me, Stan, and Clark want to go together," he answered chewing greedily on a mouthful of candy.

"Boy, you already know I don't have money to waste on that stuff. How much does it cost?"

"We only need fifty cents each," Colin exclaimed, reaching into his back pocket. He pulled out a box of Lemonheads and poured half the box into his mouth.

"Oh, I see you have money for candy but you don't have money for the game."

"Naw, I got this stuff free. Want some?" he said, offering the box to Mom.

"No, thank you," she said with a curious expression. "Fine. You can go to the game but you'd better make sure all your homework and chores are done. And I want to see your homework first. Do you hear me?"

"No problem. Thanks, Mom," he said excitedly. Colin wrapped his arms around Mom, squeezed her as hard as he could, and then stuck his tongue out at Jimmy. He began to leave the kitchen but paused, "One more thing. Who are those weird-looking ladies? There's definitely something strange about them. Did you get a load of their goofy looking hairdos? Geez, where'd they ride in from?"

"Hush your mouth. You need to mind your own business for a change! And for your information, we're in there talking about religion. That's something you need to keep learning about. Now go do your homework and let me get back to my company before your father gets home. If I hear one more smart remark out of your behind, you won't be going anywhere for a month. Do you understand me?" It was quiet for a moment. "Colin, I want you to behave for a change. Can you please try to do that, just once?"

"But Mom, look at them. Religion or no religion, there's something a little strange about those old bats. I can feel it. I was talking to you and that one lady with the mustache and whiskers was answering like she was my mother. That was rude!"

"Colin, what did I tell you? I guess you don't want to go to that game tonight after all, now do you? You can just take your little behind downstairs for the rest of the night. You don't seem to want to listen to a word I have to say. I'm sick to death of your smart mouth."

"Okay, okay. I'm sorry for being so smart," he replied, faking a look of remorse.

"Oh, shoot! I almost forgot. Clark, pick up Selvin from the bus stop. He should be there in a few minutes."

She took a deep breath, smoothed her hair back, and went into the living room.

"I'm sorry about the interruptions with the kids. They won't be back in."

"Your children seem uncomfortable with us being here," Sister Lewis commented.

"It's mostly little Colin, but it's because they're not used to me having this much company. Let's see, you were saying something about your church."

"Yes dear, we have a bus that can pick you and the children up Sunday morning around eight o'clock. After the sermon the bus will drop you off."

"It'll be good to get the kids out of here for a while."

"We shall end their inquisitiveness as well," Sister Sypher said, looking directly at me peeking around the corner.

The sisters joined hands with Alley and began praying in a hushed tone in the same manner they did upon their arrival.

"On Saturdays we usually have meetings, so you won't see us. We'll look for you Sunday, dear," Sister Cyprus said in an unwavering tone.

"I'll be there unless my husband has a problem with me going."

"You'll see to him won't you, Alley? Do not let your adversary make your rules," insisted Sister Sypher.

"It sure feels good talking to you all. I haven't had a decent conversation in a long time."

"That's simply because you are not thought of as an equal in your husband's eyes. What you have to say is meaningless. In time, you'll be amazed at how your life has changed. In time."

Ten minutes after they left, Dad was home. Mom was in her rocking chair reading one of their books when Dad strolled through the kitchen door. When he turned the corner, he found her in the living room completely focused on what she was reading. She didn't notice him standing there watching her. He snatched the book from her hands gaining her immediate attention.

"Co…Colin, when did you get in?" she asked stuttering.

"Never mind that, who gave you this shit? *Satanism*, what the *hell* is this?" He picked up another black book. *Demonology* and this shit… *Satan's*…" He took a moment and silently read the title and authors of the remaining books. He took a deep breath and exhaled blowing out steam.

"The women from the church I was telling you about."

"The women from the church," he repeated angrily. His tense jaws flexed in and out as he clenched his teeth.

"Yes," she replied submissively.

"I thought I told you I didn't want them around here! Furthermore, I don't want them bringing this sacrilegious shit into my damn house!" He opened the front door and flung the books across the lawn.

"Now just this morning—" she began.

"I told you to be wary of strangers! I don't mind you having company in my house, Alley, but I do mind strangers getting into that simple little head of yours."

"Colin. *Your* house. It's always *your* house. I can't do a damn thing in *your* house unless we get *your* permission."

"Well, *now* you're thinking. I suggest you get with the program. I don't like this shit at all. Why is it that the little things I expect you to do always seem disregarded?" he asked casually.

"What is it that you *think* I didn't do? Tell me. What is it this time?" she asked as she stood and headed for the kitchen. She took the long way around him as not to walk directly in his path.

"Should I make a long ass list or tell you the basics? For starters, do you mind telling me what's for dinner because I sure as hell don't smell a damn thing?"

He went into the kitchen and condescendingly yanked open the oven for confirmation since there weren't any pots on the stove.

"Colin, all I have to do is run the meatloaf in the oven and peel potatoes. By the time you get out of your suit and take a shower, it'll be ready. What more do you want?" she asked, smiling convincingly.

"That's not the issue. The point I'm trying to make is that while I'm at work all day what in the fuck are you doing around here besides entertaining devil worshippers? I want my damn dinner ready by the time I get home. That's what *I* want! Did you send out the light bill like I asked?"

Mom hesitated because she realized she'd forgotten.

"Colin."

"Colin, my ass. Answer the damn question."

"Yes, Colin, I sent out the damn light bill. I did it first thing this morning like *you* asked."

He raised his eyebrows and glanced at her in surprise.

"Well, at least you did something constructive today." His shoulders relaxed and he headed upstairs, still fussing. "Things have the tendency to slip your feeble little mind when you're sitting on your ass talking to weirdoes. Understand that I'm *not* going to tolerate your new friends regulating what time I eat! Do you catch my drift? Get with the program, Alley, or else." His voice faded once he shut the door to his room.

Mom pulled the ground beef, onions, peppers, and eggs out of the refrigerator. She grabbed the seasonings from the cabinet over the stove and crumpled up bread along with everything else in a large plastic bowl. She opened two cans of tomato sauce, added them to the mixture and had dinner in the oven in less than ten minutes. Afterwards, she called Clark to set the table and Stan to run the mail to the corner mailbox. Within an hour and a half, dinner was on the table. Stan brought dinner up to me and joined the boys downstairs to eat to avoid Dad since he was still agitated. The house was quiet until Mom broke the silence.

"Colin, I'm taking the children to church this Sunday."

"Look, I don't want to hear anymore about this shit. Let me enjoy my fucking dinner, which is good by the way," he added, making brief eye contact with her. "Your homemade biscuits would have been perfect with this meal. Hopefully, the next time you cook you'll make some… if you start a littler earlier."

After dinner, the boys left for the game. Dad went upstairs to his room, then called me in a few minutes later.

"Marala, were you here when those women came by for your mother?"

"Yes. I didn't feel good so Mommy told me to stay home. They got here right after you left this morning. Then they left right before you came home."

"Is that so?" he asked flipping through his mail.

"Uh-huh."

"What were they like? Were they those Jehovah's Witness people who bug the hell out of everyone in the damn neighborhood?"

"No. I don't think so because these ladies were… they were kind of strange."

"Strange? They were strange in what way? Can you elaborate?"

I had a blank look on my face. I didn't know what elaborate meant.

"What does—"

"What makes you think they were strange? Can you give me more details? A little more information," he said, motioning with his hands for me to start talking.

Afraid of getting Mom into trouble, I had to be careful with what I said. I stared at the ceiling as though my response was going to fall from it.

"They made Mommy coffee… in the kitchen."

"Kitchens are generally utilized for such things. Go on."

"They prayed different than we do."

"You mean, *differently*. How so?"

"I don't know. It's just different, I guess. I mean *differently*. You'd have to hear them."

"You had it right the first time, *different*. Is that all?"

"I guess that's all."

"You *guess* that's all," he said, sounding annoyed that I didn't have more to report. "Is there anything else I should know?" He began brushing his wavy black hair to the side while looking in the mirror over his dresser.

"I guess not, but you might want to meet them before they take us to church."

"How do you know they're taking you to church?" he asked looking down at me with a loose smile.

I shrugged. "That way you can see what you think. I already know you won't like them."

"What makes you so sure?" he asked, offering some Chicklets.

"There's something kind of weird about them," I whispered, holding out my hand hoping he'd pour more than one. This time he gave me three. I loved Chicklets. "I'm not sure exactly what it is, but there's something I don't like. And they seem kind of sneaky."

"You mean devious?"

"What's that mean?"

"Sneaky."

"Oh, then they seem devious."

He turned to study my expression for a moment, then rubbed my sweaty hair that Mom pressed and divided into three neatly braided pigtails the night before. "I must get you a dictionary. Get back to bed, sweetheart." He kissed me on the forehead. "Don't mention this little discussion to your mother."

"I won't. Night."

He winked at me and said, "Goodnight. If those women come back around, I want you to keep a close eye on them and let Dad know if anything out of the ordinary occurs."

"Okay."

"Hold on. Are you feeling any better? You still sound congested."

"Yeah, my nose is still stuffy."

"Well, if you're not feeling better, I'll tell your mother to keep you home tomorrow."

I smiled, then went across the hall to my room. The remainder of the night was serene.

―――――――

When Sunday morning rolled around, Mom made sure we were up early and dressed for church. Dad came downstairs in his dark blue pajamas and a checkered red and blue robe rubbing his glossy uncombed hair. I loved the smell of Dad's hair because the only things he put in it were Byrlcreem and hair tonic.

After abruptly clearing his throat to gain her attention, he said, "So I see you all are attending church this morning."

"Yes, we're all going to church this morning, Colin."

"Isn't it kind of early to be up? I'd like to see you this anxious to get a job."

"Colin."

"*Colin, what?*"

"I'm taking the kids to Sunday school." She adjusted her tapered green dress that hit right above the knees. Flawlessly, it fit her shapely body.

"I hope you aren't assuming that I'm going to drive you there?"

"No, the church bus is picking us up."

"Hmm, church bus? What's the name of the church?"

"Colin, it really doesn't matter. At least the kids will be somewhere peaceful this morning. If you want to know where we're going, then come. If not, I don't want to hear any further complaints from you. I'm not trying to—"

"Alley, do you really think *I'm* ignorant enough to hop on a bus and ride it to wherever it stops? Having no idea where you're going or the name of the church is absurd. You need to rethink your decision. First, you haven't known these people a full week. Second, you're attending *their* church. In my assessment of the situation, that's a serious commitment for a simpleton such as yourself. Christ, do I have to spell it out for you?" he asked throwing his hands in the air.

"Colin, I'm only taking the kids to church. Now you didn't like the Catholic Church. You don't like my sister's church. What would make you happy?"

"Boy, where do I begin? But let's start with you not being so irrational for a change. If you're taking *my* children to church, I want to know where the hell you're going. Got it?"

Just then, a horn blew a couple quick notes. Mom peeked out the living room window and announced that the bus was here. We scrambled out the door.

"If you want to know where we're going, I suggest you read the side of the bus, Colin. Got it?" As she walked away, she threw her hand up and waved without looking back at him.

Dad tightened the belt on his robe and followed us outside. When the bus pulled away, he didn't wave. He stood in front of the door with a concerned look on his face.

The bus ride took about forty-five minutes. We didn't pick anyone else up along the way. We pulled off the main road and continued a couple of miles down a narrow gravel road. It ultimately turned into a dirt road until we reached the white brick building. The church was small and intimate, yet crowded. We went inside and Mom held Selvin and Jimmy's hand. The rest of us followed closely behind.

The majority of the women wore their hair in pinned up beehive hairstyles. They all looked like Sister Cyprus in the same conforming style of dress, plain and ugly. The children were sent downstairs. Mom came with us and listened to some of the Sunday school service until Sister Sypher came to get her.

I hoped this church would be similar to other churches, but it wasn't. This church was different. The woman reading the book gave an interpretation of the passages. They didn't sound as though they were coming from the same Bible Mom or Dad read to us.

When Sunday school was over, the children received goldfish and balloons. The teacher instructed us to stay downstairs while the service began upstairs. As curious as we were, it was time for us to see what was going on. Colin and Stan slipped out the door when the attendant wasn't looking. I followed them out of sheer curiosity. As we approached the main hall upstairs, a strange ghostly noise echoed throughout the hallways. My brothers seemed somewhat alarmed but I'd heard it before, *in our house*, when the women were praying with

Mom.

Slowly, we pulled open the heavy wooden door and peeked inside. The room was packed and it was evident that the women were the dominant influence. Only women sat in the front half of the church, and the men sat in the back as if they were in a trance. Only the women were making the strange babbling sounds. For this to be a church, it was odd that there wasn't a crucifix nor a picture of the Lord displayed anywhere. The praying, if in fact it was, didn't sound normal.

"Where's Mom?" Colin asked Stan.

"There… she's over there, see?" He pointed her out.

"I hope she's not doing whatever they're doing," Colin whispered.

"Be quiet and listen," Stan whispered back, "They're talking normal now."

Just then, a tall, thin man in a black suit reached over us and pushed the door shut.

"You kids aren't supposed to be up here," he stated kindly.

"Why not? Our mother is," Colin, stated boldly.

"Let's see, you all were in Sunday school, right?"

We nodded, yes.

"And who let the three of you come up here?"

We looked at one another, but didn't answer.

"Well, then, you must go back downstairs."

"We don't want to stay down there. That's for little kids," Stan replied.

"At our church, we sit with our mother. It seems like you do things kind of backwards here, huh?" Colin asked probing.

"Follow me," he said, ignoring Colin's statement. He led us back downstairs. "You children must stay in here until the service is over."

He whispered something to the plump, brunette woman who should have been watching us, then left.

I leaned over to Colin and whispered, "This isn't a church."

"Then what is it, Marala?" Colin asked.

"I don't know, but whatever it is, it's not a church," I insisted.

"She's right. Any way you slice it, sissy *is* right about this one. We saw those people and they don't look normal to me. Didn't you hear them? Something's more than strange with this place. I mean, the people here are nice and all, but that's on the surface," Stan tried to explain.

"You guys have seen too many scary movies and they're starting to affect your little pea-sized brains. I say, screw them. If they want to be freaks, let them be freaks. They're wacko, but so what? Who cares?" Colin joked. "I don't; that's for sure."

"You should care stupid, because Mommy's up there with them. If your butt paid attention to the scary movies, this looks like the beginning of one," I said angrily.

"What are you guys yapping about," Clark asked, scooting closer to us. "Where'd you go anyways? I turned around and you jokers were gone."

"He'd be the first one gone with…" Colin snickered, while pointing at Clark, "his big red balloon and little goldfish," he blared out while laughing hysterically.

"What?" Clark asked sounding clueless.

"The bottom line, little fellow, is Manley Stanley and Ms. Fassy both think these people are messed up in the head. I kind of agree with them, but hey, what do you think, balloon boy?"

"Well, I don't think anything because you left me in here with Jimmy and Selvin. What'd I miss?"

We ignored Clark and laughed.

Hordes of women started collecting their children. Finally, the same man who returned us to the room came back with Mom. Cautiously, I observed her as if I'd expected that she changed.

"So you all couldn't sit still, I hear. Well, come on." Gently taking Jimmy and Selvin's hand, she led us upstairs. "The service is over, so let's get to the bus before it leaves and we have to call your father to pick us up. I don't have a clue where we are."

In a strange way, she appeared tranquil, as though her mind was somewhere pleasant for a change.

When we arrived home Dad was at the kitchen table finishing his lunch. He tapped his watch and looked crossly at Mom.

"I didn't know this was going to turn into an all-day retreat. What's all that junk?"

"We got it from church, see?" Clark proudly held up the bag containing six goldfish. Selvin and Jimmy held a handful of balloons each. I didn't want anything that came from that place.

"I hope they gave you food for them, too," he added, taking the last bite of his ham salad sandwich. "Alley, why are you so quiet? You couldn't wait to go, so... how was it? Tell me about the church."

"It was nice."

"What was nice about it? Can you be more specific?"

"Do you always have to be so analytical? Haven't you been to church before?"

"Look. You're the one who invites these people into my home when I'm not here. They never seem to be around when I get in from work. Then, I find your ass sitting in that damn rocking chair reading that shit they leave for your dumb ass. Therefore, if I'm inquisitive, it's because I have reason to be. You're the one who involved the kids in this secret church shit, so I'll be as analytical as I want. They're my kids, too, you know. So answer my damn question!"

"Colin, don't the kids look fine? There's nothing wrong with them. Do you think I'd ever let someone mess with *my* children? I'm not going to take them near anything or *anyone* that would hurt them. So cut it out! In fact, taking them out of this house kept them from your damn wrath. Don't ever try to make me seem unfit, Colin! You should know better than that!" She was becoming enraged but calmed down before she continued. "Listen, Colin, since you *need* to know, the service was interesting, and the people are nice. They're simply trying to help me."

"Help you... Help you how, Alley?" he asked sarcastically as if he didn't know what she was implying. "Are they trying to help you get a job or your damn driver's license? If that's the case, perhaps I should have found this church for you years ago!" His expression caused the wrinkles in his forehead to return.

"They're trying to help me deal with you! Are you satisfied?"

She opened the freezer, took out two packs of chicken, slammed them into the sink to thaw, then went upstairs.

After we changed clothes we decided to go outside and play dodgeball. Before we had the chance to leave, Dad stopped us.

"How was the service today, son?"

"Sir, fine, I guess," Clark said biting his fingernail.

"What do you mean, you guess? Weren't you there?" he asked slapping Clark's finger away from his mouth.

"Yes… I mean, no. No, sir, we were downstairs," he replied locking his hands together behind his back.

"Downstairs where?"

"The service was for adults. We couldn't go in the main hall with Mom, so they kept us downstairs in a room with the rest of the kids for Sunday school."

"That's unusual. So let me get this straight… you remained in Sunday school while the service was taking place?" he asked, directing his question to Stan as he entered the room.

"No, sir. When Sunday school was over we were told to stay downstairs, but we went up anyways and…" He caught himself because he didn't want to be the cause of a fight. He didn't mention the weird noises and how the service was set up with the men in the back of the church.

"What else? Continue," he insisted.

"They were having service, so we waited until they finished."

"You waited? Where?"

"Downstairs."

"That was all? You didn't see anything strange?"

Stan's eyes grew serious, then he shook his head no.

"Therefore, in your assessment, it was a *normal* church, nothing out of the ordinary?"

"Yes, sir," he said sounding unsure.

Stan didn't add anything and neither did anyone else.

"Fine. Where are you kids headed?"

"We're going to play dodgeball at the field down the street," Stan said.

"All right, but watch how you throw that ball around your sister."

Dad's facial expression alluded to him being in profound thought. He was noticeably uncomfortable with this church situation, and so was I.

Throughout the week, the three mysterious women came back. They always closed the heavy turquoise curtains in the living room and brought Mom tea. Their visits with her became more secretive and peculiar. Saturday was the only day they didn't return. Each Sunday she took us to church with her. After our initial venture upstairs, they tried to make sure we didn't make it up again.

After Mom had been attending the church for about five months she had changed into an entirely different woman. Nothing seemed to worry her anymore, and she became totally consumed with these women, the church, and their ways. The one thing that didn't change was Mom's hair. She didn't pin it up into an ugly beehive like the other women.

One Friday afternoon, without warning, Dad came home early. He was infuriated when he saw the three women comfortably sitting in his house studying books with Mom. The women must have known that he was coming, because they had known every other time yet chose to leave prior to his arrival. Mom was still vulnerable to Dad's authority. However, this time it was different. They were confident that they had already entangled Mom into their web of deception and had her under their wicked influence.

Intense heat trailed behind Dad as he stormed through the door. He didn't know what he would see, but he needed to understand who was causing all the changes with Mom and put an end to it. Dad had causioned her about having these women in the house. Oddly enough, even with her fear of his abusive ways, she decided to disregard this particular warning.

Upon entering the living room, they kept talking as if he weren't there. No one acknowledged him. He put his briefcase down and roughly cleared his throat, slightly gaining their attention. They didn't say anything so he cleared his throat again. The women looked up and put their books on the table. "Alley, would you care to tell me what's going on here?" he asked.

Mom didn't say anything. Instead, Sister Cyprus stood up to greet Dad.

"You must be Colin," she said sounding disingenuous with phony pleasantries. "I've heard so much about you. It's nice to place a face with the name. I'm Sister Cyprus," she said, extending her hand gracefully.

"You don't say." He didn't acknowledge her attempt to shake his hand. He looked at her crossly until she withdrew her hand. "Alley, what the hell is going on in here?"

"We're having our standard meeting with your wife," Sister Cyprus replied.

"I don't recall addressing you. Let me say it again so you can figure out to whom I'm speaking. Alley!" His voice roared and Mom looked up.

"Colin, what's the matter with you? Can't you be a little friendly for a change? These are the women I've told you about," she said trying to calm him down.

"Wrong! These are the women *I* told you *not* to have in *my house*! In addition, I recall telling you that I didn't want your little meetings here either!" Beads of perspiration formed on his angry face as he began clenching his teeth.

"Don't start, Colin. Please don't start," she said clasping her hands together as if she were praying for him not to perform.

"I'll start what in the hell I want to," he said glaring at Alley. "I don't know exactly what it is that you sit here and discuss all afternoon, but I don't particularly like what I'm sensing."

"Sensing? What are you trying to say now, Colin?" Mom asked defensively.

"So you get the gist of what I'm saying, let me be more clear for you. Hmmm, I want your new little friends to pack up their bags of tricks and break camp somewhere else. I've told you before to beware of false prophets who come to you in sheep's clothing, but inwardly they're *ravening wolves*. Something isn't right, and I don't like it! What the hell is going on here? Are you having your damn occult practices in my house?"

Sister Cyprus calmly explained, "You act as though you have something to hide, Colin," she said raising her thick eyebrows. "We haven't done anything to deserve such a display of hostility toward us. You don't know us. You haven't tried to understand what it is we want to do for your wife. Your anger concerns me greatly as it displays much unrest for your troubled soul." She took two steps toward Colin and rested her hands on her hips. There was dead silence throughout the house as their eyes locked for a few intense moments. *Her eyes turned black like oil… And so did his!*

"Look, Sister *Sinister*! I don't give a damn what concerns your fat ass," he shouted, nearly thumping his index finger on her forehead. "However, I will tell you this much… I don't know you, and I have no desire to get to know you. The way the three of you freaks have been sneaking in and out of here over the last several months, I'd say you're the ones with something to hide! This conversation is over! I want *you* and your devil worshiping cohorts to get your fucking souls, which greatly concern *me*, out of my damn house, pronto! And I don't want to catch you in it again! Is that clear? Get the hell out of here!"

The women turned toward Mom, trying to display sympathy for what she had to deal with. They quickly packed their belongings before he threw them out.

"We'll be in touch, Alley," Sister Cyprus stated boldly.

"We'll be in touch, my ass! Go touch somebody else's damn mind, but not my wife's! Don't call my damn house either!"

"You're paranoid, Colin. Listen to yourself! These people haven't done—"

"Alley, I suggest you shut your damn mouth! I'm not finished with you as it is!"

"We're not finished with Alley, and we don't fear you, Colin. She needs us. She doesn't need you. You've hurt this child enough," Sister Cyprus added as she headed for the front door.

"You motherfuckers need to mind your own damn business! You don't know who in the hell you're dealing with! Get your asses out of here! Get the hell out of my house! You're not bringing your damn bullshit into my house again! Keep your little collaboration with the devil between the three of you and away from my family!"

After shoving the three of them through the door, Dad slammed it shut, rattling the pictures on the walls. The women didn't appear discouraged by Dad's animosity. They walked down the street in their coy little fashion as if they'd won the first round. They would defiantly return, and Dad knew it.

Mom nervously began picking up the cups and saucers. She tried not to make eye contact with him, but he was staring her up and down with his burning rage.

"Didn't I tell you to keep that shit out of my house?"

"Colin, they just came by to read the Bible and talk about some things. You didn't have to act so uncivilized. There was no reason for you to treat them like that, and you know it. They just want to talk," she said faintly.

"Like hell they did! They have your ass so fucking brainwashed it's pathetic. You're mind is so foggy you can't even see that they have a hidden agenda for your stupid little ass! What was all that shit they packed up when I ran their asses out of here? What *things* do they come here to talk about that can't wait until Sunday? Enlighten me, damn it! Tell me what the hell is *really* going on with this church shit?"

"I don't have to explain a damn thing to you. You have everybody figured out all the time. So go on, figure them out, too. What's going on behind your back, Colin? Why don't you tell me since you're the one with the degree?"

"Look, idiot, don't fucking patronize me! You're too fucking dense to grasp what's going on with these women. They don't belong to a church; it sounds more like a damn cult! I asked you a question, and that ugly ass bitch answered for you while you're sitting in that damn chair like you were in a damn trance! Or better yet, perhaps you've begun to let Satan dominate your fucking mind. They seem to be contaminating your feeble ass with some satanic bullshit or something! I don't like what I see! I don't like it not one damn bit, Alley! You don't know where the church is, what religion they are. The bottom line is you haven't conveyed anything I consider acceptable!"

"You don't have to accept anything. They come here for me, Colin, not you!"

"You're damn right they come here for you. You need to figure out what that reason is. How much money do you give them?"

"Nothing! They haven't asked me for a damn dime! And you don't leave me with one either!"

"Don't you find that a tad out of the ordinary? They don't ask for money. Do they take a collection at church? I'm sure they must or how else do you suppose the church operates without getting money from the congregation, Alley? They get money from somewhere. On the other hand, are they pulling it out of their asses? That's all they really want from you anyway. Do they pray the way we do? Do they?"

"Everybody doesn't do things *your way*. They don't come here to knock me upside a damn wall or to beat the kids. They're teaching me how to handle—"

"Handle? Handle what? Who in the hell do they want you to learn how to handle; certainly not me," he replied with solid arrogance pointing at his chest. "You see, that's exactly the type of bullshit I'm talking about. I don't want them in my house trying to teach you how to run me! A... You couldn't fucking learn how to run me if your life depended upon it. And B... No one handles me! Ever! You got that? Ever!"

Her uncontrolled anxiety was towering and her eyes gave way to her fear. The more he prodded, the more she began to act like a wild animal trapped in a corner. She was pacing the room with short random steps. She would have to fight her way out.

"I'm not going to let you run me anymore, Colin! I'm not having it!" With raging hostility, she spit in his face, then wiped the back of her hand across her mouth. "If I want to go to that church, then I'll go!"

Her ferocious eyes met the anger in his as he tightened his fist and struck her directly in the left side of her head, slightly missing her temple. Her stunned body fell backwards onto the sofa. Mom had already begun training herself to accept abuse, and this was another of her sessions.

"Don't you ever fucking spit on me again! I'll kill you, bitch! You got that? And nobody... And I mean *nobody* comes into *my* house to teach your sorry ass how to handle me! Do you understand where I'm coming from? Do you, damn it?"

She staggered to her feet clutching the sofa, then unsuccessfully swung at him with weak, sloppy blows. He savagely twisted her arm behind her back and shoved her face first into the wall.

"Let go of me! Let go, you son-of-a-bitch!" She lifted her leg and kicked him as hard as she could in his knee. He quickly released her.

"Oh, shit," he moaned, grabbing his knee with both hands. "You're going to pay for that! You're really going to pay for that shit," he warned.

She stumbled up the stairs into Clark's room, trying to lock the door. He was right behind her and threw his weight against it, forcing it back open.

"So you want to play rough?" he asked as though she invited him to beat her. He pinned her against the wall by her shoulders and let his heavy hands travel up to her neck. He wrapped both hands around her throat, digging his fingers deeper into it. The pressure on her esophagus quickly cut off her air. Her cough turned to a desperate wheezing escaping from her restricted airway. She clawed at his hands frantically, trying to free herself from his insane grip until her hands dropped to her side. When he saw her nose flaring and watery eyes beginning to roll back into her head, he smiled. Her eyelids fluttered as though she was falling to sleep. With a swift and powerful jolt, he slammed her head against the wall. She dropped to the floor gasping for air. Blood oozed into her hair from the side of her head.

"That will teach you to fuck with me. You're lucky, Alley! You're awful lucky I'm in a generous mood tonight."

His long stream of obscenities continued for several minutes without a word from Mom. He ended his tirade and turned to leave the room. At that moment, her adrenaline forced her to her feet again and she lunged at him, yelling out of control. Her hoarse words were barely audible.

"I'm sick of you! I'm sick to death of your shit!"

He flung her off his back against the dresser. With a tight fist he delivered the first blow to her abdominal area. Before she could catch her breath, he followed it with another. She doubled over, spitting blood. He pinned her left shoulder against the wall and punched her so hard that when he let go, she hit the floor.

"You want to learn about control? I'll teach you! I'm the master of control around here, damn it!"

"Stanley... Colin, help me." Her weak cries lacked vigor.

"They're not stupid." He moaned, trying to catch his breath. "No one's going to help you! Call your little friends! Where are they now?

Do you feel in control? Do you? You let these people fill your head with shit, so I'll just beat the shit out of you!"

Stan, Colin, Clark, and I fearfully gathered in the doorway of my room listening to her faint cries for help. I couldn't take it.

"We have to help her," I insisted.

"It won't do any good. Look at him compared to us," Clark explained.

"At least we can try! Mommy needs us, so we have to do something! If we stick together, maybe we'll be able to stop him. We can't let her call us and not do anything," I continued.

"Like he's really going to stop. You know better. He's a monster," Clark exclaimed. "So let it rest already."

"That's what he wants… for us to be afraid of him and not do anything about it!"

"The point is—" Clark began trying to rationalize his fear.

"The point is nothing," I replied, cutting him off.

"Be realistic about this crap," Clark said.

"Well, I don't care what you guys do; I'm going to do something. Did you hear Mommy screaming in there? That sounded realistic to me! I'm not going to let her keep crying for help and not do anything. Don't forget, that's our mother he's beating!"

"Since when did you get so brave?" Clark sighed with annoyance. He glanced at his brothers and shook his head. His face was somber. He leaned against the wall and closed his eyes tightly.

I searched the room looking for something to attack Dad with, but found nothing that would hurt him. I opened the hallway closet where the vacuum was stored and firmly pulled off the long silver attachment and gripped it tightly. Without thinking, I raced into the room and swung my arms back as far as they would go, then struck him in the head as hard as I could. He turned around in complete shock when he saw me standing there with the pole. Before he had a chance to respond, Stan, Colin, and Clark bombarded him with their fists, striking him wherever they could. Mom was on the floor next to the bed coughing up blood. She could hardly lift her head as she watched with disbelief. It was the first time we'd ever attempted to help her.

"You little bastards! I'll give you until the count of three to get the hell off me and out of here! Now! Right now, damn it!"

None of us stopped. He tried hurling the boys off him one at a time. We kept fighting.

"Run, Mom… Go," we shouted out of sync.

Stan and Colin jumped on his back so she could try to make it into my room. He snatched her hair, dragging her back toward him until I smacked his hand with the pole. I was sure the pole didn't hurt him, but the fact that I did it angered him even more. I saw his manifestation and knew I was his target. Dad was going to kill me! He let go of Mom's hair, snatched the pole out my hand, and swung it in my direction, yelling violently!

"You little bitch! I'm going to tear you up! Who do you think you are? Do you hear me? I'm going to beat the daylights out of you!"

Stan, Colin, and Clark wrapped themselves around Dad as if he were a giant monster under attack.

"Run, Marala! Get out of here… Go with Mom!"

Their scared voices echoed as Dad gestured with his hands for me to try and get past him.

"Come on, bitch! You're *first* on my list!"

The pounding in my chest grew harder.

Playtime was over. He slammed Stan and Clark into the wall. Colin flew over his shoulder and crashed to the floor. He snatched the tail of my pink shirt, but it ripped, releasing me from his grip. I raced into my room for safety. Before Mom and I could shut the door, his heavy foot jammed it, giving him enough room to reach inside. Mom bit down on his hand as hard as she could until he yanked it away. She managed to turn the lock before he forced the door back open with his weight. He could have kicked the door in, but we knew he wouldn't want to pay for another one. He tried to unlock it with a bobby pin but she pushed the six-drawer dresser then my bed against the door. Panic was in control of me! My heart raced and my body trembled. I was overwhelmed with a burning anxiety. Is this happening? Was he going to kill us?

Mom quickly grabbed the bedspreads, threw them on the floor, then began pulling the white cotton sheets off the twin beds and tied them together with shaking hands.

"Help me!"

"What do you want me to do?" I asked.

She handed me one end of the bed sheet, but I dropped it.

"Pick that up and tie it around the bed real tight… Real tight." She watched me while securing her own sheets together in tight knots. "Loop it through the headboard," she instructed.

Dad's crazed pounding on the door continued.

"Why are we doing this?"

"I'm climbing out the window," she whispered.

"Why didn't you run out the door?"

"Your father would have caught me. This way, he'll think I'm still in here. By the time he realizes I'm gone, it'll be too late."

His pounding kept rattling the door and kicked our escalating fear to a new height. Our sweaty faces couldn't hide it.

"Open this damn door! Open it!"

"Leave us alone! Haven't you done enough?"

"All right, Alley! If that's the way you want it. Eventually, you'll have to bring your fucking dumb ass out here. When you do, I'll be waiting for you! I'll be waiting for the *both* of you!"

His vicious pounding rattled the weak door. I looked at Mom and cried in piercing screams with every thump. She rubbed her hand across my hair and pulled me closer to her.

"Leave Marala out of this, you fucking bastard!"

"Bring your asses out here now, and we'll see! We'll just have to wait and see, now won't we?"

"We'll see my ass… Go to hell! Go to fucking hell!"

"Marala, you have one chance to open this damn door, and I won't beat your ass. If you don't, you'll regret it like hell because eventually I'll get you! You're only making it worse for yourself. Much worse," he promised.

"Shut up, Colin! Shut up! Shut the hell up," mom yelled.

"Don't listen to your hysterical ass mother because she can't even save herself. How in the hell do you expect her to save your ignorant ass? I'm sure you're well aware of that!" He paused, then tried to continue his negotiations with more composure. "Okay, okay, here's the deal. If you open this door and let *Daddy* in, I won't hurt either of you. I'm just upset, that's all. This is between Daddy and Mommy. I won't involve you, and I won't hit your mother." His deceptive voice was unpersuasive.

"I know you're going to hit Mommy. That's why I can't let you in. I want you to stop! But I know you won't! I already know it!"

"All right, fine. You had your chance, now know this. You'd better be worried about your own ass instead of your mother's because I'm going to tear it the hell up!"

For about thirty minutes there was nothing but screaming and crying echoing from downstairs. You could hear the sounds even more clearly through the air vents. Mom looked sick over every scream. Finally, we heard the door to his room slam shut, and there was silence. Things were much too still for a few minutes. We wondered if he was up to something else. Finally, we heard the television in his room. Everything seemed settled. Mom sat on the edge of the bed for twenty minutes holding me in silence.

"Where are you going?" I asked.

"I don't know, but I have to get away from that man. That fool's crazy. He acts like he's lost his damn mind."

"Don't let him run you away from us and your home."

"Home? This is *his* house, or haven't you heard him scream it from the top of his lungs over the years? *Everything* is his! I don't have a home, and I never will as long as I'm with him!"

Mom grabbed her large blue jean purse, put the strap around her neck, then went to the window and looked up and down the street to see who was outside. She tugged the knot to make sure the sheets were tightly secured around the bed, then tossed the other end out the window. She jumped up on the ledge and straddled one leg out of it. Tears blurred her swollen eyes, and uneasiness covered her face.

"Are you leaving for good? Are you coming back for us?"

"I'll be back for you all. I promise. And thank you for defending me. It means more to me than you know."

I grabbed onto her leg and refused to release it while begging, "Please, take me with you! Please, don't leave me here! I can't stay here either! You know I can't!"

"I don't have anywhere to go. Baby, it's not safe for me to take you.

It's not safe," she said dropping tears on my face.

"And leaving me here is? You'll be gone and he's going to have a field day with me," I cried clinging tighter.

"I'll be back when I have somewhere to take you all. Now stop crying for Mommy. You have to be a big girl for me. I know your father well, and you have to trust me. He won't beat you. He'll be looking for me. It's *me* he wants!"

Mom removed my unyielding grip from her leg. She wiped her runny nose with the sleeve of her torn blouse, then threw her other leg through the small left side of the window and slid down the sheets. I pulled the sheets back inside as I watched her run across the lawn to the end of the street. Without looking back, she turned the corner and was gone.

A couple hours later, Dad came back demanding that we open the door. At this point, I knew facing him was inevitable. I twisted the end of my shirt around my fingers and paced the room, terrified at the thought of having to open the door. There was no one to protect me. I should have climbed out the window, too.

"Open the damn door before I kick it down! Do you hear me? Open it! I didn't want to, but I'm going to kick this damn door down! I'm tired of your bullshit!"

I opened the door like the doorknob was on fire and jumped back. He shoved me aside and carefully scanned the room. He pulled open the closet and pushed the clothes to one side, then lifted each bed and looked underneath. His eyes caught the chain of sheets lying on the floor, and he stared out the window in utter disbelief.

"You mean to tell me… Where's your fucking mother? Where is she?"

Hopping around in a nervous fit like I had to use the bathroom, I pointed toward the open window. He grabbed me by both arms and violently shook me back and forth, cursing like he'd gone mad.

"You let her climb out the fucking window in the middle of the damn day? You let her embarrass me like that? She needed to slide down a sheet like we live in a fucking tower! Get out of my mother fucking sight before I catapult your ugly ass out the fucking window! Get the hell out of here! Get out," he screamed, shoving me out of the room into the hallway wall.

I was too dizzy to run down the stairs so I staggered clumsily with my heart pounding at an accelerated rate to tell Stan and Colin about Mom. Stan was sitting at his desk staring at a blank piece of paper, and Colin was lying across his bed with a book in his hand. Their eyes were red and puffy.

"What happened?" I asked with my eyes welling with tears again.

Stan stood and held up his shirt displaying bloody red welts on his thin stomach and back. I knew the marks came from the buckle instead of the belt itself. Colin had them, too. Their faces were badly beaten.

"Mommy's gone."

"We know. We saw her leave, and so did the people across the street," Colin added.

"Did she say where she was going?" Stan whispered.

"No. All she said was that she had to get out of here but she'd be back for us. She said to thank you for defending her."

"See, it's like I told you guys. Anywhere's better than here. Our own mother abandoned us to get away from him. She told you, *she'd be back for us*. She left us in this house with him, and we're supposed to sit here and wait for her to come back and save us. Right? What do you think of that, Stan? Mom left us. She knew what he'd do to us, and she bolted anyway." Colin buried his face in his pillow. "She deserted us," he mumbled as he squeezed the pillow tighter. His sobs hurt me even more. After all, he was right. Since Mom finally got away from Dad, why would she come back? I was beginning to believe Colin. She wasn't coming back. Stan didn't help matters because he didn't argue Mom's point. It didn't make much sense to do so anyway.

Things remained calm around the house for the next few hours. Dad spent most of his time driving around the neighborhood looking for Mom. When he came back, he made a few telephone calls to her family. They were oblivious to what happened. He stood in the front door trying to see if Mom was wandering around the house, but she wasn't. He came downstairs and asked if we knew where the church was or where any of the women lived. We didn't know. If I had, I wouldn't have told him. The route to their church was already confusing. Besides, we never went to any of their homes, and if Mom had, it was without us. There weren't too many places she could go. She wouldn't get far without clothes, shoes, food, or money.

During that week, we went to school while Dad went to work later in the morning. He was waiting to see if Mom showed up, but she didn't. Each day we returned from school, the house was quiet, and Mom was still gone. We kept the house immaculate and did the cooking together. We did laundry and ironing on a tight schedule to avoid clothes piling up. We didn't want to give Dad any reason to be more upset than he already was.

Each time the phone rang, Dad jumped to answer the call, but it was never Mom. Even after the first week he didn't have a clue where she was. The following week began the same way, and Dad was more concerned. It didn't appear as though Mom was planning to come back at all. She didn't attempt to reach out to us, and it seemed as though Colin was right. The fights were too frequent for her to live with, so she left. I, on the other hand, couldn't fully accept that Mommy left us for good. I refused to accept it because I knew better.

Selvin and Jimmy were unusually composed because they still didn't have a clue as to what transpired. Dad told them that Mom went to visit Grandma so she could have a break. They appeared to think nothing of it, only Selvin stayed a little closer to me. I called him my little spider monkey because of the way he clung to me when I carried him on my hip and the way he hopped behind me when we walked.

The following Tuesday morning rolled around, and our routine was much the same. Each day I'd leave for school, hoping Mom would return by the time I got home. My loyalty to that thought was diminishing since she didn't call and there had been no sign of her.

After school, everything appeared to be the same, but this time something was different. I walked into the living room suspiciously lifting my nose into the air, the ends flared. I walked back into the kitchen and sniffed twice. Then I smiled. Mom had been back because the recent trace of her cigarette lingered in the air, nearly going undetected.

I noticed that when Dad asked if Mom called or anyone heard from her, Stan didn't respond. After smelling her cigarette, I knew she was somewhere nearby. That day, my disposition was better than my brothers because I knew Mom would turn up soon. Besides, Stan's birthday was a few days away. She'd *never* miss it. I had one way to confirm my suspicions.

After school the next day, light raindrops chased me down the street causing my hair to fall flat. I pulled open the kitchen door and ducked inside leaving the dark twisted clouds behind me. Stan was at the counter pulling two slices of bread from the loaf. I was positive he knew something about mom's whereabouts, and he wouldn't lie to me. I waited all day to confront him.

"Stan, can I tell you a secret?" I asked with a smile on my face and a tinge of excitement in my voice. I rested my books on the edge of the counter and tried to catch his unmoving eyes.

"Go ahead," he replied.

"Mommy's been home."

Stan's brief gaze rose to meet mine. I reached down, took off my shoes and lined them up against the wall. He reached his hand out and helped me back up, then casually asked, "What makes you think so?"

He paused, flashing a half grin. He turned around, twisted the top off the peanut butter and set it on the counter. He dug the knife into the jar and pulled out a big clump, then spread it over the bread like he was painting.

"See, after breakfast this morning I arranged everything in the refrigerator a certain way." I opened the refrigerator to show him my handiwork. He turned to look.

"So, what about it, kiddo?" he asked, trying to keep his smile from stretching. He removed the jelly from inside the door and closed the refrigerator.

"So, don't be so stupid. Only Mom uses pet milk in her coffee. And that's not all. You can smell her cigarette if you take a good whiff," I explained turning my nose up.

"You're imagining things." He shrugged. He opened the jar, held it over the bread and scooped jelly onto it. He took the knife and lightly spread the jelly, then pressed both pieces of the bread together and sighed. He dropped the knife into the sink and stared out the window watching the heavy rain.

"Well."

Stan ripped a paper towel from the holder and wrapped the sandwich in it. He leaned against the counter studying my expression, but didn't say anything.

"Fine," I said shrugging. "When Dad gets home, I'll ask if I'm imagining things. He'll know if she's been back." I was bluffing. There was no way I would mention this to Dad.

"All right, all right," Stan replied. "I'll show you something if you promise not to say anything."

"I promise," I agreed eagerly.

We heard a car door shut and peeked out the window. It was next door. Stan instructed me to follow him downstairs to the laundry room. I looked around, but didn't see anything.

"So, what are you showing me? Am I supposed to clean this room up, too? I already folded the laundry last night, and… Mommy's not down here, is she?" I asked with my eyes widening.

"Sissy, you promise?" he asked again, shaking the sandwich at me.

"I promise! You already know I wouldn't do anything to hurt Mommy. I helped her run away, remember?"

Stan shut the laundry room door and locked it. He led me behind the furnace. It was dark, smelly, dusty, and had pieces of draping cobwebs. As I began to crawl into the small space under the stairs, I noticed the cobwebs had been cleared away. The musty smell was stronger, and I heard something move. Cautiously, I looked farther inside the little cubbyhole only to find Mom crouched underneath the stairs. She looked at me with her eyes loaded with tears. Her hands were shaking as she held them out to pull me in.

"Come here, baby," she whispered softly.

I fell onto her lap, sobbing uncontrollably. She tightened her arms around me.

"Mom… I thought you weren't coming back. And… and then I saw the pet milk and I smelled your cigarettes."

"Well, then, that's not good. I'm glad your father isn't as smart as you are. I told you I'd be back. In fact, I never left."

"You were here all this time?"

"Of course I was. I had nowhere else to go." Her attempt to adjust her stiff back into a better position was unsuccessful. "I'd miss you all too much. Besides, Stan has a birthday in a couple days. I couldn't be away for that," she said smiling weakly.

"We've missed you, Mom." Stan said reaching over to hand her the sandwich.

She gave him an appreciative nod, then began devouring it.

"I know," she said swallowing hard. "I've heard you all talking, and little Colin complaining. He needs to have more faith in me. I would never think of leaving my flesh and blood." She shoved the last piece into her mouth and said, "You children are my life! Don't you know how much I love you?"

She raised the back of her hand to her quivering lips and wiped the lingering crumbs away. I was relieved to hear her say she missed us. I needed to hear that.

"Dad's been looking everywhere for you," I warned.

"Your father couldn't find me if his life depended on it. And he calls *me* stupid." She attempted a smile but the appearance quickly faded.

"The next time you run away, take us with you," I insisted.

"I'll do that if you want to share this little cubby hole." She removed a bobby pin from her hair, pulled my coarse bangs off my face, and pinned them back. "I think someone needs her hair done, don't you?"

"Mom?"

"What is it, Stanley?" she asked, reaching for his hand. He bit down on the side of his thumb trying to tear off a hangnail while giving her his other hand.

"I'm sorry you didn't have anywhere to go."

Mom dropped her head with embarrassment as tears rolled down her cheeks.

"Do you want me to make you something else to eat?" I asked.

"Thank you, baby. I'm starving, and I've hardly eaten the past few days. There haven't been any leftovers up there. I've been sneaking around trying not to mess up anything so you wouldn't know I was here. I couldn't eat much or someone would have noticed."

"Me and kiddo have to start frying the fish. I'll fix you a big plate before Dad gets in."

"Make sure Jimmy and Selvin don't swallow any bones and make sure your father gets plenty of them."

"Okay," Stan said with a slight grin.

"Try not to burn the fish so your father doesn't go crazy."

"We won't," he replied.

"Stanley, can you get me another blanket? This floor is as hard as the dickens, and it's killing my behind."

"Of course I can."

"Do you want a pillow, too? I can get one from my bed. If you need any clothes or something, I can get those, too," I said.

"I'll take a pillow as long as you get it from your bed and no one else's. I can't change out of these clothes because I know how observant your father is. Most likely, he's already counted my undergarments, clothes, and especially my shoes so he'd know if I've been here. Your father is clever. I learned the hard way not to underestimate that man. Not ever," she said, looking away from us as though reality was beginning to seep back in. On the other hand, perhaps it never left.

"We have to get back upstairs. I think Clark and Colin just came in," Stan explained as he cracked open the door and peeked around the corner. "Come on, sissy, let's start dinner. You'll have to bring Mom a pillow when those knuckleheads aren't around," he whispered.

I was relieved to know Mommy was back with us, yet disappointed that she was troubled by what Dad's reaction would be when he saw her. She wasn't ready for him to know she was home.

I was hopeful that the allegations Dad made regarding the women and their church would cause Mom to acknowledge how strange things were. I think she knew Dad was right; the technique he utilized to bring it to her attention would have thrown anyone into denial out of spite. One of Dad's shortcomings was his inability to be diplomatic and sensitive.

For the next few days, Mom continued to take refuge beneath the stairs in the tiny laundry room. At least she was temporarily free from

Dad and the church, neither of which had proven to be good for her. When she finally came out of hiding, Dad had no idea she'd been in the house the entire time, and she didn't tell him. He knew he had broken her with his interminable malevolence. His remedy was giving her time to recuperate physically, by leaving her alone. She wouldn't heal mentally. However, since his rage was uncontrolled, he stayed away as much as possible. Dad wasn't one to apologize often because that would have implied he was wrong, which he never elected to admit. Dad handled *his* mistakes by disregarding them.

Everything calmed as it always had, before the storm. Subsequently those women returned tapping on the front door with their web of deception trying to appeal to Mom's vulnerability. Heeding Dad's warnings, she didn't open the screen door. Instead, she revoked their invitation.

"Alley, it's been some time since we've seen or heard from you, dear. How are you?"

"I'm fine, thank you, but this isn't a good time for me. My husband's on his way home, and I have to get dinner started."

"You've obviously been under a lot of stress lately, and that's all the more reason we should talk," Sister Cyprus continued.

"Well, that's married life. Maybe we can talk some other time, but not now, not today. I'm sure you already know what's been going on here. You don't need to ask how I am. You never need to," she said agitatedly. "Right now I need time to think. If I want you, I'll call you."

Mom began to shut the door when Sister Cyprus yanked open the screen door and pushed it back open. She was displeased that Mom had regained some of her own strength and denied them access to her house, and mind.

"No, Alley. I came here because I know what you need, and I'm not leaving until I have a chance to talk to you. We *are* your friends, and we've been concerned about you! You were happy with us... weren't you, Alley?"

"That's beside the point. You don't understand—"

"No, you don't understand that *he* has sent us to teach you, and you're wasting our time! Colin is still controlling you! Through your own ignorance you don't realize that he has you right where he wants you. Think about what he did to you. You're as weak as a child. We're capable of giving you the things you need to defend yourself against that man! And if you turn us away, we *will not* come here again!"

"Colin doesn't want you here anyway. And to be honest, I think I should listen to him. He's not always wrong about everything, you know."

For the first time since meeting those women, Mom was genuinely concerned about Dad's accusations. She knew Dad's concerns were reasonable.

"Yes, let's not forget Colin. When we leave, *you* can worry about him on your own. Perhaps next time you won't make it beneath those stairs."

"Then maybe you all should have done something to help since you're supposed to be helping me so damn much!" Unnerved, Mom slammed the door, forcing them away. This time she resisted their evil. *It was a small victory, and I hoped it would last.*

From the beginning, these women had conspired to employ Mom for some sort of sinister plot. Their carefully spoken words, cups of tea, and phony smiles managed to identify with Mom's need for empathy and a means to escape the binds of her wretched existence.

I found these women to be a deceptive collection of evil. They alleged they wanted to assist Mom with her difficulties with Dad, yet never suggested her going to a battered women's shelter, filing a restraining order, leaving the home, or putting Dad out. They didn't offer financial assistance so she could leave and start over again. Not once did this church or the women who claimed to be her friends propose to do anything for Mom. Whatever they sought from Mom was unmistakably a crucial piece of their conspiracy. The efforts they put forth were for their own personal gain, and none of us knew what it was. Their involvement in Mom's life was causing greater problems for everyone. I was appreciative that Dad was obstinate with them. I couldn't explain it, but I was certain he did the right thing.

This spring was more ordinary than things had been for quite some time. Dad was excelling at work and making several notable accomplishments, inclusive of a promotion. It took an enormous effort, but his career seemed to be progressing well.

Dad was relentless in business. He was persistent in making the company's annual sales club and was *Man of the Month* several times that year. The problems of office politics and his race were the handicaps that obstructed his moving into a well-earned management position. Dad's high degree of intelligence continued to evolve. His boss often called him at home for advice and solutions. Although he explained that blatant discrimination existed at work, he made it clear that he couldn't show his anger there. Since the majority of his time was devoted to work, he didn't have much time to discipline us for behavioral issues.

When the powerful rays of summer returned, everything in our house was still at ease. Some of the disagreements resurfaced but it wasn't as severe. The few arguments they had were brief, merely verbal, and insignificant. The majority of them ended with passionate kissing and making-up. Dad actually appeared to be happy for a change. In the interim, Dad's salary increased, so he finally took three weeks of vacation time, and we managed to do a lot of fun activities as a family. Laughter was back in abundance and we were creating *good* memories for a change.

It was encouraging to see Dad attempt to bring the family together. He read the Bible for about an hour or so on Sunday evenings and made each of us older children read and explain the passages. His favorite books were always Proverbs and Psalms. He loved the 23rd verse of Psalms in particular and made sure each of us could recite it. In addition, Dad required everyone except Jimmy and Selvin to recite the *Lord's Prayer*. Clark had difficulty explaining the passages because he didn't pay attention.

Mom didn't join us, but oddly enough, Dad didn't complain. He found other opportunities to spend time with her. He took us go-cart racing, to Cedar Point, or the movies. Our family loved fish, so each Friday he brought fresh bass, perch, and trout home from the West Side Market in Cleveland. The smell of fresh fish in the house would have everyone waiting at the table for dinner. In addition to the fish he bought hotdog links and nasty hog head cheese. Everything else was fresh fruit and crisp vegetables.

He and Mom threw on records, cooked together, and danced intermittently with playful bouts of laughter between them. On the weekends, if Dad was resting, Mom packed a basket filled with fried chicken, Lays Potato Chips, and Fig Newtons, then took us on picnics and hikes through the Park. Mom took us on adventures all over the city, and it never mattered that we walked. *We were happy.*

Mom got her drivers license, and Dad kept his word and bought her a car. Mom cherished her little powder blue four-door car. It was used, but that didn't matter because she took us everywhere in it. Dad was proud of her. One day Mom was speeding when a police officer pulled us over.

"Good afternoon, ma'am. May I see your license and registration please?"

"Officer, I'd love to give it to you, but I'm a doctor, and I was called in for an emergency surgery at Memorial. Every second is crucial to the patient. I'm sure you understand."

"Oh, yes, of course Dr—"

"Murray. Dr. Alley Murray."

"Good luck with your patient," he said waving.

"Thank you, officer," Mom replied and drove off giggling with four of us in the backseat and two in the front.

It was amazing that Mom was able to pull off a stunt like that. She played plenty of them.

Shortly after Dad convinced Mom to get her license she got a job. She worked part-time at a nursing home, but didn't like it. After Mom had been working a few months, Dad was in his bedroom and found a brown shopping bag filled with eyeglasses, teeth, and hearing aids. He asked Mom where they came from. She replied, "Those old smelly people get on my damn nerves! They want, want, want all the damn time, and I'm sick to death of it!"

"So what do these have to do with anything?" he asked, pulling a pair of glasses from the bag, followed by a hearing aid.

"I took their glasses so they can't see me! Then, I took their damn hearing aids so they can't hear me coming!"

"Alley, you took their teeth! Teeth, Alley?" he asked with a look of bewilderment on his face. "Why the hell would you take their teeth? How are they going to eat?"

"They can eat with their gums, the same way your mother does," she said laughing. "Oh, and the reason I took their teeth is so they can't complain about shit. I just tell them I don't understand what they're trying to say and to call me when they find their teeth. Those old people get on my nerves."

"Get on your nerves?"

"Yes. Get on my nerves. That's what I said, isn't it?"

"You have to return these items. Those people need these things. Besides, you're supposed to be helping them, not hurting them."

"Well, they hurt me every damn time I have to change their diapers and smell that shit!"

"I wouldn't be so harsh if I were you. One day, Alley, if you live that long, it'll be *you* having your diapers changed!"

"Not before your behind, Colin. You know you're older than me."

———

In the middle of summer, we were outside, enjoying the afternoon warmth. Selvin and Jimmy were trying to catch grasshoppers in the corner of our fenced yard while my other brothers and I were playing wiffle ball. Whenever Jimmy and Selvin were around, that's the only bat and ball we were allowed to play with. The thick carpet of grass was still moist from the heavy overnight rain. Colin took a flying leap to catch the ball and when he landed behind the pitcher's mound, his foot sank deep into the soil. Quickly, he tried to yank his leg out as the ground beneath him began to cave in. Stan helped pull him up, and we concluded our game until Dad came home from work.

The next day, our neighbor Mr. Kelly helped Dad dig around the loose earth to determine the width and depth of the hole. It was a manufactured well. When they dropped rocks down the well, we couldn't hear them hit the bottom. Dad and Mr. Kelly bought a couple large pieces of plywood, covered the well, and that's how it stayed. Dad instructed us to stay clear of the hole and not to remove the covering.

Periodically, Colin and Clark removed the plywood before it rained to see if the well filled after a heavy downpour, but it never did. The well made it difficult for us to play ball games because it was near the center of the yard, so we played at the recreation center.

The mysterious incident with the well appeared to be a portal to something, perhaps hell. Did the other yards have one, too? It was odd that the women couldn't capture Mom's attention, then the *well* emerged. Immediately afterwards, we learned that nothing lasts forever. Subsequently, everything reverted to the way it used to be. Work became increasingly demanding for Dad. The fights erupted again, and their arguments twisted into ferocious physical battles. *The fire was beginning to burn out of control.*

———————

The brilliant rays from the sun that warmed us throughout the week had disappeared leaving dark clouds to pollute the sky. This was the day the evil returned, refusing to let their principal constituent to their wicked plan escape their clutches. Trying to shield a black eye and several bruises with her hair and makeup, Mom was no longer reluctant to let them in. Instead, submissively she welcomed them inside.

They resumed their customary bloodcurdling routine and began with their forum. An innate insight provided them with the duration of time they had to work within before Dad came home. It appeared that every moment was valuable. They'd immediately toil like witches brewing a lethal potion. Sister Cyprus closed the curtains, and Sister Sypher made some of her tainted herbal tea. They erupted into the same uncanny babbling that I couldn't decipher, nor did I want to. This meeting was riveting because they made it clear to Mom that they had to recover from lost time.

Sister Cyprus pulled several candles from her bag and lit them. Sister Lewis and Sister Sypher removed several statues from their bags and set them on the coffee table. There were monkeys with wings, dragons with multiple heads, and statues with grotesque shapes, among others. The women joined hands while an animated Sister Cyprus recited phrases in words foreign to me. The temperature in the room decreased, and Mom's expression altered as though she were being seduced by spiritual evil. Without warning, the house filled with the same discriminating and daunting sensation I felt previously when they chanted and implored *something* to come!

There was an impetuous manifestation spawning dozens of demons into our living room for some form of a demonic gathering. Mom threw her hands up, surrendering to the evil, and discharged the most terrifying voices. As clearly as Mom spoke to us, these things were conversing *with* her and the women. I heard coinciding voices from undetectable people. The voices, using archaic languages, were comparatively dissimilar and angry. These women contaminated my mother with wickedness, then used her to release evil omens. The evil they had been hiding in our house, inside mom, was now being exposed!

At the stage where I resigned to the fact that I was living an ill-fated destiny with my father, this thrust me into an inconceivable realm. I'd considered life with Dad as hell, but I was mistaken… this was it! Was this a séance, and why were these demons communicating from beyond? After hearing more than my frail nerves could handle, I snatched my book, raced down the stairs and out the kitchen door, appearing as if I hadn't noticed them at all. I fled to the only safe place I knew of: the park.

I was cold with fear. I collapsed on the merry-go-round with my heart thumping from the terror. I was afraid to turn my back in any one position, so I kept pushing it around with my right foot. I couldn't make sense of this; it was too much for my *juvenile* mind. I was already trying to escape the destructive rage that Dad brought home. When he was gone, we were safe. Now, there wasn't a safe corner in our house, and this was all I had, a merry-go-round at a park. I put my head down and cried for the longest time, trying to empty the confusion inside of me, but it didn't work. I was certain something iniquitous would happen. I saw it coming, and now it was here. I tried to deny it, however, it was too conspicuous. This was beyond the boundaries of reason. Inside of our mother was an unforeseeable and disturbing multiplicity of demons discharging from her.

My older brothers were picking green peppers on a farm down the road, leaving me no one to turn to for an explanation of this ominous occurrence. Jimmy and Selvin were next door at Robbie's house oblivious to what Mom was doing. For whatever reason, I was always near her madness. I didn't want to become whatever she had. I didn't want that evil *around me,* let alone *in me!*

Around seven that evening Dad pulled into the driveway. I was waiting for him on the curb with my book in my hand and my legs rocking without control. The women were gone. I had to tell him what I'd heard, but wondered if he'd believe me. Anxiously, I approached him as he swung open his car door. I knew he didn't like talking to anyone that was in frenzy, so I had to compose myself and make my point. Although I tried to act normal, he detected my discomfort.

"Hey, Dad. How was work?"

His eyebrows scrunched together, bringing wrinkles between them. Examining my face, he asked, "What's wrong now?"

"Nothing, really." I shrugged.

"Nothing? Then what's with the strange look on your face?"

"Well."

"Well what? Marala, if you have something to say, spit it out. What is it?"

He loosened his red and white striped tie and unfastened the top two buttons on his shirt while continuing to study my facial expressions.

"Well, today I... I—"

I still displayed a hint of confusion as I tried to find, and then form, the words.

"I... I... I... what! Cut the small talk and spit it out," he insisted mocking me. He swung the keys around his index finger and shoved them into his pocket.

"It's Mommy! Today those same creepy women came here and started that stuff again. They brought candles and statues, then—"

"Look, save it. The last time I got involved, if I recall correctly, you children thought *I* was the bad guy. This time, I *don't* want to hear it. If your mother let's those women come here and fuck up her head... So what? Let her sit and listen to their bullshit all she wants, but, hey, I'm through with it."

He reached into the backseat for his suit jacket and black

briefcase.

"I have a feeling that something's wrong because today was different. It was really scary, and I'm afraid that—"

"I told you, Marala, from here on out that's between your mother and her new fucking friends. Like it or not, I'm out of that shit. I have more pressing things on my mind. If she wants to deal with those fruitcakes, then so be it."

He threw up his hand and went in the house.

Although Dad made it clear from that point on he didn't care about Mom's relationship with the women, I could tell it bothered him, but he didn't know how to handle what was happening, so he disregarded it. Taking into account Mom's physical and mental state, you couldn't help but notice she was shrouded in mystery.

I persisted in taking my annotations and concerns to Dad regardless of his lack of interest. I knew if I supplied him with sufficient facts I'd build a case against these women. Sooner or later he'd have to intervene. I was certain something worse was bound to happen and steal his attention. The atmosphere in our house was overly alarming and inexplicable. We had nowhere to turn. Neighbors must have detected that something was wrong, but we didn't speak about it. We didn't want them afraid or passing judgment, so we kept it locked inside, with us.

———

Approximately two months passed, and Mom continued going to church, taking us with her. It was surprising that she wanted us there, particularly after she had become a magnet for spirits. Their practices were now unconcealed. I didn't ask questions, but did manage to sneak upstairs and monitor the service more often.

I refused to pay attention to what they taught in Sunday school, nor was I willing to become brainwashed the way Mom and the others apparently had been. The reason I went to that church was because Mom made us go. *My* only justification was to look out for Mom. If anything bizarre happened that I could unquestionably link to the church, Dad would have to consider doing something. At the very least he would stop her from taking us. It was evident that he wasn't doing anything about her iniquity at home. However, if something happened outside of our house, it *would* destroy the perception people had of him. He didn't witness every gripping moment because he was seldom home but her conversion was distinct, and he saw it.

The ceremony in the main section of the church had discussions on the adversary of God, humanity, as well as demons, prophetic signs, supernatural rituals, the occult, and other inscrutable topics. I'd never heard any positive mention of God, and the formation in the church didn't change. It was impossible to differentiate what was good from evil, so I deemed that it was all evil. The more time Mom spent with them, we became less of a priority to her. Most of the time she wasn't mindful of our presence. My younger brothers felt the impact more than the rest of us and showed it.

To ensure that Mom's unresponsive demeanor didn't become a situation tackled by Dad's abuse, we continued working the routine we created for ourselves as though we were running the household void of both parents. My brothers and I did the cleaning and nearly all of the cooking.

Dad demanded that our house was always in "ship shape" as he called it. He wanted the beds made first thing in the morning, so if he bounced a quarter off it, he could. Regardless of the weather, he wanted the curtains open and windows cracked for fresh air. Closets and drawers were always neatly organized and the house vacuumed daily. We kept the kitchen mopped every night and left nothing on the counters, stove, or in the sink. At times the house became a complete mess with six children and two adults, but it didn't stay that way for longer than a few hours.

Dad's room was off limits after we cleaned it. Mom didn't spend much time in there either. His dresser had a particular order that Mom kept up for years, which became our chore. The top drawer held a few inexpensive ties; second drawer t-shirts; third drawer underwear folded in half; the last drawer had casual clothing items on half the drawer and socks folded like little ships on the other side. His area of the closet was immaculate. He kept his nine suits together by color on wooden hangers, followed by ten heavily starched and pressed white shirts. His pants hung on the same type of hangers adjusted to the identical length, facing the same direction. Everything was spaced precisely four inches apart. His belt rack held two black belts and one brown belt. When you slid Dad's closet doors open and the light hit his Florsheim shoes, they sparkled. Each pair had a hardwearing polish, spit shine, and wooden shoetrees resting in them. Nothing was out of order for Dad's personal items.

Mom's clothing hung unevenly on wire hangers with no particular order and were shoved to the other end of the closet as not to disturb Dad's things. They had a strong musty smell. We were surprised he left it that way.

He kept several books in the headboard of his bed. Most of them were psychology, medical, or history books. He loved to read. He had a few books on Western literature such as *The Iliad*. His dresser held a bottle of his good cologne and the faithful bottle of Old Spice, which was always my favorite scent. His bristle brush, black comb, and money tray were all that he kept on top of his Pledge-waxed dresser. The money tray was a hand-carved almost heart-shaped tray that Stan made in his shop class. He had given it to Dad as a birthday present. If anything was out of place, he knew it. Keeping the house in order meant giving him one less cause for being discontented. We did a first-rate job.

***

After church one Sunday Mom proudly announced that she was going to be *baptized* the following week. To some degree, this caught Dad off guard. He knew Mom was becoming more involved with this church, but hadn't predicted *this* narration. He looked at me as if I should have informed him, but all I could do was throw *my* hands up because I *had*. Dad simply chose to ignore my mounting concerns. Boy, was he in for a treat!

After clearing his voice he turned his undivided attention to Mom.

In a serious yet non-aggressive tone he asked, "So when's this big event supposed to take place?"

"This coming Sunday," she replied, sounding elated as she placed an herbal teabag into a cup and poured hot water over it.

"Who decided that?"

He removed his glasses and rubbed his eyes.

"What do you mean, *who* decided that? I decided *that,* Colin," she retorted calmly as she leaned against the counter, bouncing the teabag in the cup a few times before taking a sip. "Or don't you have faith in the fact that I can *think* for myself now?"

She opened the refrigerator and took out a dish with a piece of leftover chicken and bit down, tearing off a large piece.

"You don't say, Alley. Well, that's news to me! Nevertheless, I *think* I would like to go to your little baptism. Do you have any objections?" he asked as he put his glasses back on.

"Now, correct me if I'm mistaken… Aren't you the same person who threw *Sister Sinister* and her *devil worshiping cohorts* out of *your* home? Now you're telling me that *you* want to go to *their* church! You don't make any sense, Colin, not that you ever do. I don't know why you'd want to go in the first place since you don't like those people," she stated while taking another sip of her steaming tea. "The only reason you'd go is to show out," she joked.

"Come on, Alley, get real! I'm not going to show out at a baptism. I'm not boorish like some people I know. I'd like to be there. That's all there is to it, right? It's *simply* a baptism," he asked inquiringly.

"Well… we'll see, Colin," she replied, producing a halfhearted smile at the thought that her husband might finally be accepting her newfound religion. "And to answer your clever little question, yes, it's simply a baptism."

She finished devouring her chicken and went out back after refreshing her tea. Dad returned to reading his newspaper without inciting an argument.

During that week, Mom spent a lot of time away from home and at Sister Cyprus's house. Mom appeared to have quite a few things to learn before being baptized. She was especially distant from us and kept to herself in a secretive way. She became aggravated and defensive when anyone asked her about the church and was vigilant not to engage in any conversation that would divulge information.

When Sunday morning arrived, I was anxious to see what was going to happen. Surprisingly, Dad was dressed to go. It bothered me that I knew this church had an abnormal hold on Mommy and he let her keep attending their services. They were extraordinarily persistent about having Mom in their grasp even when she declined their involvement in her life. They knew too much about things they shouldn't have known, and realizing this, we went to witness her being sacrificed without opposition. To satisfy our own curiosity, we watched them welcome *our mother* into their evil congregation.

Mom rode to church with Sister Cyprus. As usual, the bus came to pick us up. Dad never intended to ride that bus, not knowing where it was going, as he'd told Mom before. Instead, he followed it. At last, Dad would finally know where this church was located. Upon entering the church they began to usher us downstairs like always.

"Dad, can I stay with you? I don't want to go down there."

I was afraid he'd leave me with those evil brainwashers.

"Of course you can," he replied firmly. "In fact, I want all of you to stay with me."

He instructed my brothers to follow him.

When we entered the main hall, I clenched his hand as tightly as I could. I saw the same nonconforming setup I'd seen before. The men sat in the back pews, and the women seated themselves in the front half of the church. A man directed Dad to the back part of the church, but he declined to sit there.

"I'd like to sit closer to the front," Dad demanded as he flashed a stern look to a man wearing a cheap black suit with a black clip-on tie. By the look of his hair, which was seventy-five percent gray, this man was in his late fifties or early sixties. The wrinkles covering his pale white face gave another clue to his age. His once erect posture was beginning to slump unless he had a serious case of scoliosis.

"I'm sorry, sir, but we're set up a little differently here. I apologize, but we don't allow children in the main hall," the man replied.

"Well, today you do, since that's not my concern. My wife is being baptized, and I'd like to be able to see it. I'm *not* a member of this place, and I *don't* intend on following *your* rules! Got that?"

"Yes, sir, I fully understand. However—"

"Good, then we'll sit right over there!"

Dad walked away before the man could say anything else. We sat five aisles back in the center of the room. Astonishment blanketed everyone's face, and the whispers began. Dad intentionally broke two of their sanctimonious rules. They didn't allow children upstairs, and the men sat in the back section of the church. Before the service ended, I was sure he'd break a few more rules.

When the service began, Dad was extremely attentive. Each time they prayed he didn't close his eyes. Instead, he scanned the room and observed everyone, including me. I wasn't stupid. I kept my eyes wide open! He definitely didn't appear comfortable with his observations, and neither was I. After my own surveillance, I leaned over and whispered to him. "Dad, look around this place. Do you see what's missing?" I asked as I took a piece of tissue, tore it in half and twisted it into a cross.

"There aren't any crosses or blacks," he whispered, sounding insulted that I asked.

Dad prided himself on being astute, yet Mom said he was just plain *stupid*. Well, not this time.

I was astonished that he noticed so quickly, especially with all the pandemonium taking place. I hummed in my head to block out what they were saying. I'd seen enough scary movies with my brothers to know that I could easily be brainwashed without realizing it. I wasn't about to go out like that, not here! I held the paper cross in my hand for protection.

Unexpectedly, everyone stood and the women began chanting loudly in somebody's tongues. They placed Mom on a stage draped in a plain white robe with a white towel covering her beautiful head of hair. The chanting was bizarre and frightening. When Dad looked behind him, he noticed the men were standing, but not saying a word. They weren't babbling; they looked like they were in a trance. Dad didn't stand.

A white woman with a heavy frame, black hair displaying streaks of gray, dark evil eyes, a black cape, and black dress approached the podium to speak. She was the leader, I'd seen her before in our house. My older brothers watched attentively. I assumed that all of the women were like Sister Cyprus. Jimmy and Selvin held onto the seat in front of them trying to peer over the women, but they couldn't see anything.

"Today, we're adding a new member to our flock whom all of

you know. We sought after our sister a few years ago and taught her our ways. Alley has experienced the boundless outreach of *his* higher power! She has experienced what *he* has allowed us to do through *him*! She's the link we need to obtain our goals. She has great powers. Alley has accepted our way of life and agreed to become a part of our amity. We grow stronger as we add to our congregation and must acknowledge those with special gifts and bring them here where they belong."

Applause echoed throughout the church until the leader nodded, signaling for it to halt. I glanced at Dad, already knowing his question. What special gifts did Mom have? Everyone in the pews sat down and followed the service as it continued. Arcane in thought, Dad sat motionless, staring at Mom. I was waiting for him to rescue her, but he didn't move.

"Are you ready, Alley?" the leader asked. Anxiously, Mom nodded in agreement.

The woman began to speak louder as two others took Mom and led her in front of a pool. With a firm grip, they grabbed her arms and the minister shouted, "We baptize you in our *father's* name." They dunked Mom into the pool headfirst and pulled her out by her arms. I watched fervently without batting an eyelid.

"We cleanse you in the name of our *father* so that you may have a rebirth with us."

The woman at the podium babbled outlandish words, then forcefully motioned for Mom's submergence once again. This time they held her underwater for a longer duration. The people on the platform around Mom chanted words that I couldn't understand. Dad slid to the edge of his seat listening.

"We welcome you into our *father's* embrace and *his* spirits and powers are bestowed upon you! Your gifts are beyond measure, and you're a significant part of our union."

They submerged Mom a third time. When they pulled her up, she gasped for air, then violently burst into the babbling or speaking in their tongues that the women had beforehand. She hopped around in the water, shrieking louder and louder with no sense of control, suggesting an animated force was controlling her. Everyone listened and applauded, but I took Dad's lead and sat still. Throughout the church, women joined hands and babbled in their jargon, oblivious to Dad's presence. When the praying stopped, the woman at the podium continued.

"Sister Alley, you belong to us and nothing comes before this sect. Do you accept us as your new family?"

Mom was aware Dad was there, but she didn't look at him or us. Without hesitation, she nodded *yes*. It was obvious they had acquired what they needed for the past two years. The entire church gave Mom a standing ovation, which grew intense. The atmosphere was disturbing. It felt as though they'd summoned some type of spirit. It reminded me of home, and I wanted to leave.

Subsequent to what we witnessed, there was nothing left to question. We had at least two hundred or more shifty eyes gazing at us. One of the men kindly notified Dad that Mom wouldn't be riding home with us, so we left the church. Upon leaving, Dad didn't converse with anyone else. He was noticeably troubled and anxious to leave. The problem with Mom had been right in front of our faces but because dad ignored it, *we had bigger problems now!*

The drive home proved to be somewhat of a challenge as well. It wasn't because he had six children whispering in the car at one time, but because he made several wrong turns. Eventually, we made it. Dad slammed his keys on the counter, loosened his tie, and glanced around the room. His expression was utter bewilderment coupled with a hefty dose of fear. This alliance was disturbing. Mom had a desperate need to have something greater to combat Dad's abuse. Whatever the woman wanted to give Mom, she now appeared to have.

I could tell by his tense face that his theological interpretations and intellectual mind was processing what he'd witnessed. Even after deep thought, I was certain his logic failed him.

Apparently, the strange things I had witnessed, and the disturbing feelings I was having about all of this, weren't figments of my imagination. The demonic invasion captured Mom and finally, Dad acknowledged that it was conceivable. I wondered if it was too late to do anything about it. *Our house became an open gateway to hell!*

Dad paced the living room floor reflecting upon everything

that led us to this implausible scenario. He took the information I'd provided over the past several months with what he observed and realized what I'd been *trying* to say. I was the one who spent two years trying to convince Dad that it was time for him to do something about the situation, but I didn't want him to beat my mother over it. Each time they argued and fought that gave her more of a reason to seek support from the church. Yet, those who try to utilize Satan to alleviate their problems are only exchanging one for another. Now that Dad actually went to their church, I was interested in his thoughts.

I followed him into the kitchen, grabbed two cookies from the jar, and sat at the table.

"Dad?"

"What is it, Marala?"

"Why'd you finally go to that church?"

"Why?"

"A-huh."

He sighed and said, "Let's see. You told me a few weeks ago that you saw a woman make your mother pass out during the service. That raised a red flag. And for the record, I knew something was wrong, especially after meeting that Sister… whatever her name is."

"Cyprus," I said.

He nodded.

"Consequently, that led me to evaluating the hold these women have on your mother. She's walking around here in a fucking trance most of the time. Then, with this baptism popping up out of the clear blue… I don't know," he said shaking his head. "I guess it was a multitude of things." He leaned back in the chair, rubbing his forehead.

"I wish you had listened to me sooner."

"Well, Marala, we all *wish* for things, yet the fact remains that your mother has always been stubborn. I can't tell her anything without her debating it. That's why we fight all the time. You kids don't understand because you only hear the fights or see what you want to see. It's hard for daddy to work, support all six of you… seven including your mother, by myself. By the time I get home, I have to deal with your mother's shit *and* the problems with you kids."

"Then instead of staying mad all the time, why don't you leave us like Mommy said? Why'd you have so many of us?"

"Don't you think I've asked myself that question numerous times? Nevertheless, if I left you all, tell me, who would take care of you? Who would pay all the damn bills and feed your asses? Have you ever thought about that?"

"No," I said softly.

"Well, your mother doesn't want to drive. She doesn't want to work. She doesn't take care of the house or you kids. The point is, your mother doesn't want to do shit." He opened the refrigerator, grabbed a can of Genesee beer, pulled the tab off, and took a long drink. "I didn't want so many kids, but like I've told you all before, it was your mother. She didn't believe in abortions."

"What's that mean? Abortions?" I asked with a puzzled look on my face.

"Never mind," he snapped. "I only hope that one day you'll be smart enough to know when to have one!"

He was annoyed that I couldn't comprehend his comment. I refrained from continuing that dialogue and changed the subject. He got up from the table and entered the kitchen. He looked in the sink and huffed.

"Do you want me to start dinner?" I asked.

"It doesn't appear as though your mother's going to do it. She didn't take anything out for dinner so figure something out. Find your brothers and tell them I said to help you. I'm going to watch the game and forget about this bullshit for now."

He reached in the refrigerator, grabbed another beer, then headed upstairs to his room.

"By the way, make me a liverwurst sandwich and bring it up when you're finished. Thanks."

———

By the time she came home, dinner was over, everything was cleaned up, and we were in bed. Dad was sitting at the table waiting for her. As soon as the door shut, the yelling began.

"Where the hell have you been all this damn time? Dinner's been over, the kids are asleep, and here you come strolling in when you feel like it!"

"Nobody's strolling in," she replied, taking off her shoes. "Can't you leave me alone tonight? I don't want to fight with you, Colin. Today was a special occasion, and I want to have a peaceful evening," she said dryly.

"Tell me, Alley, what's so special about today besides the obvious fact that you were baptized into a satanic cult of some sort? You have the nerve to say that you want to have a peaceful evening? Hell, the evening is over," he said pointing out the window at the black sky.

He put his elbow on the table, balled up his right fist, and rested it under his chin. His eyes narrowed as he watched her pull a glass out of the cabinet and fill it with ice.

"What the hell happened in church today? What have you gotten yourself into, Alley?" he asked cocking his head slightly to the right.

"Nothing," she said lacking expression.

"Nothing? I was there! I saw the whole fucking thing! What is that place?"

She didn't respond. She pulled the tab on a can of Pepsi and poured it over the ice.

"You didn't acknowledge us as your family," he continued.

"Who'd want to claim you, Colin?"

"So they turned you into a fucking comedian now? These people have fucked up your head and *now* your priorities! At the very least you could have called! Perhaps we wanted to take you out for dinner."

"Colin, you haven't taken me out to dinner in … I don't know how long. Look, I was out; now I'm back, so drop it. I don't feel like fighting with you again. Please, drop it."

"I'll drop it when I feel like it! Let me tell you a few things first!"

She picked up her glass and went upstairs into their bedroom. He followed taking long strides behind her.

"I said I don't want to hear this."

"You're going to hear it whether you want to or not! Those ugly ass bitches are fucking devil worshippers and you know it! I don't like them, not one fucking bit! You don't have a fucking clue what you're getting yourself into, not one damn clue! Didn't you pay attention to that shit about reincarnation? Did you hear that bitch asking why God... if he's such a loving God, let evil persist? The only evil that persists around here is *them!* They have some fucking nerve preaching that shit! Satan is the master of deception... Well he sure as hell deceived your dumb ass!" He pulled back the beige and white bedspread, fluffed his pillow on the right side of the bed, and sat on it.

"No, Colin, *you're* the master of deception and you damn well know it," she said with a slight pitch in her voice.

"Alley, you've been brainwashed by those fucking false prophets. It's more than obvious that you were involved in a satanic baptism today or hadn't you noticed? What in the hell were those monkeys with wings and statues with distorted faces all about? What was that shit, huh? Can you even attempt to explain that bullshit to me? Come on, Alley, please... enlighten me." He paused for a moment, then said, "For the last damn time, I don't trust nor do I like those damn freaks."

"They don't like you either. Nobody does," she shouted, then slammed her dresser drawer shut rattling the items on top.

"And that place we went to today... it's no fucking church! There's no damn way!"

"Then what, Colin? What is it?" she asked facing him.

"If you need me to put it in simple terms so you understand me, pay fucking attention. What I'm saying is... I... don't... think... those... people... believe... in... *God!* Did you grasp that? Perhaps I need to repeat it slower. What *they* teach is not what we've been taught, and you know it! I'm telling you, Alley, those people look more like a pack of devil worshippers in a cult than a church. Furthermore, good judgment tells me you already knew it!"

She took a deep breath and analyzed him. To his surprise she laughed for a few moments, smiled, and said calmly, "You know, Colin, maybe for once you're finally right about something."

This time, there was no trace of sarcasm in her voice. She turned and gave him an evil stare just as he'd always given her. She took a wire hanger from the closet and laid it on the bed, then pulled open her bottom drawer and grabbed a pair of gray sweatpants and a white t-shirt. After slamming it shut she went into the bathroom and closed the door. When she returned, she hung up her clothes, trying to avoid eye contact with him.

"Look, bitch, as it is, you haven't been acting like my fucking wife! This coming in and going out when you feel like it shit is going to end! You should have had your lazy ass here cooking dinner instead of Marala and the boys. Jimmy and Selvin went to bed not knowing where their fucking mother was! You neglect those kids as if they're invisible. I think—"

"Damn it, Colin! There you go again with *I think, I think!* I'm sick of your ass talking down to me like I'm a damn child. Don't tell me what I should have done around here! If you want something done *I think* you should do it! *I think you* should have cooked dinner for the kids!"

"My, my, my, don't we sound mighty *Christian* for someone who was baptized today!"

"Go to hell!"

"What was that?"

"I said, go to hell," she blurted with more aggravation.

"Why don't you and your fucking devil worshipping friends lead the way? I'm sure they've been there before! Go on, call them and ask."

He picked up the phone and put it in her face.

"Stop it, Colin!"

She snatched the phone out of his hand and slammed it back on the receiver.

"What I find amusing is how those ugly bitches can control your damn mind so easily, and I can't seem to get you to come home in time to cook a fucking meal for your family! Since you don't like being told what to do around here, I think you should take your lazy ass out and find another job. Let's see how you handle someone else giving you orders. That's why you quit that damn nursing home. What happened? Refresh my memory. You stole their shit so they couldn't tell you what they needed! You despise being told what to do because you're fucking lazy! You don't do shit around this place as it is, and I'm sure as hell not going to sit by and watch you start doing less! You got that? You're fucking possessed and don't even realize it! Or do you?"

"Why don't you shut the hell up for a change? I'm sick and tired of your damn mouth. I've been taking your shit for too long, and it's finally going to stop! You got that?" she asked slamming her hand down on the dresser.

"Don't be cynical with me, bitch! If you'd listen to a fucking word I have to say instead of running your damn mouth all the time, perhaps you'd see my point of view. And for the record... *I'm* sick to death of these people messing with your mind. And if *you're* sick to death of my shit, then drop dead!" he said passionately. He slid to the edge of his bed and observed her angry movements for a few minutes. He composed himself and tried reasoning with her. "Can't you start acting like a wife and stop all this bullshit before it's too late?" He sounded convincing and was shocked that his mouth even formed those words.

"Too late? Colin, it's been too late," she said, laughing. "Or haven't you noticed?"

"Great, I'm happy to hear that! Just remember *you* said it, and that's all I needed to know," he smirked.

She went into the bathroom and began rummaging through the drawers, slamming each of them shut. A moment later, she went downstairs into the kitchen. He followed.

"Can't you see what's going on here?" he asked leaning against the counter.

"I don't need to *see* what's going on. What's *unseen* is eternal. Have you ever thought of that?"

She opened a drawer looking for something then slammed it and walked away.

"You don't make any fucking sense! And I don't give a damn about the *unseen*. But what *is seen* is the difference in your behavior. Even the fucking kids see it."

She stopped and turned around angrily. They locked eyes for a few seconds without a word being spoken. She pointed at him while shaking her head as though she was trying to force out her thoughts. Her sad eyes welled with heavy, stinging tears.

"Leave the kids out of it! Don't say a damn word about *my* kids," she shouted in an emotional outrage tightly clenching her jaws. "*This,*

Colin… All of this is about my kids! It's because of you that I have to do this to protect my kids!"

She turned and ran up the stairs, two at a time, with him right behind her. He wouldn't let it go.

"You're doing this devil shit to protect *our* kids and you want me to leave them out of it? Are you nuts? Oh, I think we've already established that! Nonetheless, they're not out of it, not when you have this shit going on around them. They're afraid of those damn people. Don't you think they see what's going on here? Can't you see the kids are afraid?"

"You're a piece of work! Can *I* see the kids are afraid? I've watched you terrorize our kids for years and years, Colin! Don't ever tell me that my kids are afraid and imply that it's *of me*!"

She turned her back and whispered something.

"What's that? Speak up!"

"They've lived in fear of you their whole life! These people aren't going to do anything to the kids! It's *you* who should be worried," she shouted.

"Look, damn it! Don't threaten me in my fucking house!"

With quick steps, she positioned her thin body in front of him. Her clothes were draped loosely on her petite frame.

"Go ahead, hit me, and it will be the last time you do," she threatened. "Hit me, Colin! I'd love to see you try it this time! And try to lay a hand on *my* children!"

She gritted her teeth and turned her cheek to the side, placing her hands defenselessly on her hips. Her attempt to provoke him was calculated. She knew he wouldn't swing, and strangely enough, he didn't. He looked closely at her as if he wanted to knock her into the next room, but he didn't touch her. This courage emerged without warning. His newfound fear of Mom derived out of thin air.

"You and your friends are a pack of fucking fanatical bitches! You know what? I don't want your crazy ass sleeping next to me anymore! There's no telling *what* might jump into me! Get your shit packed and get out of my damn room! I don't want you around me! This is it! This shit ends tonight! Get the fuck out of my room, you loony ass bitch! As for hitting you… if you're so damn miserable, why don't you *hit* something... *the road*, damn it," he yelled, pulling clothes from her drawers and throwing them into the hallway.

"This is *my* house, too. If you don't like it, *you* hit the damn road, Colin! Nobody wants your abusive ass! Nobody wants you at all! I'm surprised you haven't noticed... I haven't slept next to you in months!"

"Let's keep it that way! Let your fucking little friends with all their little rituals and shit fuck up your head some more! I could care less! At least you can ask them to do me a favor and brainwash your ass into cleaning this damn house! You've made this fucking room smell like shit," he snapped angrily. "And by the way, if you actually think that no one would want me, then you're crazier than I thought! I'm prime stock, baby! One hundred percent, fucking prime stock! I'd have no problem replacing your nappy-headed, uneducated ass," he shouted while snatching more clothes from the closet. He balled them up and threw them into the hallway.

"You think this world revolves around you! Everything revolves around the great Colin Murray!"

"As it should!"

"Well, there's more to it," she insisted.

"Go on," he said inquisitively.

She stared at him for a moment.

"In this world, there exist two powerful entities."

"I'd like to hear this," he said, rubbing his chin. "What are they? Go ahead, humor me." He folded his hands across his chest and chuckled.

"This isn't meant to be amusing," she replied sternly.

"I'm listening," he said with a smile.

"God," she said, looking up. Then she looked down at the floor and added, "And Satan."

"Is that so?" She didn't respond. "Well, for your information, the two powerful entities you speak of... *God* and Satan... They're unequal! Guess which one is greater?" he asked pointing at the ceiling. "*God!* Not your pal down there," he snapped, tapping on the floor with his foot. "You're weak! I told you that years ago. So go ahead and let Satan take over your little useless mind. He'll find out he wasted his damn time with you, that's for sure," he smirked.

She confiscated a handful of items from her dresser drawer, then stormed into my room slamming the door behind her.

"Put your brother in your bed for now! Let him sleep with you," she snapped. "Tomorrow he can start sharing a room with Clark and Jimmy! I'll sleep in here from now on." She dropped her clothes in a pile on the floor and plopped down at the foot of Selvin's bed, then started talking to *them*.

That was exactly what Dad wanted. He took the cowardly way to get the profound wickedness out of his room. He allowed the sacrifice of two people today, first Mom, now me!

———————

The following afternoon, we came in from school. I didn't recognize seven of the twelve churchwomen crowded in the living room. They got uglier as I scanned their pale white faces. The room had books and statues everywhere. They were conversing and sipping tea. When my brothers and I were in sight they laid unfriendly eyes on us, then grew silent. My brothers went to change out of their school clothes, and I went to do the same.

Upon opening the door, I took two steps backwards before I slowly made my way into the room. I found candles and statues crowding the dresser and surrounding Selvin's bed. There were books on the occult, Satan, witchcraft, Bali, Buddhism, and various religions scattered about. This room didn't look anything like mine.

After changing my clothes, I went to get Clark and showed him my room. All of Mom's things were in there. The closet had clothes shoved everywhere. My bedroom was the only space her cigarette smoke didn't shroud me, until now. The nauseating haze of smoke owned this room, too.

"Look at this junk… and take a whiff of the room. It stinks," I shouted in a tantrum. "I can't sit in here and do homework! Geez…" I huffed. "And I definitely can't sleep with this odor," I complained, dragging Clark into the hallway before we choked. The clothes that she shoved in the corner, under the bed, and in the closet were dirty, and they reeked. The foul smell was body odor with a heavy mixture of cigarette smoke.

"Pew," he said, covering his nose. "What's that about?"

"I don't know, but I don't want her junk in there. Oh, God, please... please don't let this be happening," I prayed.

I placed my hands over my eyes hoping when I removed them, the room would be back to normal. It wasn't.

"Better in there than in my room," he joked. "That room looks like *hell!*"

He went back in the room and walked around laughing. I covered my nose and followed.

"Can't you be serious for a minute? You sound like Colin."

"All right, all right, just cool it. I'm sorry," he said, putting his hands on my shoulder. "It does look nuts in here. If I were you, I'd see what Dad thinks when he gets home. It won't hurt to show him this place, that's for sure! As obsessively neat as he is, he won't like it. He'll have it cleaned up in a jiffy. But I wonder why he didn't smell this stuff when it was in his room? That's weird," he said opening the window.

"She's in here because he doesn't want to deal with it. And he doesn't want the smell either," I complained. "What do you think he's going to do? Nothing!"

Clark dropped his head and replied in a hushed tone, "You're probably right."

"I can't deal with this. I just can't—"

"You'd better do something. And take my advice, you'd better do it quickly," he warned sadly.

"I wish I knew what to do about Mom, let alone this room."

"Like I said, just show him the room. Remember, he hasn't seen it yet. You have to think positive. If you don't believe he'll do anything, then you're already screwed! Just see! See what he has to say," he said taking hold of my hand. "For your sake I hope he does something." He kissed the back of my hand and gave it a squeeze. "It's not just you, I wouldn't want to be in here either," he said compassionately.

He let go of my hand and picked up a little statue on the dresser, then shook it. "I'd be scared, too."

"Put that down," I ordered while shoving him away from the dresser.

"Why?"

"You don't know what the heck that is! It could be cursed for all you know. Do you want those things to get you, too?"

Clark dropped the statue.

We glanced around the room once more, then went outside to take in some fresh air. We walked down the street in silence until he'd asked softly, "Are you all right?" I didn't respond. I kept my hands buried in my pockets and shrugged. My brain was scrambled. By the time we returned home, the women were gone. The kitchen had several plates and forks tossed into the sink. The living room was messy. A half plate of ham salad sandwiches with the bread becoming stale was left on the table next to seven empty coffee cups and a half full glass of Pepsi.

Mom was rocking in her chair with a cigarette in one hand, flipping through a book on her lap. She mumbled some words and made gestures with her hands as if she were drawing something in the air. I knew better than to disturb her. I let her finish whatever she was doing and went to start dinner.

Until this point, nightfall brought temporary relief. Although it didn't guarantee safety from one of Dad's abusive episodes, it was as close as we could get. I often lay in bed constantly rocking my legs back and forth until they grew weary, and I drifted off to sleep filling my head with screams and chilling nightmares because of Dad. Now, the tint of the sky fading to black created an entirely different ambience. The more Mom learned from the church, the more cautious and fearful I became.

My brothers and father slept comfortably in their beds with the door to their rooms locked. Dad kept company with a heavy metal pole about three and a half feet long on the side of his bed for additional security. They locked out their fears and left me confined with them. My nights grew longer and longer as my sleep became less and less. Madness ran a twenty-four-hour shift *in our house*. Mom functioned with little sleep. She sat on her bed Indian-style, smoked, read, chanted, and talked to herself and to the demons *every single night!*

My mind was shattered from an inordinate fear of the demons. Nothing made sense. I didn't believe any of this could be possible. Demons existing inside Mom… inside that room! Had my mother entered into an agreement with Satan? Do *they* know what I'm thinking? Do *they* know I'm afraid? Am I the next victim? I had many unanswered questions.

The baptism unleashed more doors to a harrowing revelation. She spent several hours at a time at the homes of the women in her new family. Often, it was the entire day. They kept Mom isolated from us as much as possible. Their efforts were insidious. Whatever it was they were exposing her to definitely had an effect.

Practically out of thin air came a chilling twist to this already sick situation. Mom was trapped with the demons inside of her. All she did every waking day was talk with several demons. In the beginning she had intervals where she would stop talking to *them*. Even if it were to read, she could at least stop. Sometimes I could only hear her talking to herself. But now, this was different. When Mom was home, her conversations with *them* were in-depth. The appearance of her talking to us instead of to herself was over. Seeing as this was constant, we couldn't hide it.

Mom sat in her rocking chair for hours on end reading passages from a book and discussing them with the angry demons. Some of them sounded as though they were evil, tormenting demons that owned her soul, battling good spirits. Some of their conversations were difficult to decipher. The demons spoke with her freely because they lived in our house, too. We dealt with this for so long it became part of our daily life. If she cooked, she kept talking. If she tried to watch television, *they* constantly interrupted her. I'd pass the bathroom, and she was in there talking. Anywhere she went, she never stopped talking with *them*. Anyone who went near her could hear their constant roar. She wasn't worried about who saw or heard her except when it came to Dad, only because he tried to listen. For some unknown reason, she or *they* didn't want him to hear.

My days were already challenging enough, yet they became more agonizing. It was difficult to concentrate in school due to my acute lack of sleep. I was in the fifth grade and thin for my age. I no longer had the flexibility to enjoy recreational activities because of the housework. My brothers and I continued to share in the long list of chores, but they were beginning to have their own social life, especially with

Dad's perpetual disappearance. There was still a great deal to do, and Jimmy and Selvin, who were now six and eight, needed looking after. I reminded them to take a bath, selected their school clothes for the next day, and made their lunches. Jimmy needed help with his homework, and I had mine to do, not that I could concentrate.

At the end of my day the house grew dark and I went to hell. Once Mom entered the room, the smoke began to asphyxiate me. I lay dead in my bed, trying with great difficulty to refrain from rocking my restless legs. I didn't want Mom to think I stayed awake to listen to her, so I faked being asleep until sleep captured my consciousness, which usually happened around three or four in the morning. My nerves became frail as the fear from Mom's abnormal transitions weakened them. No one seemed to notice. No one seemed to care.

As the months passed, Mom's style of dress was defiant and eccentric. She no longer wore the neatly tapered slacks with a matching blouse or pretty skirt and sweater. Mom's original personality was gone. She dressed like a gypsy whose style was often masculine. Most of the time Mom wore mixed-matched clothing. She loved Indian clothing and moccasins in particular. If she wasn't wearing moccasins, she wore boots. Sometimes she wore black military boots. It was as if a separate personality selected her attire each day.

Often she changed her appearance several times throughout the day. She had two or three rings on *each* finger, ten or more necklaces clanking around her neck, four or more watches, and ten or more bracelets on each wrist. Most of the time she'd tie a scarf around her head for a headband. She didn't bathe or shampoo her hair regularly. Her skin evolved from silky smooth to dirty skin that peeled if I hugged or touched her when she sweat. Her fingernails were turning yellow, and her face became thin and sunken as the smoothness in her cheeks turned into sticky wrinkles. Her lips stayed dry and cracked. Mom wasn't the same. The demons were devouring her soul and shaping her physical appearance.

When Mom walked down the street, people stared, pointed, or snickered at her, but she didn't pay them any attention nor was she embarrassed. Her nonsensical gibberish was endless. She never put her head down. The sad part of it all was that Mom didn't ask for what was happening to her; it just happened, like a horrible fate. She was tricked into servicing Satan by hosting his demons once her curiosity caused her to embrace the spirit world.

No one showed any sort of compassion or concern for her. They were too busy concocting hurtful, malicious comments. I don't know what people thought of Mom or if it hurt her, but it upset me. Occasionally, when she walked to the store, I straggled behind her. When we left our house, I tried to make it seem as if she were talking with me instead of the spirits. It was difficult to get that close to Mom and not be afraid. At times, I had to shorten my stride and fall behind because I was afraid, of *them*. My efforts to support her didn't erase the look of despair and confusion that dwelled in her eyes.

———

Dad didn't have an idea of how to cope with Mom. His theory was that she was in the hub of demonic possession because of the church. That was original! One evening he took Jimmy, Selvin, and me to visit his friend. His name was Pastor William, but Dad called him Bill. He was kind, sincere, and always embraced Dad when he opened his door. He was five foot seven, wearing a white shirt with a clip-on tie and neatly pressed dress pants. His salt-and-pepper hair was thinning at the top.

He welcomed us into his home, went into the kitchen, pulled out cheese puffs, Cokes, then popped a big bowl of popcorn and took it into the family room where we sat quietly in front of the television. We watched *I Love Lucy* while he and Dad conversed.

Dad had several concerns regarding Mom and hoped his friend could enlighten him. Surprisingly, when Dad told him the name of the church, alarm plagued Bill's face. He couldn't believe these people had maneuvered their way into our lives.

"Colin, these people practice evil wrongdoings and mind control. They have a hidden agenda. What it is, I don't know," he said throwing his hands up. "But I assure you, that place is *not* a church! They're more like a cult, and I'm sure you know what that entails. They have control tactics that'll take hold of Alley," he said tightening his grip and shaking his fist in front of Dad. "And you won't have a chance.

This is an underground full of false prophets. They use people for their own purpose. It's my understanding that they have disciples. And from what you've explained, it appears that Alley's become one of them. The only way you'd be able to help her is…" He stopped talking for a moment and shook his head. "Colin, I don't know. These people persuade their followers not to communicate with their family because *you're* the outsider. I can assure you, this will definitely cause problems for you and your children. The authoritarian is a self-appointed messianic person who claims to have a special mission in life, which is far beyond what we could ever imagine! My friend, I advise you to do whatever you have to. Get your wife away from those people as quickly as possible!"

The two sat quietly for a few minutes. Only the sound of the television interrupted their silence. Bill appeared to know far more than what he shared with dad. How did he know about these people in the first place?

"Bill," Dad began in a rough voice, "Alley's already involved herself with those freaks," he exclaimed, folding his hands together. "Don't you think I've already tried to discourage her from having anything to do with those people? She doesn't want to discuss it. We've fought about it for the past few years, and it hasn't made a difference. All we do is co-exist in that house because she's consumed with that crap. Alley does her own thing and there's absolutely no rationalization with her. I had to move her out of *our* bedroom because she made *me* uncomfortable! Come on, Bill, what does that tell you?"

"Had you thought about the two of you seeking marital or spiritual counseling before it got to this point?"

"For what? She won't admit there's anything wrong with her!"

"There must have been something that pushed her toward those people. What could it have been?" he asked. "The only thing I can advise you to do is find some way to pull her away from them, now! To be honest, I wish you'd come to me sooner. Those people are coercive. You'll have to combat too many variables. It may already be too late as it is," he said shrugging sadly.

"I've been spending so much time at work with meetings, handling accounts and presentations, that I really didn't see it coming. I mean, sure, in retrospect, considering everything leading up to this maybe I should have taken the whole thing a little more serious. But who can tell about these things?"

"Don't allow this problem to persist. These people are into something that could cause serious harm to Alley, if they haven't already. They're shaping her. Keep in mind what's best for her and your children. Speaking of the children, how is this affecting them?" he asked, glancing into the family room at us.

"Well, all I can say is that it's taking its toll on all of us."

"I'm sure that you're well aware that God permits the devil to try and destroy man."

"Yes. I'm aware of that."

"*Well, then you should know that this is a test of our faithfulness to God.*"

CHAPTER FIVE

So that no one would be disturbed by these afflictions; for you yourselves know that we have been destined for this.

I Thessalonians 3:3
New American Standard

Early in the morning on a sweltering and hazy weekday in July, the evil trilogy of Sister Cyprus and her two associates invaded our house and spoke with Mom for quite some time. They wanted to introduce her to more people. When she agreed to have a discussion with them, they left and returned within an hour. They brought two evil looking women. They secured their privacy in the manner they always had by closing the curtains and doors. However, this time they lit candles and sat on the floor in a perfect circle. Sister Cyprus introduced Mom to the two women, Adele and Francis.

With much composure and bearing deception, Sister Cyprus explained, "There's a reason we've drawn closer to you as we welcomed you into our church. We need *your* gifts, Alley. And now it's time for you to utilize them to your fullest capacity. With the help of these women, we'll enable you to do so. Don't be afraid. You are doing *his* work."

Alley sat with her legs folded Indian-style giving the impression that she was in command. She rested the cigarette between her lips and puffed lightly, as they spoke.

Sister Cyprus stood and scanned the room, then told Alley, "We need to summon a demon who has a superior knowledge than we do and *he* will speak through you and become a part of you for counsel."

Ironically, Alley was no longer full of the curiosity and questions she once had. Now she appeared absorbed and calm.

"Let us join hands," she continued.

Alley smashed her cigarette into the ashtray and joined hands with the women sitting in the circle.

They began babbling as if they were contacting someone from the dead, by séance. The louder the sounds, the more irritating it became. Although the atmosphere converted to tense and actively frightening, none of the women showed fear. I couldn't understand the words they used, and I'd doubt if anyone outside of their circle could. At the point they reached their elevation in their summoning, without warning... out of the mouth of *my* mother erupted a numerous collection of the most terrifying voices I'd ever heard. The voices continued to multiply and speak at once with overlapping tones and diverse patterns of speech and languages. These demons were undeniably different. These demons shouted horrible railings against God.

The climax in the scenario that I'd felt mounting was irrefutably *here!* On previous occasions, I heard voices of demons derive from Mom, but I couldn't see them. This atmosphere created the ultimate terrifying effect. It was starting to come together. These apparitions sought out residency in the body of my mother engaging her in what appeared to be empty conversation and causing me, at times, to doubt my own lucidity for sensing their presence. *This was not my imagination!* These women released the evil they had been brewing inside of Mom. Satan gladly provided Mom with her needs in exchange for her housing his demons. *No one seemed to realize that Dad wasn't abusing Mom or us any longer. He was still verbally abusive, but the physical abuse came to an end.*

I sat in the hallway at the top of the stairway with my hands gripping the rail. My slinky rested on my lap and I became petrified beyond words. Nothing could have prepared me for this. I was hesitant to move because I didn't want *them* to hear me. I was afraid of what was going to happen next. At that thought, the voices calmed, revealing a demon with a heavy accent from another country in some other period. It demanded a response.

Adele spoke up for the first time saying, "We come to you asking assistance in a matter beyond our powers. It is necessary that we call upon you for resolutions."

"Speak!" the angry voice demanded again as the echoing screeching of other demons continued.

I sprung to my feet, unaware that I allowed the slinky to roll from my lap and tumble down the stairs. The threatening tone triggered my fear, and I fled into the spine-chilling bedroom, locking the door behind me. I sat on the floor trying to determine why this was happening. I thought about all the changes that were taking place and how they were connected. My intuition scared me because everything that was happening had a warning. The warning was there for all of us.

A few days prior I returned from a weekend with my cousin in

Detroit. I came to a complete standstill upon reaching my bedroom. Mom had painted it! It looked like she had taken several buckets of blood and splattered them all over the walls! The clean white walls were now bloodstained and white! The room looked nuts, and I was even more afraid to sleep in there after that, but Dad made me. He said that I should, "Enjoy a little color for a change," although he, too, came across as being confused and disgusted with what she had done.

I dealt with the terror in my room and heard more than I cared to. The frequency of my nightmares increased, as did my fear. I couldn't remember all of them, but Dad said he heard me screaming all the time. My brothers got used to it. I always wondered why no one took under consideration that something may have been happening to me. No one ever rushed in the room to check on me. I accepted that, as long as it wasn't them, who cared?

"Dad, where are you?" I mumbled.

The voices downstairs echoed throughout the house for at least a half hour before I heard knocking on the door.

"Marala… Marala, open up. It's me, Colin," he called out, with urgency.

"How do I know it's you?"

"Because I'm not one of those crackpots downstairs," he whispered through the door, laughing.

Dad had choked Colin so much that his laugh was one of a kind. I don't think the demons could have imitated it. I opened the door, let him in, and quickly locked the door behind him.

"You're scared, huh?" he asked, hugging me. "This is some situation we have here! I don't know what they did to Mom, but that sure as heck isn't her down there. How long have they been here?"

"The usual trilogy got here right after you guys left this morning." I picked up my alarm clock on the side of my bed and said, "It's two twenty-five now."

"Did you hear those crazy voices? Man, it sounds nuts down there. Who'd believe this crap? Wow!"

His laugh was obnoxious and he was insensitive.

"Brother, it's not funny! It makes me mad when you keep joking about this stuff! You laugh about Mommy like its no big deal, but it is... How many times do I have to tell you this isn't funny? There's something wrong with *you* if you think it is," I snapped poking him in the chest. "Look at this room! Dad put me smack dead in the middle of this mess. If those things don't drive me nuts, being in *this room* will!"

"No, don't think like that! You have to be stronger! Maybe all the beatings we get from Dad are supposed to make us resilient so we can tolerate this crap," he joked again. I didn't know what resilient meant, but I didn't care to ask him. "Of course it's not funny, sissy. It's just that I never thought she'd get this bad. None of us want to think about mom being like that. I mean, at first, yeah, I thought she had some kind of multiple personality thing, but we know it's more than that now. I'd say she has about fifteen of those suckers in there. At least that. And I don't know how they're talking at the same time. I haven't figured that out yet," he said sighing heavily. "They're the real deal and that's why I don't say anything to her. She scares me, too." Then, to sustain his tough image, he quickly added, "I mean, sometimes she scares me. The only way for me to deal with Mom being like that is to joke about it or I'd go nuts."

"But she's always like that," I said falling back onto my bed.

"Tell me something I don't know," he said looking around the room stealthily.

"Well," I began.

"Well what? Well, the *well* in the backyard. Or are you going to say something?"

"That's how she—"

"How she what?"

"Nothing."

He rubbed his chin and studied my eyes. Colin looked so much like Dad it was scary. He had his expressions and movement.

"How she what?"

"It's nothing; just forget it."

"Come on, if you're going to bring it up, then say it."

"Let it go. That's what you do best!"

"Sissy, talk to me. What's going on?"

It was rare to see Colin genuinely concerned.

"I don't want to talk in here," I replied, nodding at the statues with discomfort while biting my fingernails. "*They'll* know that we're talking about *them,* and *they* might get us! *They* watch me," I whispered. "Can we call Dad to come home? I want to call Dad," I said, whimpering.

Colin sat beside me, took his sleeve, and wiped the tears from my eyes, then wrapped his arms around me. I felt safe, at least for that moment.

"And say what? Can you come home? Mom has a bunch of demons hanging around the house, and *they're* eating all the food! Sissy, I hate to break it to you but Dad knows what's going on. That's why he's been staying away from this place," he said watching my eyes descend. "I have a better idea. Come on, let's go outside," he insisted, trying to sound enthusiastic.

He grabbed both of my hands and pulled me off the bed.

"No! No..." I said, resisting him. "I don't want *them* to know I was up here."

"I told you to come on. You don't want to be in here because *they* might get us, so let's get the heck out of here! No one's going to mess with my baby sister... You got it! They can't do anything to us anyway because they're just spirits... demons... ghosts... whatever you want to call those jokers. But *they* can sit and run their mouths with Mom. Like I said, what can they do to us? Nothing. Now quit being such a crybaby because you're doing exactly what they want you to do, fear them! And sissy... since they *are* demons, I think they already know we're up here," he said, with a big smile showing his perfect white teeth. "Besides, isn't that *your* slinky laying at the bottom of the stairs?"

"But—"

"But nothing. You believe in God, right? I mean... *our* God," he said, pointing up at the ceiling.

"Yeah, but..."

"Do you believe in God or not?"

"You know I do."

"Then start acting like it! Have faith in *Him,* and *He'll* protect you."

"Then what happened to Mom?"

"That's another story because right now, you have to worry about yourself. Have some faith, and don't waste your time and energy being afraid of *those* jokers! The only person you need to worry about fearing is *God*. Look at me," he demanded, grabbing my shoulder, "I'm not afraid of Dad anymore. I used to be. But then I realized that, sure, he can hurt my body and beat the crap out of me all he wants… not that I want him to… but he can't touch my soul and neither can those things. Have some faith, and you'll be fine. We can't sit here and wonder why that stuff happened to Mom, because it did. It just did! Yeah, it's sad, but if you don't get over it and let it go, it'll consume you, and you'll end up as crazy as they are," he said, pointing at the floor. "I've had to learn how to let go of a lot of stuff. I'm suggesting that you get wise and do the same. Come on, let's get out of here. Hold my hand."

He grabbed my hand, led me downstairs past the women and out the kitchen door. We didn't look in their direction, and they didn't acknowledge us. They were far too involved in the oration from the demons. Colin and I walked down the street without uttering a word until we reached the park. We sat on the swings next to each other, then I had a surge of words flying out my mouth.

"What happened to her?" I asked, kicking the dirt, making a large dusty cloud. "She's not the same as before. I want her back the way she was! Those people took Mommy. They just took her from us! Why'd they do this to *our* mother? Why didn't they get somebody else's?"

"Sometimes strange things happen that none of us can explain. We knew these women were weird to begin with because that wasn't a normal church. I don't know what they did to Mom or even why, but what can we do about it? Nothing. For starters, we don't exactly know what's wrong with her. When we get to the point that we think we do, she changes again like she did today. None of us have a clue where to begin with this whole screwed up situation. Yeah, she's possessed, but by how many now? Who are they? Are they staying, going, or what's the deal?" he asked. "It's hard to adjust to this situation."

"Are we supposed to live in that madhouse wondering what's going to happen next?"

"Apparently dad seems to think so," Colin explained. "I don't mean to sound like I don't care, but after you've gone through the stuff

I have, you learn to take things with a grain of salt. You'll see what I mean when you get older. When I was your age, I learned things would get worse—"

"Before they get better," I said, interrupting him with a trace of hope in my voice.

"Naw. I learned things would get worse, and they did. I had to be realistic and see things for what they are. You have to ignore the negative because we don't have any options. Have we ever? Trust me; it kills me to see all this junk happening to Mom, but—"

"There has to be somebody who can help us. Maybe we're not trying hard enough."

"What do you mean?"

"Maybe we're just hoping this goes away on its own."

"Who's going to believe something like this? Our mother sits around puffing on two or three packs of cigarettes a day, talking to spirits in her little rocking chair. Maybe some of them are smoking her cigarettes and that's why she goes through so many," he joked.

"So what now?"

"Wise up and get used to it or you'll never make it to my age. Tell somebody what's happening in our house and you'll end up in a nuthouse. Why do you think Dad hasn't told anyone? They'd think he's crazy! That's why. You know Dad finds a solution to everything. But he's not touching this one."

His laughter grew harder and louder. He held his stomach and doubled over.

"Will you talk to Dad and ask him to get me out of that room? Can you ask him to do that for me?" He shook his head, no. "I won't ask you to do anything else. I have to get out of there!"

I put my hands in prayer position and sobbed.

"Nope."

"Why not?"

"You expect *me* to talk to Dad? Are you forgetting the loving father-son relationship we have? Our father loves to beat me! I think this stuff with Mom scared him enough to leave us the heck alone because he doesn't know what she might do to him. And honestly, I've never had this much of a break from him beating me and I'm not going to give him a reason. We don't talk much. I do my chores, homework, and stay out of his way."

"But this is different. Maybe this time he'll listen."

"As soon as I open my mouth, he'll knock me right in it. It's not that I don't care because I do. It's that the one thing I try to do is stay away from him. I don't say a word to him unless it's absolutely necessary. That's the way he wants it, and so do I."

"I understand. This is just hard."

"As far as your room's concerned ..." He paused. "He'll get you out of there at some point. Look at it this way; hopefully he'll have sense enough to see things for himself. It's his wife! He won't deal with it right now because he doesn't know what to do. He doesn't have time." He grabbed my hand and pulled me off the merry-go-round. Slowly, we made our way back down the street toward the house. My head began to throb, and my stomach became queasy as it always had when I returned to our house. Colin said he felt exactly the same way.

The one thing I *wouldn't* adjust to was that bedroom. Mom spent more time in the room than in the living room. She spoke openly to the statues and reacted as if they responded to her. I never touched nor looked at them for long. I wasn't sure if they did anything or not, but I wasn't curious enough to find out.

She had an unyielding infatuation with certain statues and pieces of jewelry. One piece in particular was a ring with a black stone in it. She seldom removed it. Her personal belongings were off-limits to all of us. They weren't to be touched or moved, especially the spine-tingling statues. Most of her things looked like junk to me, but to each his own. Sometimes when she acquired a new piece of jewelry, she'd polish it and hold it in her hands for a long time. Once, I asked her why she did that.

"I can tell who it belonged to and what kind of life they had," she replied with certainty.

"What if it belonged to a lot of different people?"

"It doesn't matter. I know that, too."

"What if they died?"

"Then I can tell if they went to hell, now, can't I! Go on! Leave me alone… I don't want you in here! Get out of my room!"

Whenever she didn't want me in the room, I left without protest!

———————————————

Months passed, bringing many strange occurrences. Mom began to use her Ouija board more often, among other things. None of her actions had a logical explanation. It was clear she was fascinated with the outcome of her mystical efforts. Mom's appetite for power was increasing. Occasionally, she showed off her new abilities, appearing to instill more fear into us. Stan was afraid of the Ouija board since he saw what she did with it. Mom had me terrified of that thing! Oddly enough, throughout all of this, she didn't hurt us… and she hadn't let *them. At least, not yet!*

I hated being in that room because it reeked terribly. Mom rarely showered, bathed, or washed her clothes. Piles of her dirty clothing were shoved into the closet and the corner of the room. Shoes were everywhere. She bought most of the items from garage sales. Not only did Mom's stench fill the room, but I had the odor of a bunch of other people in there since she didn't wash the items she bought. Mom didn't shave her legs or under her arms. Hygiene wasn't a priority to her like before. Her teeth were plaque-stained and her hair turned grayer. She wasn't the same.

Since she spent so much time in the room, she kept packs of cookies, pumpernickel bread, and cans of food under her bed. I'm surprised we didn't get bugs. I understood why she kept the food, but it was disgusting. There were times that Dad wouldn't buy groceries, as punishment or oversight. Mom would take his payroll checks, sign his name, and cash them before he knew it, then she'd buy food. When he caught her, he had his checks sent to another address and took her off his bank account. Mom continued to keep food under the bed that remained available to us; however, my older brothers preferred the shoplifting sprees *for food*. At this point, we couldn't hide the obvious problems. They stood out like Clark's lack of eyebrows or Colin in my dress!

———————————————

I was sitting in the family room watching *The Day the Earth Stood Still* when she called me upstairs for a demonstration of her clairvoyant powers. My brothers were already asleep, but I couldn't because I made a conscious effort to stay out of that room as much as possible.

"Marala, get up here," she called enthusiastically.

Afraid to upset her, I headed upstairs. When I reached the doorway to the room, I froze. She was sitting on her bed with books, statues, and other junk scattered around her.

"Yes," I replied.

She was strange, different than when I left her earlier.

"I want to show you something. Get me a deck of cards from the kitchen."

"But I was watching—"

"I don't care! Get them," she demanded angrily.

I jogged down the stairs only to return with a red and white pack of cards from the drawer. She was standing in the hallway. I gave her the cards and she shoved her ashtray into my hand, then snapped, "Hold this."

Her impatience showed as she slid the cards out of the pack and quickly shuffled them several times. Not once did she look at the faces.

"Here, now you do it." She snatched the astray from me and shoved the cards back into my hand, then leaned over and flicked on the hall light. "Sit down. You'll want to see this," she said folding her legs Indian-style on the floor.

"I really don't," I replied unwilling to participate.

Her eyes grew narrow and angry, then her voice turned rough.

"I say you do! Now, sit down, child!"

She placed the ashtray next to her, and took a deep breath while digging for her cigarettes and lighter buried in the pocket of her wrinkled shirt.

"What are you waiting for? Shuffle the damn cards," she snapped.

Mom was beginning to scare me so I scooted back until my back hit the wall. I shuffled the cards four times, then handed them to her. She shoved them back at me.

"No, *you* keep them! Hold the deck so I can't see the cards! I don't need to see them!" She lit her cigarette and took a long drag. "I'll tell you what the cards are. Don't let me see them." Her words were rushed as she began speaking. "Nine of clubs."

I looked at the card. It was a nine of clubs. Okay, I thought, along with everything else, now Mommy can do tricks.

"Three of hearts, eight of diamonds, queen of hearts…" Her eyes were disturbing.

She had already gone through the deck once.

"Shuffle them again," she demanded.

She was noticeably amused with her accuracy. I shuffled the cards eight times and started over again. She didn't miss one, not one! She didn't hesitate or hope to get them right, *she did!*

"How do you know what the cards are?" I was stunned.

She didn't answer. Instead, she continued naming the cards with complete accuracy before I peeled it up to look at it. There was an abrupt change in her voice and the intonation was now that of a man. Before I could blink the voices were of numerous men but her eyes were as evil as I'd ever seen them. She continued identifying the cards without error. They fell from my hands as I sprung to my feet. Half-crazed, I pounded on the door to Dad's room until he answered. I didn't care that she knew what the cards were… Those weren't Mom's eyes!

"What? What is it?"

"Let me in," I screamed still pounding.

An even more sinister smile emerged on Mom's face and she vanished back into the room. I heard Dad unlock the door and, before he could open it, I turned the knob and forced my way past him. He peeked into the hallway, then shut and locked the door. He sat on the bed with his briefcase and paperwork scattered in front of him. He cast a perplexed look and tilted his glasses while examining my frantic demeanor.

"What seems to be the problem? Every time I try to get something done around here, I have one of you knuckleheads interrupting me. Can't you see I'm busy? Christ, someone has to work around here."

"I know you don't want to hear anymore about Mommy, but she's acting really weird and I'm scared!"

He pushed his paperwork aside, clasped his hands together, giving his undivided attention.

"What did she do this time?"

"She told me to shuffle the cards and not let her see them."

"Okay. There's no harm in that."

"Dad, she named every card correctly!"

"So what? Your mother's been practicing card tricks. That goes to prove she doesn't do shit around here. I've been saying that for years! What's your point?"

"She couldn't see any of the cards."

"Marala. I don't have time to talk about card tricks."

"Her voice changed like a man, then like a lot of men. She started naming the cards faster and faster, and she kept getting them right! She didn't miss one! I saw her! There's no way she saw the cards!"

"Then what?" he asked, curiously.

"Then I banged on your door because she scared me. She didn't look like Mommy," I said shaking my head. "I promise she didn't! Her eyes, Dad! You should have seen her eyes! They weren't Mom's."

"Oh, come on, that's absurd. There's obviously a logical explanation," he said firmly.

"Then can you go find it? *I* was holding the cards and *I* saw her eyes!"

"Really now."

"I promise."

He stared as if he were looking right through me, searching for the truth. I'd just given it to him. It was evident that ever since Mom became part of the church, he evaded having confrontations with her. For the most part, Dad neglected everything going on in our house. He wasn't stupid; he knew what was happening.

"Listen, your mother isn't a psychic. A *nut* maybe, but not a damn psychic. She must have learned a new trick from her weird little friends."

"What about her voice changing like that, huh? What about that? You can't explain it. You should have seen her face. It was her expression! Her eyes!"

For a brief second, he was at a complete loss for words. Of course, he didn't want to admit it, but he knew something was wrong.

"She's trying to scare you, and it worked. Your mother's learned how to do that ventriloquist thing. She used to get me with her jokes and tricks when we were kids."

"Jokes? Tricks? Have you ever seen Mommy change her voice before?"

"Actually, I have. But as soon as she senses I'm around, she stops... or *they* stop. I'm not curious enough to figure out how she does it. Whatever it is, she's found a way to scare you, and that's all there is to it," he lied. "I don't think we should dwell on this subject because it'll make you crazy trying to figure her out."

"Why would Mommy want to scare me? That doesn't make sense. Go see for yourself," I said, pointing at the door. "Have her do it for you. She always has voices coming out of her and there's more than one. There's a ton of *them,* and they're all creepy! I don't think she can control it. Those things talk by themselves when they get ready. And they're ready all the time. Samuel, Joseph... all of them! What do you think this is doing to Jimmy and Selvin? You come home to sleep sometimes but we're the ones stuck here! And I'm the one stuck in there with her," I said pointing at the door. "Don't you care about any of us? Can't you see what's happening?"

After a few seconds of silence something registered with Dad. He saw and knew more about the situation than he led us to believe. Normally he would have spit an array of obscenities at me and thrown me out of the room for questioning him. What else is there to say? Either he'll do something or he won't. If he doesn't, I'm definitely a goner. After some deliberation, he got up and crept into the hallway. Hesitantly, I followed behind him, grasping onto the back of his white t-shirt. I didn't want to be left alone.

"Alley!"

There was no answer. He pushed the door to *the room* halfway open, took one step inside, and looked around. She was sitting next to her bed while her shadow mysteriously scaled the wall. His mouth dropped open when he glanced around the room in shock. He stepped back into the hallway.

"What the hell did you do to this room? It smells in here," he said, fanning the odor away from his nose.

She continued puffing on her cigarette with her back to us.

"Alley? Can't you fucking answer when I call you? What's all this shit about you scaring Marala? Don't you have anything better to do?"

"No one's scaring that girl. She scared herself," she replied without turning around.

"What happened in here?" he asked trying to sound stern.

"Whatever the child told you is what happened," Mom replied boldly in a mixture of voices.

"Then bring your ass over here and show me your sick little trick. What are you, a damn witch now?"

Mom slowly stood and walked over to Dad. He took three steps away from her as she sat down in front of him. I let go of his shirt, backed into his room, and stood in the doorway.

"Go ahead, Colin, mix up the cards so you know it's not a trick," she said with a daring grin.

She stared at the floor as he shuffled the cards seven or eight times, then cut the deck twice.

"Now what?"

"Queen of hearts."

He looked at the top card. It was the queen of hearts.

"So, that doesn't fucking prove shit." Dad was incensed. He held the cards down so tight that he could barely see them. He stumbled backwards until his back was against the wall.

She continued getting every card right. He ripped his hand over her head and flung the deck across the room in a rage.

"Go back to practicing your damn tricks and leave the kids alone! Better yet, if you want to do this shit, then join the damn circus!"

"Tricks, Colin?"

Her laugh was scathing. Her eyes were darker.

"Yes, tricks! Why don't you do that thing with your voice Marala was talking about? Apparently, everyone's seen you do it all damn day except for me! Is that what you were doing in there? Come on, Alley; let me hear the little demons. Oooohhh," he joked nervously, trying to cut through the thick bloodcurdling tension. "On the other hand, have they gone home for the night?" he asked, waiting for a response. She didn't provide one, so he continued, chastising her. "They probably wanted out of this smelly ass room," he complained, "And I think you're full of shit!"

Mom took out another cigarette and lit it. She took two long drags.

"I don't think you'd like it, Colin," she hissed.

"For your damn information, I've heard your ass before! Am I supposed to be amazed? Oooohhh! I don't know what the fuck kind of tricks you're playing, but cut the bullshit! Cut it the fuck out!"

"Why don't you tell *them*, Colin? Tell *them*. They're waiting."

This time Mom responded more ardently. Several voices flushed out of her mouth and said in repetitive chants, "Tell us... Tell us... Tell us!"

"You're fucking nuts! You know that? You're a fucking nut! Look at what that cult did to your ass! Look at yourself! Do what in the hell you want, but keep your shit away from the kids! You got that? Do you, damn it?"

The swarm of voices continued, "You know, I think *you're* finally starting to *get it*! Do what in the hell you want, but stay out of *our* way!"

The angry demons were from another era. That wasn't my mother! It wasn't his wife!

Without another word, she got up and went back inside the room, slamming the door behind her. As Dad turned to look at me, I examined his face as he shook his head in disbelief.

"Now do you see what I have to deal with?"

He staggered into his room wearing a bare expression. Beads of sweat slid down his face.

"Let's get some fresh air," he suggested.

Dad picked up a thin black bobby pin from his dresser and put it in his pocket. He locked his door from the inside, pulled it shut, then led me downstairs. This had become his usual routine when he left his room, and that little routine couldn't help him if *they* decided to get him. What was he hiding, or hiding from?

I grabbed our jackets from the front closet. We went outside and headed down the dimly lit street with a few minutes of silence. Finally, Dad spoke.

"Are you hungry?"

"No."

"Don't let your mother scare you. I think that's exactly what she wants to do. She's having fun, that's all."

"Having fun? Is that the best you can come up with? Besides, why would Mommy want to scare me? Does she scare you? Tell the truth, does she?" I asked looking up to study his face.

He gave careful consideration to his response and replied, "Honestly, *yes*. Sometimes your mother does scare me." Trying to break the mood with a mild tone, he continued, "Your mother's going through something that even I don't understand. Unfortunately, we can't help her until she wakes up and realizes that she needs some type of help. I think we need to pray for her because at this point I'm not confident she feels there's anything wrong with the behavior she's been displaying. Regardless…" He reached for my hand and tried to sound sincere, "Your mother would never hurt any of you kids, not in a million years."

"Maybe that's what *you* believe, but you don't know for sure. I mean, I know Mommy wouldn't hurt me, but it's not Mommy I'm worried about."

"If Alley wanted to hurt you kids, she would have already done it. Whatever the hell is inside your mother… spirits, demons, ghosts, goblins… I don't know what to call it, but they can't hurt anyone. They're not tangible objects, so they won't affect you. Do you know what tangible means?"

"I think so."

"Tangible means discernible by touch, or possible to touch, like that tree over there. Tangible is something concrete. You can't touch a spirit, so how can it hurt you? They can talk all they want, but when it comes down to it, they can't harm you. Look at it as noise coming from your mother. It's like listening to a radio."

"It's not like listening to a radio because you can turn a radio off. You *can't* turn Mommy off, and those things are hurting her. Look at her. She keeps changing. There's no telling what she'll do to any of us when she's completely changed. And I don't know what *they* might make her do to herself. I'm afraid for her, and nobody seems to care."

Except for the crickets, there was a long silence between us. There wasn't a cloud in the sky and this night was as serene and beautiful as I'd seen it in a long time. The stars were out dancing and I wanted to wish on every one of them. The air was fresh, not polluted. I held my head back and inhaled. We took a few more steps; Dad turned around and headed back to the house. Instantly, the pain in my stomach started stabbing at me. I tried to ignore it by looking at the lights inside the other houses. I just kept looking and wondering. *What's going on in their house?*

"So you seem to think she's getting worse?"

"Of course she's getting worse. I'm the one who shares that room with her! Why do you think I was banging on your door like that? I'm locked in there night after night, afraid of those things. I can't explain the voices and I know you can't. She can't fake that. Not the way *they* sound. Ask Colin and Stan. I keep trying to tell you about those things and I know you don't want to hear it."

We walked in silence for a little while longer. Dad was taking it all in, but I had to get it all out. I'd been dealing with this torment for too long.

"Are you getting cold?" he asked.

"No. I'm okay."

"Are you finished?"

I looked up at him again.

"Not yet." I took in a deep breath and said, "Jimmy and Selvin don't understand what's going on. They don't want to go near Mommy half the time. They're always with me. They don't have a mother anymore! I mean, they do, but they don't. If you came home a little earlier sometimes, you'd be surprised at what you'd see in *your* house. She used to play with that Ouija board all the time talking to spirits and stuff. But now, she doesn't even need it! They talk to her all the time! This has been going on for over two years, and you never say anything. You stay gone so you don't have to deal with it."

"I threw that damn Ouija board away!"

"Yeah, I know. But guess what? It's back. You're gone all the time, so you don't know what's there or what isn't! You don't see what we deal with. That's not my mother."

"And that's not my wife," he added with a brief pause. "I think what happened is your mother has been under a lot of stress raising all *six* of you kids... and then there's me. But honestly, I think you kids have been a tremendous strain on her. It could be that she started having a nervous breakdown, then that church most likely caused the rest of that shit!"

I looked at him for a minute. I never pegged my father for stupid until now. Did he even listen to me? He had a lot of nerve suggesting that *we* had anything to do with what was happening to Mom. I think what he did was beat her senseless, and those people got what was left of her. Between those women and Dad, the devil didn't have much work to do.

"Call it what you want, but that's a lot more than a nervous breakdown."

"Then what would you call it, little Miss Freud? Huh? What analysis have you come up with?"

"You might think I don't know what I'm talking about, but I think she's possessed and so do my brothers. That's all there is to it."

"And why is that?"

"Because Mommy didn't have *time* to have a nervous breakdown. She was too busy taking care of us."

"Maybe she is possessed," Dad said, looking at the dark sky as if he was searching for answers.

"But you just said she's having a nervous breakdown. Which is it? You can't say maybe she is to shut me up."

"What is there to say on the subject? I've never seen anything like this before. I'm certainly not a doctor, so I can't properly make a diagnosis. What's wrong with her? Hell, I don't know what happened to Alley. She should have listened to me. I agree with the fact that your mother is possessed. All right! But I don't want to scare you. Yet you seem to know *precisely* what's going on."

"Yeah, I know what's going on. How could I not? But what gets me is that nobody wants to deal with this stuff. My brothers ignore her, or at least try to because there's nothing they can do about it. I can't ignore it because I hear her talking and chanting all night long. Her spirits even have names. Do you want to know what they are? Matthew, Luke, Mark, John, Peter, Samuel, Melek, and a whole bunch more. I hear that stuff at night *and* throughout the day. She talks and talks, and guess what? *They* all talk back! It's like one big demon party taking place twenty-four hours a day. This stuff replays over and over again in my head. When I go to school it's still replaying!"

"Matthew, Luke, Mark... Hold on a minute! They're *the apostles of Christ*. No, that can't be right! That's Satan trying to confuse your mother. I tried to explain to her a long time ago that Satan is the master of deception! But she didn't listen, and now she's being deceived again!"

"Look at me, Dad! Look at my weight. I have dark circles around my eyes. I can't deal with this anymore!"

"Marala, calm down. We're outside, and people could be watching. Now, obviously I care or I wouldn't be talking to you about this topic."

"Yeah, a few years later!"

"Watch your damn mouth before I slap you in it!"

"Don't you understand that—"

"Calm down or I'm going to end this little dialogue and finish my work. I can't deal with this shit anymore either!"

"All I'm asking is that you understand where I'm coming from!"

"And what I'm suggesting that you do is ignore her! I don't have any answers. I know these people did something to your mother, but I don't know what. So until I determine how to handle it, stay away from her! Quit listening and spying on her. Leave her alone!"

"I'm not asking her to show me that creepy stuff. She just does it, like she did with the Ouija board. She made that thing move by itself, and none of us were dumb enough to get near it. Seeing that thing move is creepy! I can't help but see it. You're the one who always says, *you're a product of your environment*, so don't forget she's in my room now! What do you think is going to happen to me? Do you ever wonder about that? On the other hand, does it even matter to you? Am I going to become a product of my environment? Don't you think those things can get into me just as easily as they got into Mommy? Or do you want me to be the next sacrifice in our house?"

"Are you worshipping the devil with her?" he snapped.

"No!"

"Well, then, the best advice I can give you is to shut it out of your mind and don't dwell on it when she's in *your* room! Simply go to sleep!"

"I don't want to be in there anymore! I don't want to share that room with her! I can't sleep because I'm afraid *they'll* get me! If it's so easy to ignore it, why isn't she in there with you?" I asked.

I tried my best to refrain from having an outburst but it wasn't working. This was too hot of a topic not to show emotion.

"Look, smart ass, she's not with me because I pay all the fucking bills and no longer want to deal with that shit!" He paused and took a deep breath, then said, "You know what? You're exactly right, there's no telling what she's capable of, and I don't want *them* or *her* in my room!"

"So instead of dealing with it, you just pass the problem... *them* or *her*, across the hall to me."

"Well, shit, I let Selvin sleep at the foot of my bed at times. What more do you want me to do, lock all of you in with me? Besides, you can continue to keep an eye on her for me."

I looked at him crossly absorbing his contradictory words.

"You don't care about anybody," I shouted. "Didn't you just tell me to ignore it and stop spying on her?"

"I'll tell you what, smart ass. You'd better watch your fucking tone! If you don't like it, that's tough! Now I'm going to get back to my work, and that's enough of this shit for now. You know what to do. Ignore it! Go in the family room and read a book until you pass out since you don't like being in that room!"

Dad went inside, grabbed a beer from the refrigerator, a bag of pretzels from the cabinet, and went back to *his* room. That was that. I looked around the dark, quiet kitchen and leaned against the counter. I wanted to run away from this horrible place, but like Mom, I, too, had nowhere to go. I couldn't face the nights with Mom and *them* collectively. I went downstairs into open territory.

Like Mom, I had my own ritual at night. Hers was to sit on her bed or the floor and talk to the spirits, channel them, read from her stacks of books, or talk in tongues or other strange languages while chain-smoking. My ritual was taking my blanket and tucking all of the loose sides securely beneath my thin body. Then I covered my head, leaving only a small area to breathe the contaminated air. Mom never left the door open, especially if she was in the room.

I imagined the blanket was a cocoon that the demons couldn't penetrate. As long as I remained tightly wrapped, I'd be okay. I wouldn't let so much as my toe or finger stick out of the blanket for fear of the demons taking possession of my body, too. My brothers were locked in their rooms, unaffected by the demons, so I pretended that I had locked myself in my cocoon. I believed that this was my innovative way of protection from the evil invading my body the way it had Mom. Oddly enough, I came to learn that Stan and Colin both wrapped themselves in their own cocoons at night.

At daybreak, I examined myself to see if *they* conquered my soul when I slept. I was fearful that someday I'd gaze into the mirror and find the identical sinister look that my mother had erupting in my eyes. Was I sane or long gone? Maybe I was already crazy and didn't even know it. Perhaps everyone in the house could hear the demons because we were all like Mom, but it wasn't showing yet. I wondered if it was a lucid dream or a dream that I was destined never to awaken from. It could be that I wasn't able to separate reality from fiction. I was questioning my own sanity, or lack of it. Perhaps that's the reason Dad left me in hell with Mom. In all probability, he must have deemed me infested by the spirits. Dad selfishly abandoned me to battle insanity and hell with Mom. Why didn't he save me? Why didn't my own father protect me from her… them… and insanity? He must have a tremendous degree of hate to subject his only daughter to this private torture while no one else was that close to the flames.

Nightly, I gathered false courage so that I could step into that room. I was never convinced that it would end. Mom and her demons were building momentum, and they had no plans of departing from her. Once safely inside my cocoon, I prayed to be spared from the awful fate my mother had met. I prayed until the thought of God protecting me serenely consumed my thoughts.

With Mom getting worse, my faith couldn't waver. God knew my prayers and faith were sincere or I would have stopped believing a long time ago. *I didn't realize it then, but now I am certain that I was covered with the blood of Christ because I woke up every morning.*

For three years, the desire to be done with that life and simply die climbed in and out of my mind, but no one knew. When I went to school, I was hopeful that some sort of an accident would terminate my life. I wasn't desperate enough to take my own life and be stuck with the same fate I already had. Why would I want to live in hell for eternity? I had to believe that one day there would be something better. I needed to know that my life would have meaning, even if it were just a little.

Regardless of my struggles the 23rd verse of Psalms still seemed to comfort me and temporarily flush the negative thoughts away. It was when I forgot to pray that I became vulnerable. I had to remember, even in the midst of madness that, *The Lord is my shepherd, I shall not want.*

As long as Mom was in that room, I never went to sleep without safeguarding myself the best I could. I tried not to become familiar with her latest beliefs, conversations, or plans, nor did I read her books or touch her statues. I didn't *want* to hear her, and I didn't want *them* to think I was interested; nevertheless, I had no alternative since I was surrounded by it. When the demons spoke to Mom, I froze as if I were in a comatose state at night. There was always the profound presence of evil in the room, which became Mom's place of retreat to learn more about her demons. She studied and read more than I had ever known her to. Language barriers weren't a problem for her. She appeared to understand them completely, regardless of any language they spoke. When a demon spoke to Mom in a particular language, she replied in what sounded like their same language with the same accent.

Periodically, throughout these episodes Mom moved toward me to see if I was asleep or not. She knew when I wasn't, and that was her way of warning me to go there. It was the most disturbing thing to hear her talk to *them*, as though they were actual people, and to hear many demons talking to Mom as though they were sitting in front of her. My fears escalated to an unfathomable degree.

While Dad now slept away from home we locked down the asylum, and I was in the padded cell. The room represented the most horrid component of my life because I slept in what seemed to be a hellish nightmare, sharing a cell with demonic spirits inside my possessed mother. It didn't take long for me to realize that demons and spirits existed. I often perceived *their* presence presiding over or around me. I came to believe that the demons must be invited inside, one way or another, and I refused to show any sort of curiosity in *them*. I refused to let *them* in.

My prayers were intense, heartfelt and the only thing between lunacy and me. I would have had little doubt that I was in the midst of a nervous breakdown myself if my older brothers and Dad hadn't validated the demonic possession of our mother.

Every disturbing night I spent in that room seemed to push me closer to the brink of insanity. For some peculiar reason, I was convinced that was an element of my father's plan, and the stage had already been set. He'd let Mom eradicate herself and one of his children along with her. The walls with paint splattered on them like blood, demons' in horrifying conversations, and their threats to harm Dad was enough to drive anyone mad. I continued questioning my sanity the majority of time. Was this some sort of outrageous joke, or had I created this in my head? I tried to manufacture resistance to these demons ambushing me, yet was uncertain if it was working.

No one could imagine the terror that the hours of darkness brought to me. My days began as a charade. Like everyone else, I went to school interacting like normal with other kids and teachers. I looked somewhat unkempt, but I did my best with Jimmy and Selvin. In reality, our house was packed with dysfunction, but I couldn't disclose that to anyone. As unnerved as I had become, I was disappointed that no one outside of our house had detected it. I couldn't sit still without fidgeting, tapping on something, or rocking my legs back and forth, even in school. Often, while sitting, my legs rocked uncontrollably without me realizing it until I looked down at them. I persisted in biting my fingernails to the skin, with traces of blood ready to trickle out while my mind played looped images of my life inside my head.

I always thought the torment in my own life would be eternal. Satan had sabotaged my mother's life. He kept chipping away at her with great persistence. I was exhausted from living that way, but God's faith in me, for whatever reason, pushed me along and kept me going. What would I be like if I made it out of here with a tinge of sanity? If only. God must have a reason for this madness; I just couldn't figure out what it was, not yet. I had nothing but prayers, and I had to believe in something. Realistically, I understood the cocoon I created wasn't what was protecting me. That's why my prayers began with, "Father, have mercy on me," because I knew he did!

As time continued, Mom didn't attend the church as frequently as she once had. The women came to her for instruction and resolutions. There were demons they sought, and Mom was the connection. Each time she summoned demons, her destruction was evident because it added *another* to the existing collection. Her abilities increased, and now it seemed as if they controlled her. She enjoyed her newly discovered vitality and appeared to crave additional knowledge. Then, everything stopped! *Mom was autonomous and persistent in her endeavors to allow this unbound evil to continue.*

Finally, we had a peaceful Saturday morning while Dad was home. Mom was away and Dad wanted the house quiet so he could work on a presentation he had to deliver the following Monday. After breakfast and our chores, he sent us to the recreation center to play. Stan, Colin, and I rode our bikes back home to grab something for lunch. Clark stayed to watch Selvin and Jimmy while they were playing so we could get back faster. We hoped Dad was finished so he wouldn't become upset that we came back, however, his car wasn't in the driveway. We peeked into the living room window. The curtains were shut, but the window was open.

"Sshhh! Listen," Colin whispered.

"Can you see anything?" Stan whispered back.

"Naw. But there's a lot of people in there," Colin replied, lowering his voice. "Sshhh! Quiet for a sec, I want to hear what those freaks are saying." He snickered.

Guardedly, we listened at the window and heard numerous voices overlapping one another in heated dialogue. Some were in a sundry of languages, others we could discern. The voices escalated into an aggressive manner.

"Tell me what's going on," Stan asked Colin, curiously looking over his shoulder.

"I can't make out everything they're saying, but it sure sounds like the demons are in rare form today, buddy," Colin joked.

Cupping his hands around his eyes, he put his face up to the screened window trying to see inside, but it was useless. The heavy drapes blocked the slightest view.

"I'm not afraid of anything! You all can't intimidate me either," Mom retorted angrily.

The voices filled the room, sounding like responses. Colin looked at us with a terrified expression blanketing his sweaty face, bronzed from the sun.

"Man, forget the food! Let's go back to the center and leave *them* alone," Stan insisted.

"Yeah, we need to leave them alone, all right. Why would I want to be in there with them? I get enough at night," I protested.

I backed away from the window and knocked over my pink bicycle.

"You're going to be the reason they hear us," Colin said, frowning at me. "Now come on, let's check it out. Stan, are you with me, bro?"

"Man, I don't know about this. Maybe Marala's right. What if—"

"*What if? What if nothing,* sissy boy! Let's see what's in there, is all I'm saying! Don't be such a wuss!"

"I'm not a wuss, butthead. It's just none of our business is all."

"What do you mean, it's none of *our* business? Man, this is *our* house, and that's *our* mother. I don't care who's in there; we've got the right to be in there, too," he said twisting his mouth into a nasty frown. "Forget it! You're a little punk. I'll go by myself. You wusses can wait here."

"Colin, you know I've got your back, man. I'm with you, brother," Stan responded trying to sound brave.

"Sissy, you can wait here if you want to chance it, but you never know what's going to happen around here. We'll come back with the grub," Colin announced smugly.

"Nope, you guys aren't leaving me out here by myself. I'll go, but I'm *not* going in first, and you better not leave me!"

"I got you, kiddo, just follow me," Stan added, securely grabbing my hand.

A burning knot of tension twisted in my stomach.

Colin pulled open the white screen door on the side of the house, then pushed open the other door, and we tiptoed inside the kitchen. Colin grabbed a full loaf of white bread from the counter and some bologna from the refrigerator. Stan grabbed two handfuls of cookies from the cookie jar and wrapped them in paper napkins. I didn't move. The voices continued in their tumultuous tone. Colin gripped the wall and peeked around the corner into the living room with Stan standing over his shoulders. Before either could say anything, they fled from the house yelling and screaming like fools. Without hesitation I shot out behind them. We jumped on our bikes and raced back to the park.

Before we went inside the center, we leaned against the building and caught our breath. Colin kept looking down the street as if he expected something had followed us. Maybe he was trying to scare me even more than I already was. Perhaps he was scared this time. His pupils were dilated, and a black hole of fear swirled inside of them.

"That's messed up! That's so messed up," Colin blurted. "I mean, her *mind* is completely gone! She's nutty! Whacked out! Possessed! Something!"

Colin shook his head in disbelief, laughing wildly.

"You're a moron," I shouted, pushing him as hard as I could. He didn't budge.

"Seeing Mom in that condition isn't funny. And I have a bad feeling that she's worse off than any of us expected, which is hard enough to deal with. I'll give you that, she's messed up, but all you ever do is laugh like a hyena! That's not cool," Stan argued.

"If you want to know what I find funny, I'll tell you," Colin began in his partially hoarse voice. "I'm not laughing at Mom. I'm laughing at the reality of this madness being an everyday part of our life! First, our hateful father's trying to beat us to death! And when you don't think it can *possibly* get any worse, we have this crap going on with Mom. She's trapped with a bunch of dead people talking to her. Think about it! How many people get to walk into their house and have it filled with creepy demons? Brother, I thought that stuff only happened on television. Who would have thought?" he asked, still laughing. "Horror originated in our house! You go there and lock down the asylum, a lunatic starves you for days, beats you to a pulp, and the demons run the show with Mom! Admit it, she's batty," he said, holding his stomach laughing as hard as he could.

"Man, shut up," Stan shouted. "I'm not going to sit here and let you talk about Mom like that!" His fists tightened, and anger blanketed his face.

"Naw, I'm not shutting up because we need to face the facts. It is what it is. And what it is… *is* messed up!"

"So what? You don't have to make a stinking joke about it," Stan snapped.

"Brother, you can laugh about this situation or vanish in the madness. I look at it that way. You can't blame me for being real. Tell me if anything I've said is a lie." He paused and threw his hands in the air, waiting for a response from Stan. "You can't, because it's true. If you think I'm exaggerating, then take your brave butt back down there and help her. Go right ahead, buddy boy, but don't come running back here for my help. She doesn't want help, and she can't help us anymore. Learn to laugh when you're away from home, because you're sure as heck going to be screaming or crying for some reason or another when you're back there."

Colin was right. I sat on the ground and tried to drown out their words. I couldn't handle another conversation without a solution.

"Look what you're doing to sissy," he said pointing at me biting my nails. "At least we're not in that room. We don't know what she has to deal with! So do you really think she can handle hearing you cracking jokes about this?"

Colin leaned over and flashed a broad smile. "Damn skippy she can handle it, right, sis? If she knows what's best for her she'd try cracking a few herself," he added. Then he socked me in the arm. "I deal with things the way I need to and I don't appreciate you trying to make me handle this crap any other way. One day maybe we'll make it out and maybe we won't, but I know one thing for sure; all of us better pray like hell that we do. Our stats for survival aren't that high, you know. Some of us are going to die in there, and it's not going to be me if I can help it!"

They glanced over to find my eyes pooled with tears. I quivered from the reality of Colin's accuracy. That's what threw me awry. I couldn't cope with the abrasive details of my life. In essence, what he was saying was true. This was our reality. None of us had alternatives. I knew in my heart that Colin meant well, but I refused to accept that things were destined to stay that way. God wouldn't put us here to deal with this for the rest of our lives, at least not without a purpose. I couldn't imagine what any of us could have done to warrant this. Colin's motive for being cynical about our family life was to toughen us up. His intentions were meant to help us because he wanted us to survive this.

"You know I love you, but there's nothing any of us can do, sis. You have to stop getting upset over this crap. Mom made her choice to go to that church and deal with those freaks. We went over this before. Remember?"

I looked at Colin with derision and stated, "Mommy didn't know what she was getting herself into. Are you saying she asked for that? Did she want to be possessed and controlled by those things?"

"Come on, Colin, lighten up," Stan interjected defensively. "You have an arsenal of insults, don't you, brother? Keep it up and one day that crap's going to fire right back at you."

Stan always tried to contain his anger, but it was there. Stan reacted to the slightest provocation when it came to Mom. Although Colin knew how to trigger a reaction, he was aware of his boundaries.

"Well, they didn't exactly put a gun to her head, now did they? We all make choices, brother! I make mine, you make yours, and hers was just messed up. At some point, Mom knew what those freaks in that church were doing, and she still let them infect her mind. The first time a demon appeared, she should have cut it off and gotten rid of them. What can I say? That stuff back there's too deep for me to get involved in because I don't understand it. It doesn't mean I love

Mom any less than you guys. All I'm saying is we're screwed. I'm just a realist," he said passionately.

"You're *just* like—"

"I'm just like who?"

"Forget it," Stan snapped.

"Who? Say it! Who?"

"I said forget it!"

"Naw. I'm not forgetting anything. At least have the guts to finish your sentence. So answer me. I'm just like who?"

"Well, let's just say his name begins with … *Dad!*"

"You little—"

"Shut up! You wanted to know who you're like. Go look in the mirror, and you'll see him. You disrespect Mom just like him. You're always—"

"Don't start your crap with me because I won't take it! I'm nothing like dad!"

"Yeah, well, that's why you're so concerned about Mom, right?"

I knew they were headed into a fight. Once in a while they got into it with one another and fought over trivial things. Sometimes Stan won and sometimes it was Colin, but when Dad found out, he made them fight until someone was hurt and they couldn't fight anymore. Then he'd whip the winner. That way, both of them were beaten. I tried to change the direction of the conversation and shift the focus to stop their fueling altercation.

"Hey, you guys, when those demons leave mom, where do they go? Are they still in our house?"

"They probably go back to wherever they came from." Stan said sounding uncertain. "Or maybe they just get quiet for a while."

"I don't think they ever leave the house because sometimes they're in the room at night," I continued.

"Why? Do you see anything?" Stan asked.

Colin moved closer with greater interest, too.

"No. It just feels like people are watching me. I don't mean they're staring at me from inside Mommy. It feels like they come out of her."

"So you're saying these things come outside of Mom's body? You actually see them?" Colin asked with more curiosity.

"No, I told you that I don't *see* them, not that I want to, but I can tell. It's like they want me to know they're there or something."

"For real?" Colin asked.

"Naw, for fake! Of course, for real," I said with an attitude.

"I understand the situation's tough, but try to be sympathetic for a change. Think about everything Mom's done for us over the years, then think about everything Dad's put her through. I wouldn't be surprised if we helped drive her to this state or at least to that church. Man, Mom was trying to find a way to protect us from Dad. She was trying to protect *us*. When she got to the point that she couldn't do it on her own, that's when…" Stan looked away from both me and Colin. He paused for a moment before he began again. "Have you really forgotten what Mom's been through for us? Do you think she deserves having her son say *she made her choice*?"

"Bro, remember I'm dealing with it my way," Colin said with more compassion. "I feel the same way you do, but I'm afraid that there's nothing we can do about it. It's hard for me to dwell on the subject."

His eyes welled with tears. This conversation was difficult to discuss without some display of emotion. I couldn't say anything because my heart was heavy, and I had a lump in my throat that wouldn't go away.

Colin smiled and tossed the loaf of bread to Stan.

"Where you going?" Stan asked.

"To get something to eat, maggot. That crap won't be enough to fill my belly!"

Colin jumped on his gray ten-speed bike and peddled toward the corner store a few blocks away to pocket some food.

Stan and I went inside the recreation center to take lunch to our brothers. Afterwards they played air hockey and basketball while I sat in a folding chair thinking about Mom. At least the center still provided a place we could escape to and have temporary peace of mind. Sometimes we hung out there practically all day and played basketball, games, or listened to music. It was our home away from hell. For the most part, it kept some of us busy and out of trouble since we weren't as tightly supervised as we once were. I, on the other hand, didn't have as much time as before to enjoy the center.

Mom continued to grow distant from us. We no longer engaged in quality activities with her or talked the way we once had. Although she still spoke to us, it was usually to send someone to the corner store for a pack of cigarettes with a letter allowing permission for them to be sold to us. Other than that, she sent us outside to play. The damage was primarily to her, but awarded us an enormous void and psychological challenges. Regardless, I believed she loved us and that Mommy was still there... *somewhere*.

———— ————

Dad arrived at the point where he no longer ate at home. He brought groceries, paid the bills, and stayed away as much as possible, but not for more than a few days at a time. He felt Mom's mental instability might cause her to poison him or something else. Dad concluded that the dominance the women had over the men in the church wasn't going to be his fate. He wasn't leaving himself open to be subjected to any method of mind control.

When I told him about the tea they gave to Mom, he instantly made a connection. He felt they would try to render him submissive, so he removed himself from their plans without notice. He wasn't going to allow himself to become a pawn in their sadistic game. He didn't want to play because he'd finally met his match, but it was too late; the game had already begun... long ago.

After cooking dinner with my brothers one evening, I took Mom a plate of fried chicken, cabbage, and boiled potatoes. I found her sitting on her bed in a pair of baggy blue jeans and an orange and blue sweater that was too big for her. Mom was already petite but she'd lost about ten pounds. Her black hair with traces of gray was matted into a messy afro that had a slight odor. Her face was extremely drawn and weary from lack of sleep. Dark circles hung comfortably under her eyes, which had a mystical gaze about them.

An ashtray filled with at least twenty cigarette butts sat in front of her along with a variety of books on various religions, Satan, and others scattered about. She was reading passages in the Bible and looked for what appeared to be opposing points in the other books. I handed her the plate, but she ignored me and picked up one of the statues, firmly held it, then closed her eyes as though she were meditating.

Dramatically she recited phrases and observed the figure in detail. The sculpted bronze figure was of a man. It was different from the rest of her collection. When she finished with the statue, she smiled and placed it back on the dresser as if she had accomplished something extraordinary. She began moving her hands in all kinds of ways as if she were wrapping the evil around her. It seemed as though she didn't know I was there so I set the plate on my bed and left the room, pulling the door shut behind me.

Her inexplicable collection of statues denoted a diverse array of religions. She gained knowledge of their history and appeared to worship them at times. The women brought statues to use in their meetings, some of which weren't of a human form; these were of beastly creatures that found refuge in our room as well.

Everything that happened directly affected Dad even though he seemed to think he could abandon *his* house. He didn't have control over his wife the way he once had for the duration of their fifteen years of marriage. His violent temper was still evident, but he was warned to keep his hands off her, and he did.

Our fear of Dad was still in tack as it had always been. The issues with Mom and her demons kept Dad from being as abusive. If Mom were gone, Dad was his usual self. When she was home, she was a clear distraction from his explosive temper.

There were countless times when Colin Jr. was caught stealing. On a specific occasion, he was caught shoplifting from the corner convenience store. Upon his return home by the police, Dad beat Colin in the same ugly manner as always. When he fell to the floor, Dad repeatedly slammed his forehead into the ground, staining the kitchen floor with puddles of blood as he had many times before. Mom walked through the door and spoke up more wrathfully than we had ever heard her.

"If I ever see you lay another hand on that boy, Colin, it'll be the last time you ever hit another soul!"

She stared at him in an inexplicably profound manner while she inhaled her cigarette and flicked the ashes to the floor. There wasn't a single trace of fear in her voice. Dad stood and lunged at Mom, but before he could reach her, chest pains crippled his movement. He stumbled back, falling into a chair, gripping his chest until the pain subsided without speaking a single word. After that incidence, it was a long time before he laid a hand on any of us.

━━━━━━━━━━━

Around four in the afternoon, Dad called to inform us that he was on his way home. At this point, he typically slept at home once a week. For the most part he'd let me know when he was planning to do grocery shopping so I could help prepare a list. It was after ten o'clock that evening and there was still no sign of Dad. I waited for him because if he didn't show I was going to sleep at the foot of his bed. He didn't want anyone in his room, but I would rather have been punished for not obeying him than to be in that room knowing he wasn't across the hall to protect me. I'd sneak into his room, turn back his bedspread, then climb in bed and surrender to sleep. This night, I was in *the room* with the door wide open rocking my legs. Other than Mom in her whispers of conversation downstairs, the house was still and everyone was in bed.

Eventually Dad made it home, well after midnight. She greeted him in the pitch-black living room. The only sound escaped from the soft movement of the rocking chair. He put down his briefcase, loosened his tie, and cautiously moved toward the black kitchen searching for the light switch.

"I see you finally made it home," she said, catching him off guard.

Startled, he turned to face her, but he didn't know where she was. Gradually his fingers made their way to the light switch and flicked it upward. It didn't come on.

"Don't worry about it. You could care less as long as the fucking bills are paid," he retorted, lacking confidence in his tone.

The orange burning tip of the cigarette moved closer and the smell of her cigarette became stronger as if she were standing directly in front of him. Still, she was invisible.

"So," she said calmly.

"So what?"

"So you've been in a car accident. Tell me what happened," she asked inquiringly.

"What makes you so damn sure I've been in an accident?"

"I don't know, Colin. Just a feeling."

"Perhaps you're feeling is wrong."

"I'd bet my life on it."

The cigarette smoke was exhaled in his face but you could still hear the soft rocking of the chair.

"Get that shit out of my face," he snapped fanning the smoke. "I hate the smell," he said talking with a heavy lisp. He reached his hands out to move her away but there was no one there. He reached for the lamp on the end table and quickly turned it on. *She* was rocking in her chair with her legs crossed, exhaling cigarette smoke. He had a fresh row of stitches directly below his bottom lip, bruises, and scrapes on his face and his two front teeth were broken where his head hit the dashboard. "Did you do this, Alley?"

She smiled coyly without responding.

"I'm going to bed. I don't have time to sit and play little mind games with the likes of you. If you have something to say, then say it! If not, then keep your little comments to yourself!"

"You'd better learn to be more careful in a car or you'll do more than knock your teeth out," she warned.

"How did you know about the accident, Alley? What are you doing now, practicing voodoo or something?"

Without another word, she went upstairs with a look of gratification covering her thin face. Trepidation spread over his.

I wasn't worried about what the women from the church were teaching Mom... it was what she was teaching herself!

━━━━━━━━

The light from small white candles faintly illuminated the hot, musty room. Wax melted into the top of the cluttered dresser and candles were carelessly lit around her unmade bed. Multiple shadows danced on the bloodstained walls as demons played in the thick haze of smoke. A few feet away, the demonic spirits inside of my mother were engaged in disturbing but blended dialogue, some leading to searing arguments. *This* night in particular was strangely different. The simultaneous angry outbursts and chattering was unbearable. The diversity in languages discharging around me was petrifying, especially when coupled with the relentless crashing thunder from outside.

My pounding head felt like it was going to explode at any second while my aching heart thumped recklessly inside my chest, trying to force its way out. There was nothing I could do about the stabbing pain in my stomach because the sharp knife being jabbed in and out repeatedly was random. I felt every burning twinge of my nerves. I closed my eyes as tightly as I could and clamped down on my teeth at each twisted spasm in my legs. My unnerved body didn't attempt to adjust to *this* formidable environment. I couldn't shake off the fear because I was teetering. I couldn't wrap my mind around this madness any longer and I couldn't purge this madness from my head.

I prayed that she'd extinguish the candles. Whenever the stench from them grew faint, I knew *they* were finished for the night. This time, it didn't seem as though it were going to happen too soon. Tonight she was talking with some of the typical spirits, John, Luke, Peter, Paul, Samuel, and Mark among others. They were always present. The others were the demons that insolently argued with them.

Anyone else may have believed that some of the demons possessing her were good and some were bad. But I decisively alleged that all of those things were evil. She believed *they* knew what was best for her because *they* were given to her, like a gift, for counsel by some unassailable higher entity. She was enthralled by the wisdom *they* seemed to communicate to her. She was mesmerized by the power they claimed to have.

At times she held her rosary and studied the Bible. Leviticus was of particular interest. If she touched a crucifix, it didn't burn in her hand, as I would have expected. She wasn't afraid of what dwelled inside her, and she never let us talk to *them*. Not that I would have. Colin Jr. may have, because he wasn't as afraid as I was. The only aspect that remained the same with Mom was her chain-smoking habit of at least three packs a day.

Over the past three years I'd witnessed such a variety of unfolding revelations with Mom that it was impossible to diagnose any part of her behavior conclusively and without questioning my own sanity. It was tormenting to observe it helplessly day after day after day.

The tone was extremely uncompromising and disturbing as the demons continued their chilling dispute amongst themselves. I couldn't do anything to stop or avoid it. It had already trapped my fears. This novel sense of terror remained unexplainable. My brothers were asleep, and Dad was home locked into his refuge. It was nearly dawn and they were *still* conversing.

I was swaddled in my cocoon when I realized *I* had become the focal point of the enraged evil in their bizarre conversations. The persistent thunderous blast and the howling rain crashing against my window didn't help matters. *I hated thunderstorms!* The sound of them made my heart pound and enhanced my fear.

"She knows of us! It's time," an evil voice said speaking above the rest.

"Ignore that girl. She's asleep anyway," Mom said aimlessly. "She's fine; she doesn't pay you all any attention. None of them do. They think I'm talking to myself because I'm crazy or something," Mom continued, trying *not* to lead to her defensiveness over me. It sounded as if my mother was trying to protect me.

"We must *not* have interference," a demon demanded angrily.

"We must rid ourselves of the child," insisted another.

"She has nothing to do with us," Mom tried to whisper in a worried tone. "Nothing at all! Now let's leave it at that! You all have me; what more do you want? Don't be so damn greedy," she insisted, pacing the floor with heavy steps.

A violent flow of incensed voices filled the air. Whatever was inside Mom brought supplementary supernatural spirits into the cold and threatening room. *Tonight* the presence of her demons existed in the room and not merely their voices. This time, *they* were discussing *me!* Bloodcurdling evil was hovering around me, and its intrinsic presence reigned. I was terrified to experience this madness any further.

My mind was struggling with a way to get out of the room. I can make it, I thought to myself. The door's only a few feet away. They're going to get me if I don't get out of here now! On the count of three, run. I began counting. One... two... three! My body wouldn't move because panic was climbing up my legs. The door's ten feet away, and Dad's another three. I can make it. I can make it thirteen feet, I thought. I knew I had to try again. One, I counted. Two. I can do this. Reluctantly trying to convince myself, I finished my count. Three…

As fast as possible, I threw my legs over the side of my bed and jumped up, clinging securely to my cocoon for temporary protection and sanity. I threw open the door and savagely beat on Dad's door, ordering him to unlock it and let me in. If he didn't I was going to kick it down! The unfaltering ghostly echoes from the room rang out behind me as the invisible arcane approached my backside.

"Open the door! Let me in! Hurry up, Dad," I yelled as loud as I could. His door vibrated with every blow to it.

"What's wrong now?" he asked in an alarmed tone, without opening the door.

"Hurry up! Let me in! Let me in," I shouted, afraid to look behind me.

"How do I know it's you?" he replied with a great degree of uncertainty emerging from his own startled voice.

"It's me! You know it's me!"

I couldn't think of anything rational to say. Hurriedly, he opened his door, visibly shaken, holding the metal pole in his hand.

"So what's all the yelling about this time?" he asked, looking nervously over my head, trying to peek into the dark hallway.

"It's *them*! It's all of *them*!" I pointed into *the room* without looking behind me.

"What? What did she do now?"

"It's… It's…"

"It's what? What?" he asked, rushing me to explain my terror.

"It's them… *they* want me! They told Mommy I know about *them*… and they don't like it!"

"Get in here! Come on!" He yanked me by my arm into his room. "Calm down, I'll be right back."

"You don't want to go out there," I said grabbing him by his arm.

My nerves had me jumping around as if I was walking on hot coals.

"Why not? Why wouldn't I want to go in there this time?" he asked releasing my grip.

"*They* might get you! *They* don't like you either! Just leave *them* alone! Please don't make it worse!"

"I'll be right back. Stay here," he demanded, stubbornly.

"But Dad..."

"Just stay here!"

A loud crash of thunder struck a tree in the yard and made the both of us jump! The lights flickered on and off. Rain mixed with large hail was mauling our house. Using the tip of his pole, he pushed the door to the room completely open and timidly looked inside, only to find her *gone*. The candles were extinguished and the noise halted. The rage of the storm amplified.

"Dad," I whispered.

He ignored me and continued his slow expedition.

"Alley!"

There was no reply. The hall was dark, and the light didn't go on when he flicked the switch. The orange tip of a cigarette appeared to float up the stairs. Dad flicked the switch again as her cigarette drew closer. It came on but no one was there! This time, he didn't look for her and he wasn't curious to find out where she was. The one thing he was certain of is that she wasn't with her cigarette! There was no possible way! He checked the door to Clark's room to make sure it was locked. He swiftly backed into his room and closed the door, locking it again. He placed his ear on the door and listened. At first, he didn't hear anything, but a few minutes later she returned to the room and resumed her demonic conference.

"Shit! It sounds like she has a room full of people in there!"

He moved away from the door and nervously sat on the end of his bed.

"She does. You just can't see *them*! *They're* always in there! *They* live here, too, you know!" I started rocking back and forth, trying to understand why all this evil existed in our house. "Remember last time... Well, since you didn't do anything, she got worse," I explained.

"Sshhh... There's no point in crying," he said, pulling me closer to him. "Stop rocking and calm down. You're safe in here," he said, unconvincingly.

He tried pressing his heavy hands on my legs to stop them from trembling. As soon as he removed them, they started again.

"I can't take it in that room anymore! I can't take it! I'm afraid of *them*, and now I'm afraid of Mommy, too! Can't she see what *they're* doing to her? Doesn't she see it?"

"Your mother can't stop what's happening. It's too late."

"I'm not sleeping in there! *They'll* get me if I go back! I know it! I can feel it! And I'm not crazy! I'm not!"

I tried to explain the evil swirling around me because no one felt it the way I had. *No one!*

"Sshhh, try to calm down. You're making things worse. Let me think about the situation for a minute. I can't do it with you in a frenzy," he said staring at the door.

"Okay... okay," I promised.

He got up, went over to the door, gently placed his hand on it, and tried turning the doorknob to make sure it was still locked. Then he checked the door to his adjoining bathroom.

"I know you're there, Colin. Why don't you come out?" she asked invitingly in an eerie tone.

"I don't feel like it! Why don't you take your sick ass to bed? In fact, all of you take your asses to sleep!"

It was quiet again. This time Dad didn't seem too enthusiastic to confront her. His insecurity showed. The thunder crashed and he jumped again.

"Do you know if Stan locked his door?" he asked, sounding concerned.

"He always locks it."

"Good! This shit is ridiculous! Fucking ridiculous," he admitted.

"You're not going to make me go back in there, are you?" I whispered, still trying to control myself.

"Use some common sense for a change. Unless you can fit through that hole on the knob, I'm not opening that damn door tonight!"

He realized how harsh his words sounded and looked at me with sensitivity. He folded back the bottom of his bedspread, then tossed me a white pillow while I climbed under his blanket and top sheet *with my cocoon.* Maybe now he'll start to care.

I triple-checked my cocoon. I wanted it securely wrapped and tucked under my body. I curled into a powerless fetal position, placed my head on the pillow, and stared beneath the door to see if anything was trying to slide underneath it. All I saw was her shadow. Ironically, Dad sat on the edge of the bed with a black Bible in his hands without speaking a word. I knew he was searching for answers, or a way to rebuke the demons, which suggested he was trying to keep *them* out of his room and out of himself. I laid there still trying to figure out why this was happening, but my mind was foggy, and the fog was dense. This, I couldn't handle. All these years I tried to get used to this problem with Mom, but never could. Now, any chance of trying was over. Dad and I heard Mom's heavy pacing in the hallway for some time before unconsciousness finally consumed me.

A few hours later I awakened not knowing what I would find. I looked out the window and saw several broken branches from the storm randomly scattered on the ground. I checked Clark's door and found it was still locked. Watchfully, I crept downstairs shortly after Dad had ventured out of his room only to find him dipping a Lipton teabag into a cup of steaming water. It was apparent he was thinking through his options to determine how he could put an end to this situation with Mom.

The sun had barely risen and she was nowhere to be found. With his teacup in hand, Dad walked into the living room, I followed and quietly sat on the sofa. He looked at the piles of books on the coffee table and shook his head. His expression was perplexed. He took a few sips of his tea before setting it down. He knelt on one knee and pulled opened the cabinet door to the end table. With reservation, he searched inside and carefully observed the statues he removed. He continued removing books, reading the titles of each. He noticed a ceramic ashtray shoved underneath the table so he slid it out and set it on the coffee table. It was overflowing with cigarette butts and a few of them fell on the carpet. He picked them up and sighed.

"Dad," I began, interrupting his thought. "Have you seen Mom this—"

"How long has your mother been buying books like these?" he asked sternly.

"I guess it's been about three years, give or take a few months."

"Where does she get them?" he asked without making eye contact.

"She buys some of them in stores, others come from garage sales around here, and the rest came from those church people."

"Garage sales?"

"Uh-huh."

"What kinds of people keep books like these in their home?" he mumbled under his breath.

The next book he picked up caught his attention. He began reading the first few pages, sighing as he continued. He skimmed through the book and stopped at a page that appeared troublesome, then threw the book on the table with the others.

"Maybe they have the same problem Mommy does. You never know," I suggested timidly.

"Have those fucking church freaks been sneaking their asses around here lately?"

"I haven't seen them in weeks. But if I'm not here or in school, I don't know what she does. The only thing I can tell you is what I see or hear."

"Do they call?"

"Not that I know of, but I don't listen to her conversations if I can help it."

"Does *anyone* come by to pick her up?"

"Not really."

"Which is it? Yes or no? Give me a definitive answer! I asked if *anyone* comes by to pick her up?"

His irritation was abrupt.

"No. And the only reason I said *not really* is because I'm not here every minute of the day."

"I'm well aware of that, smart ass," he snapped slamming a book on the table.

"And…" I began.

"And what?"

"Mom walks everywhere she goes. She still doesn't drive much. I used to follow her to make sure she was okay, but I don't do that anymore."

"You used to follow her?"

"Uh-huh."

I folded my arms and rocked back and forth in place. I sensed something, but I wasn't sure what it was. It wasn't supposed to be there. Dad observed my uneasiness, then continued his questioning.

"Then where did she go?" he asked looking around.

"Like I told you before, garage sales and stuff. She likes to buy jewelry, books, statues, and clothes."

With growing discomfort, I scanned the room and let my eyes scale the ceiling.

"Shit, you'd think I was making enough money so my wife wouldn't have to buy leftovers from our fucking neighbors. That shit's embarrassing. Neighbor's talk, you know. They already think blacks don't have shit anyway." He took a deep breath to take it all in. An intense look formed on his face, and then he asked, "Have you adapted to the environment in your room?"

"What does adapt—"

"Have you *adjusted* to your surroundings? Are you *used* to *them*? Are there any *modifications* that you've witnessed? Need I go on?" he asked rolling his hand in little circles.

I thought for a moment, then said, "No."

"Are you sure about that?"

I tightened my arms snuggly across my chest and replied, "Yes, I'm sure about that. I haven't gotten used to *that room*. Nobody could get used to that!"

"No one?" he asked with a heavy huff.

"Yes, that's what I meant. *No one.*"

"Are you concerned that your mother will harm you in any way?"

I began to fidget with the end of my shirt. I wasn't sure how to answer this question. My throat grew tight and I spoke in a low voice.

"To be honest," I began, dropping my head as though I was ashamed to admit it. "Last night was the first time I was afraid of Mommy. *They* scared me, but *she* didn't," I added trying to protect her.

The reality this time was that *they* scared me and so did *she*!

"How so?"

"I mean, it's just that this was the first time I felt like those things were going to get me. I didn't know if they were going to kill me, get inside me, or what! Either way, I wasn't willing to find out. But *Mommy* wasn't trying to hurt me. She was trying to protect me from *them*. But if something happened to me… it would have looked like Mommy did it. Does that make sense?"

"Hmm. That's an interesting concept. Actually, I do understand your point of view. Go on."

"What else do you want to know?"

"Are you all right?"

"I think so," I lied. I wasn't all right. I still felt the frenzied palpitations in my chest but I knew he wasn't going to do anything about it.

"Exactly how long have those demons been floating around the house like that?"

I thought for a moment trying to recall the timeframe.

"Do you need me to explain what *exactly* means or do you have this one on your own for a change?"

"I know what it means. I was thinking about your question because I want to be *precise*." I suspended my thought, then replied, "Well, I kind of think *they've* been living with us for about two and a half out of the past three years. I've heard her talking with them for that long. If you want me to give you a *precise* time frame…" I began counting in my head, "Yeah about in seventy-three, that's around the time it all started. But you already knew that. I'll be thirteen, so that's right."

"Jimmy's nine," he added.

"Selvin's seven, Colin's sixteen, and Stan turns seventeen," I said helping him.

"Clark turned fourteen five months ago." He stood and let out a long yawn and then stretched his arms as wide as he could. He sat down on the sofa and continued, "This shit started pretty early." He removed his glasses and massaged his face with both hands. "How did I ever get myself into this?" he asked himself.

"Most of the time she's able to control those things, but lately *they* seem to be getting strong enough to come out on their own. And now, I can feel *them* hovering above me at night. And I can tell when *they're* in the room. Before, all they did was talk to her or they'd talk amongst themselves. But I told you about that a while ago. Remember?"

"I don't need you to jog my memory with what I'm already cognizant of. I want an update! Got it?" he snapped. He replaced his glasses and took another sip of his tea.

"Yes, sir," I said, fidgeting with my hands again.

"Now, what else can you tell me?"

"She can speak a bunch of languages."

"I've heard her."

"Well, that's about it," I said trying to end the interrogation since he was irate. "All I can say is, Mommy's been that way for so long that I avoid her for the most part."

"Just so we're clear, let's recap," he said studying my eyes. "Answer this question again. Has your mother *ever* tried to harm you?"

"No. Never," I answered defensively. I knew where he was going with this question. "Dad, *Mommy's* never tried to hurt any of us."

The question saddened me. He never asked if *he'd* hurt any of us.

"Well, at any rate, that's good," he conceded.

"Do you… I mean, do you *think* she might try?" I asked, feeling that his question was implying he'd experienced something or was unusually suspicious.

Was he aware of something that I wasn't? He didn't answer. He positioned himself like his *Thinker* statue for a few moments without uttering a word. Stan was making his way into the kitchen and caught Dad's attention.

"Wake your brothers and get in here," he instructed firmly.

Within seconds, Jimmy, Selvin, Clark, Colin, and Stan quickly gathered in front of Dad. Jimmy and Selvin came and slithered onto the sofa next to me after I patted the cushions. Jimmy was snuggled in a pair of faded racecar pajamas and tan slippers on his little feet. His eyes could hardly stay open and he had bits of crust resting in the corners. His reddish-brown hair held small pieces of lint tangled in his curls. It was too early for him to sit erect. He hunched over when he leaned on my arm, staring glumly at the carpet. Generally, Jimmy was quiet and didn't say much. However, I could ascertain he'd begin taking mental notes on everything that was going on, especially when his thin little eyebrows scrunched together and vaulted. He wasn't impetuous, but he did have a concealed temper that intermittently surfaced. His expressions often spoke for him.

"Is everybody all right?" Dad asked while observing each of us. We nodded yes.

"Clark, did your mother enter your room last night?" he asked.

Struggling for an answer, Clark replied, "Sir, I wouldn't know. I was asleep. But our door was still locked when I woke up."

"That doesn't imply anything. I should have known you wouldn't have a clue," he said shaking his head annoyingly. "What about you, Jimmy? How are you doing?"

"I guess I'm okay. How are you?" Jimmy asked sounding insincere.

"Dad's fine," he answered in third person as he did from time to time.

"Come here, Selvin."

Selvin was lying on my lap. He tightened his grip around my waist.

"He's still tired," I said hugging him closer.

Due to the circumstances in our house, Selvin was closer to me than Mom. I spent a great deal of time taking care of him. If he had a cold or fever, I knew before anyone else and usually told Dad so he could give him medicine. When it was time to get him dressed, I made sure his clothes were clean and ironed. When we played, most of the time he stayed with me. If I was busy, he was with Stan. Selvin was like my son.

Selvin had beautiful cinnamon eyes that complimented his light almond skin. His hair was a natural black with tiny ringlet curls. He reminded me of Mom every time I looked at him. He had her high cheekbones and well-defined, yet perfect nose. He was a curious little boy who always asked questions and giggled when anyone corrected his mispronounced words. Selvin couldn't pronounce his favorite meal properly, which was spaghetti. Instead, he'd clap his little hands together and yell, "Umm... basketti, basketti!" I knew just what he wanted.

Selvin was extremely obedient. It was rare that he needed scolding or told to do something twice. If I instructed him to take a nap, he did it without resistance. Similar to Mom, Selvin constantly lit up the room when he smiled. Regrettably, it wasn't as often as I would have wanted. He was chubby as a baby, but became slender with age.

He had a large scar on his thigh, which spread to part of his stomach. When he was a baby Mom was making coffee with the cord to the pot carelessly hanging off the counter. Selvin grabbed hold of the cord, pulling over the metal coffee pot, badly burning his thigh and part of his stomach when it fell on him.

Dad reached over and tied Selvin's blue robe then scooped him from my lap and sat him on his own as he crowded next to me. Selvin leaned his head against Dad's chest and closed his eyes. He didn't appear affected by our conversations whenever he was in the room, but I never knew for certain. Most of the time he was asleep when one or all of us were being beaten. If he empathized with our plight, he didn't act like it. Selvin behaved as though he was detached from the problems and evil that plagued our house.

Dad turned to Stan and Colin, then said, "Let's have it. What did you two clowns hear last night?"

Stan and Colin looked at one another before answering.

"Sir, we heard Mom, if that's what you're asking," Colin replied.

"Do you mind being a little more specific? I'm sure you *heard* your mother, but what else can you add?"

"Sir, all I can comment on is what I heard. And I didn't leave the room except to use the bathroom. That was about eleven."

"So you finally decided to stop wetting the bed," he said cutting his eyes at him. "Go on."

"Around two or two-thirty is when it started getting noisy upstairs... but with the storm last night I couldn't hear any particulars. And I'm not trying to be disrespectful but we're used to accepting that anything can happen around here. That's why we don't react to things as easily as you might. Besides," Colin shrugged, "you told us to mind our own business, so I went back to sleep, sir."

"Oh, now you want to mind your business, huh? What about you, Stan?"

"Sir, the storm was so loud, Colin's right, I couldn't hear the specifics either. Since we're used to hearing noises and Mom talking, maybe I inadvertently blocked it out."

"Inadvertently. Wow, that's a big word for you, isn't it? How the hell do you block out something that abnormal?" he asked angrily.

"Sir, no disrespect, but if you were around here as much as we are, you wouldn't have a choice but to get used to what goes on or you'd crack up," Clark admitted.

"Well, it's not feasible for me to stay here all the time, smart ass! I need to concentrate on my job so I can pay the damn bills and feed your asses." He shoved Selvin back on my lap and stood. "I can't deal with this shit at night and give a presentation or participate in a sales meeting the next morning. Besides, *you* never seem to hear anything, so I'd be amazed if you even realized your mother had anything wrong with her. I'm sure she doesn't know that I'm gone half the damn time anyway."

We were aware of why Dad was gone most nights. It was because of his affair with the woman he called his Aunt Bronzella. Mom was right about that being the real reason he wasn't home much for the past year. Dad lived in an apartment with his mistress approximately five miles from us, off Route 57. He kept pictures of the two of them in a shelf on his headboard, narrowly hidden inside the pages of a book. As meticulous as we were, he should have known we'd find the pictures while cleaning. It's possible he wanted us to. They slipped out of a book when Colin dusted the shelving. In a few photos they were embracing one another as they kissed. She appeared to be several years older than Dad. In all honesty, it bothered me, but there were bigger issues to contend with, so I didn't dwell on it.

"Sir, is everything going to be all right with Mom?" Stan asked.

"Does everything look all right to you moron?" he snapped. "What do you think? Your mother hasn't been *all right* for quite some time. Do you think she can pull that possessed shit, then become normal overnight? Let me answer that for you so there's no confusion. *No*, she's not going to be *all right*! So all of you are clear on this, last night was the end of it! Any further questions?"

None of us responded, but what did he mean, *that was the end of it?*

"Okay since there aren't any questions, Colin, Stan, and Marala, I want you three to get breakfast ready. Marala, get your brothers dressed afterwards. We'll discuss this matter later. I have more pressing matters I need to contend with." Dad walked into the kitchen, pulled open the drawer, and grabbed the phone book. He rubbed my hair, then disappeared upstairs.

Colin opened the refrigerator and stood glaring into the light. "Make breakfast? Out of what?" he asked with a silly grin.

"Let's have cereal," Clark suggested, opening the cabinet left of the sink. He hunted through it and announced cheerfully, "Wow, we really lucked out. There's a bag of rice in here." His grin became wider.

"Yeah, but there's no milk. How's he expect us to eat if there's no food in this place? I'm tired of this crap," Colin complained, slamming the refrigerator door.

Clark shrugged without responding.

Stan grabbed Colin by the shoulder and said, "Brother, don't make an issue out of it. Let it go for once. Just be grateful we have something to eat as opposed to nothing! Right?" He turned his attention to me and asked, "Hey, kiddo, put some water on."

"Okay," I replied and began digging in the cabinet for a pot.

"How do you suppose we eat a big bowl of rice without milk?" Colin barked.

"Eat it with chopsticks, moron. Go pull a couple twigs off the tree outside," Clark retorted sarcastically. "And sharpen the ends with your abrasive attitude."

"Come on, guys, cut it out before we piss him off again. We'll put butter and sugar on it. It's not as if we haven't eaten this before. Be happy we have rice," Stan joked.

"Stan, can you get some clothes for me so I can get dressed after breakfast?"

"Sure, kiddo. What do you want me to get?"

"I need a shirt, blue jeans, my pink tennis shoes, and a pair of panties from my second drawer. My socks should be next to them. And can you try to make my clothes match?"

He nodded.

"You should come with me to make sure I get the right stuff. You can wait in the hall if you want, but you shouldn't let those things run you out of your room," Stan suggested. "I'll make sure you're okay."

He wrapped his arms around me and tried to force a smile.

"Yeah, it's easy for you to say but I don't want to be in there when she gets back. And for the record, it's not my room anymore or haven't you noticed. It's *their* room!"

"All right, all right, calm down. I got you," he said consolably. "Wait for me downstairs."

After breakfast we cleaned the kitchen. Shortly thereafter, Mom entered the kitchen wearing the same clothing she had on the day before. Trying not to let my eyes touch hers, I left the kitchen and went downstairs to change in the bathroom. Afterwards, I sat in the family room and watched Stan draw.

After the previous night, Dad made a smart decision and didn't interrogate Mom. Whenever she entered the same room as him, he walked away. Arguments were pointless, and he was afraid. Mom didn't have the temperament to harm anyone. If she did, Dad would have been dead before these women ever entered her life. Nevertheless, the question was not if Mom would or wouldn't entertain the idea, it was whether the evil spirits would instruct her to get rid of *Dad, or any of us*! Last night, they wanted to eradicate *me!*

———

The events that continually took place were traumatizing. Throughout the years of this accumulating insanity, I had to accept it as my fate. Still, the pain feasted on my interior. Normalcy was dead in our house. Dad always reminded us that we were lucky we had a roof over our heads and food on the table. To him, we had no right to complain about anything. He told me that I should be more grateful. Of what, I thought, to exist in hell?

I never stopped wondering about what went on in other houses. Each time I saw a house, that very question consumed me. Were their mothers possessed? Did they, too, experience excessive forms of abuse? Were the children beaten? Were the wives regularly beaten? Did all women wear sunglasses because they were hiding a black eye? Was there suffering in *everyone's* home, yet *no one* chose to talk about it when they left *their house*? What else was out there? How many people lived like this? Were there any families that didn't suffer abuse, verbal or otherwise? If so, who was privileged to live in one of those homes? Did their neighbors abandon their screams and cries?

CHAPTER SIX

Do not judge, and you will not be judged; and do
not condemn, and you will not be condemned;
pardon, and you will be pardoned.

Luke 6:37
New American Standard

A few weeks later, on an emotional and unforgettable Saturday afternoon, Dad put a devastating end to the lunacy with our mother. The boys were downstairs playing monopoly and watching *Super Host* on television. I was at the dining room table reading. The heat from the furnace was slowly turning the room into a sauna. A violent outburst of arguing echoed from upstairs.

"I've had enough of this shit! I'm through with it! Do you understand me, Alley? You sit in this filthy ass room talking with fucking demons all day! When you walk down the street, the neighbors see you talking to your fucking self and think you're as nutty as a damn fruitcake! You don't clean, you don't cook... you're a fucking possessed mess!"

"Do you really think I give a damn about these neighbors or what anyone thinks of me? Those people don't know me! They don't know one damn thing about me, so don't go making an issue out of nothing! Just get the hell out of here before I..."

The demons began talking with her and Dad observed bravely.

"Before you what? Go on and finish your damn sentence! Before you what, Alley? Put a spell on me? Poison me? Before you what?"

"There's no telling what I might do if you don't leave me the hell alone. Just try me. I dare you. Try me, Colin! No one's afraid of you anymore! We aren't afraid of shit!"

The demons spoke to her again.

"That's precisely the reason I'm getting rid of your sick ass! You're finally off your damn rocker!"

"What the hell are you talking about? Get rid of me? You can't get rid of me! I'll get rid of *you* first!"

Without realizing it, she was on her own. The demons stopped talking. They stopped!

"Watch me. Just watch me. It'll be a piece of cake. I've had it with your crazy witchcraft or whatever the hell you call it. Look at yourself; you don't see anything wrong, do you? What happened to that church you were so involved with? Where'd your fucking cohorts go? What the fuck happened to you, Alley? Tell me, what?"

"What the fuck happened to you, Colin? Examine your damn self. You're a fine one to talk!"

She picked up a book and abruptly turned the pages.

"They fucked you up and left! That's what happened!"

"Those people aren't for me. They're all crazy. They just want to use me. Everybody wants to use me! I'm sick of it!" She slammed the book shut and flung it on the bed like a Frisbee.

"That's pretty damn ironic. You're finally acknowledging they're crazy, *too*! So then, tell me, what makes *you* so sane? You were baptized by those fruitcakes!"

"I don't want to talk about them! I'm sick to death of those damn people!"

"Well, you're going to! You let them in our lives! The devil has to be invited in some way or another! And you let him in!"

"No, Colin! You let him have your soul a long, long time ago! And what about this house? You turned this into Satan's playground! You let Satan inside of you and walked him into this house! It was you who did this to me! You invited him in! You did this to our children!"

His eyes descended and he was rendered speechless as she stared through him. He began to leave the room, but turned around to address her again. He rolled his shoulders back and cracked them to reset mentally, then he confidently stiffened his posture. He couldn't let her have the last true word.

"You know what, Alley? Don't try and manipulate the situation and blame all this shit on me! They came here, fucked up your simple little head, then split. Now, you're the fucking idiot trapped with a bunch of damn demons telling you what in the hell to do. Sister fucking Cyprus and her band of witches have flown off to fuck up someone else's mind! Maybe they took a sabbatical. Who knows?" He threw his hands in the air. "Look around this room! Statues... " He picked up one of the ceramic statues of a man with snakes draped around his feet and dropped it back in its place on her dresser. "Books on spells and spirits... candles, piles of junk jewelry, shit, shit, and more shit everywhere! Where did this come from? The fucking room even smells like shit! Look at all those clothes stuffed in the closet and shoved in the corner over there!"

"These are my things, Colin! *My things!* They aren't yours, so don't worry about *what* they are or *where* they came from! You're getting on my damn nerves! Since this room smells like shit, get out! Go on, get out," she shouted hysterically.

Her speech was rapid and erratic. She intermittently yelled at him and spoke to the demons but *they* gave no response.

"You're getting on my fucking nerves, too! The children are afraid of *you!* They don't have friends because parents don't want them around your crazy ass! And to top it off, you don't act like a wife! We haven't slept in the same bed in God knows how long! Not that I'd want to! Are you aware that I can divorce your ass on those grounds alone?"

"Divorce my ass then! Do you really think I'd give a damn? Who the hell cares anyway?"

"Believe it or not, I care, Alley! I've waited too long and let this insanity get out of hand! Ouija boards, spirits, or demons... There's no telling what else has been going on around here that I haven't seen. Maybe that fucking *well* out back has something to do with all this! I don't know. I can't explain what happened to you and perhaps somehow, some of it *is* my fault, but I'm not going to let you run our lives anymore. I'm not going to watch you ignore the kids any longer. I've heard Selvin call for you repetitively... Mommy, Mommy, Mommy and you don't say a fucking word to the kid! He can stand there and tap on your shoulder a hundred damn times and you don't move. You don't even acknowledge him. Look how thin Marala is! She doesn't sleep! She's terrified of *you!* She has no choice but to hear your fucking babbling and carrying on all hours of the night, then all *fucking* day to boot! It's over, Alley! This shit is fucking over! I've been waiting for you to come to your senses, but instead, I've finally come to mine. I'm done!" There was always a reason for his summarizing statement because he never alluded to his next twist until he was ready.

"You think you're perfect, don't you, Colin! You're fucking perfect! The great *Colin* can do no wrong! Don't you *dare* go blaming me for Marala being that damn thin because you're the cause of that! You're the reason I went to that damn church in the first place! I went to get away from your abusive ass! I'm tired of this shit, too! How about that! You blame everyone around you for your fucking mistakes! You beat those boys when you feel like it, and you blame it on them! You beat me and let the kids watch! How do you think they're going to end up? *Like you*, beating their wives and children! Just like you! And the thought of it makes me sick! They might not even want kids because of you! Those children detest you because you've made their lives a living hell! Then you turn around and call it discipline! You hateful son-of-a—"

"That's right, it is discipline! They deserve everything they get! My disciplining them is why this house has been running so damn smoothly without their batty ass mother! *Pardon me*, Mrs. Smart Ass, but you're the one who exposed them to *hell* with your fucking demons," he said adjusting his pants. "What about Selvin and Jimmy? Who's been raising them? It sure the hell hasn't been *you* for the past few years! I can divorce your ass for gross neglect! Boy, I have a hundred reasons to get rid of your ass! How about—"

"How about *you* get the hell out of my sight? Don't you stand there telling me what I haven't done for *my* damn kids! Those are my babies, and they're fine! Just fine! They never deserved a father like you! Go look at the knots you put on little Colin's head! Look at the welts on Stanley and Colin! Go look, you fucking four-eyed bastard! Before you go blaming me, you'd better take your ass straight to the mirror and see the monster that you are! One day they'll be glad to be rid of your ass! You'll see! Now get the hell out of my room, Colin! I can't stand the sight of you!"

"Wrong, Alley! Your deranged ass is about to get the hell out of *my* damn house. You're on your way to the fucking funny farm! Then you and your damn demons can perform all you want! You can put on nice little shows for the nuts! Since you want to be such a hard ass and blame me for everything that's wrong around here, then go right ahead. I don't give a shit. I'll be the bad guy. How's that sound? But let's just see what happens after they get a load of your crazy ass. Let's just wait and see what they think, shall we? They'll probably lock you up forever! Let's get this shit over and done with," he announced, lightly dusting his hands off of one another.

"Those people can't do shit to me! Go ahead, let them try!"

"Oh, yeah?"

"Yeah!"

"We'll find out then, won't we? Remember the business associate I had over here last week. Well he was a fucking psychiatrist. He watched you walking around talking to your little invisible pals. He heard them mumbling back at you. He saw you neglecting the kids. He saw how filthy you are. He even saw this room. He saw everything he needed to see to lock your ass the fuck up!"

Their arguing was interrupted by the sound of a small white truck pulling in the driveway. Three doors slammed shut, causing Dad to quickly compose himself before the heavy pounding hit the front door. Colin Jr. and Stan went upstairs to answer it when Dad ran down the stairs, headed them off, and instructed them to return to the family room.

"I've got it, boys. They're here for your mother," he said calmly while wiping the heavy perspiration off his forehead.

He tried to maintain his composure, but it was difficult.

I watched silently while he opened the door and invited three men wearing white clothing inside.

"Mr. Murray?"

"Yes."

"Hello, sir, my name is Tom. This is Bob, and that's John. Dr. Warren sent us here today for Alley Murray. Is that correct?"

"That's correct, and you're right on time. She's upstairs in the first bedroom to the left. I'm Colin, her husband," he said extending his hand to each of the men. "I've been to see Dr. Warren at the State Hospital over the past few weeks."

"Yes, sir. We have the report," he said, holding a clipboard while flipping through a few pages. "It states that she's been talking to spirits and that she's extremely violent. We were informed that this has been going on for some time," Tom explained.

"Yes, that's about the gist of it," Dad replied confidently.

Tom was a large white man standing about six feet four and two hundred fifty pounds. He was wearing a carefully pressed pair of white slacks with a white button up short-sleeved shirt, neatly tucked into them. His pants were locked around his waist by a white belt with a polished brass buckle. His arms were large and muscular with visible scratch marks. He was clean-shaven and had thick wavy blond hair with serious light-blue eyes.

"Is it okay to go up and talk to her? Or how do you suggest we handle the situation, sir?"

"You guys are welcome to go right upstairs and determine that for yourselves," he replied while pointing in the direction of the stairs. "She's highly agitated and irrational. Trust me when I say she won't want to talk with you. You'll see. She's pretty far gone, delusional even. But don't mistake what you see for schizophrenia," he warned persuasively.

"Are there any weapons in the house, sir?" Tom asked while the other two men cautiously observed their surroundings.

"No, we don't keep weapons around, you know, with the children and all. It wouldn't be prudent, especially given the state of mind she's in," Dad replied. He neatly tucked his plaid shirt into his blue jeans, took a deep breath, and put his foot on the first step to lead the three men up the stairs when Tom tapped him on his shoulder after glancing over at me.

"Would you mind if we asked you to have the children leave? Is there someone that can take them until we handle this situation?" Tom asked.

Dad winked at me and said, "It's not necessary. They've been dealing with this for years. It's time that they see it's being handled so they can finally feel safe around here."

By the time they reached the room Mom had locked the door. Dad took a bobby pin from the ledge above the door and unlocked it. He entered the room to find her crouching on the floor by the side of her bed extinguishing a cigarette into a Pepsi bottle.

"Alley, there are people here to talk to you," he said calmly, with the men standing behind him.

"I already told you to get the hell away from me," she said with her voice escalating passionately. "I don't want to talk to anyone! Let alone to your ass!" In a highly agitated state she motioned her hand for them to leave. "Get out of here, all of you! Go on, get!"

"Alley, they're from the State *Mental* Hospital. Remember? The one we were discussing a few moments ago."

"I said, get out of here!"

"Well, see that's a problem because they can't without… you," he said smiling affectionately.

"Let them leave here with your ass!"

He turned to face the men, then shook his head with disgust.

"Alley, you've been having some major problems, and I'm going to see to it that you get the help you need. I know this must be difficult for you to handle, honey, but trust me, you'll thank me later. Why don't we talk like adults and you can tell these gentlemen what's been going on with you," he insisted with care. "Tell these gentlemen all about the demons and spirits you talk with. Tell them about the church and your little friends."

"Shut up! Shut the hell up!"

"They want to know what happened, Alley."

"Shut up! I said shut the hell up!"

"Explain to them how you don't do anything around here because the spirits take up all your time."

"I said shut the hell up! Get your crazy ass away from me! Get away from me, Colin! I hate your sorry ass!"

"Tell them how you've neglected the *kids*. Go on, tell them, Alley! Tell them about all the threats and your little late night sessions with your friends."

She sprang to her feet and started stomping and yelling even louder. "I hate you, Colin! I hate you! So get away from me! I don't have anything to talk about! Stay the hell away from me you bastard!"

He wanted to evoke a violent reaction from Mom, and he did it, effortlessly. He was satisfied.

He'd always known how to get a hostile reaction out of Mom. Demons or not, dad could do it! The three men observed Mom launching the Pepsi bottle across the room. They watched it crash into the wall, narrowly missing Dad, as he quickly ducked to avoid it! He pushed every button he could. One after another she violently hurled her books and statues at Dad, screaming as she aimed for his head.

Mom had on a pair of blue and green striped nylon pants with a dingy white t-shirt, a brown turtleneck layered by a blue sweater vest with lint balls covering it, and a button-up sweater. Her face was thin and drawn. Her once beautiful jet-black hair was cut into a sloppy short afro with a fair amount of gray beginning to glisten. She had a sweaty blue and white bandanna as a headband. Twelve bracelets dangled from her right arm and six different watches for men hung loosely on the other. Twelve or more necklaces with various charms were draped around her thin neck. Each finger held two or three gaudy rings. The metal from the rings stained her fingers green. Her once long, manicured fingernails were bitten to the skin. Her ear lobes hung low with the holes torn larger than usual because of the excessive weight of the earrings. Her white socks and old tan moccasins covered her little crusty feet. Sadly, Mom appeared extremely unstable.

"I think you boys are going to need some sort of restraints with her," Dad suggested.

"Sir, we'd like to try and talk with her first," Tom explained.

"Be my guest, but you're wasting your time," Dad firmly added.

He backed into the hallway and let Tom go to work.

"Ma'am, my name is Tom, and I'm from the State Mental Hospital. I understand that you and your husband are having some problems. We're here to discuss what's been going on with *you*. Is it okay if I call you Alley?"

"Don't call me shit," she shouted.

"Call her Alley," Dad callously interrupted with a smirk.

With a large statue in her hand, she backed her frail body into a corner panicking like a wild animal. She was talking to her spirits, yet they continued to abandon this fight.

Tom calmly continued, "Alley, are you listening to me?" She continued yelling for her demons to answer. "Alley, do you hear me?" Tom asked again.

"I hear your ass! Stop talking to me like I'm crazy! He's not my husband," she shouted angrily. "The only problem I have is *him*," she said, pointing a large statue at Dad.

"She's irrational," he said crossly. "Alley, you don't remember marrying me sixteen years ago? Well, aren't you the lucky one. I wish I couldn't remember that either."

"Sir, we have this under control. Can you let us handle it? We'll probably be more effective."

"Effective, my ass! I told you he's not my husband, *so* he's not my damn husband! And he can't do this to me!"

"Well, he says he's your husband, Alley, and we have the documents here to confirm it."

"Well, he's not! He's a damn liar! He made that shit up himself! He sells copiers and computers and that's what he did. He printed it at work," she screamed.

"Then why do you live here?" Tom asked. She didn't answer. She was incapable of correcting contradictions. "Alley, do you mind coming out here to talk to me? I'll have Colin leave. How's that sound?"

"Good! You do that! Have Colin leave, and you go with him! Get the hell out of here and leave me alone! I'm not bothering you people! I don't have anything to say to you!"

Tom leaned back and whispered to Bob, "Irrational, and anxiety." Then he returned his attention toward her. "That's not going to happen until I have a chance to talk with you and find out what's going on. Now he claims you've been talking to yourself and to some sort of demons or spirits. Are you talking to anyone in particular who maybe *he* doesn't know about? Do you care to share that with me, Alley?"

"That's none of your damn business! Who in the hell do you think you are to question me like this? I don't go to your home asking you fucking questions! You don't know me! Do you hear me, Thomas Parker! You don't know anything about me, so don't come up in this house asking who I've been talking to! You don't know anything about me!"

Her erratic outburst of anger was coupled with fear.

Astonished, Tom tried pulling himself together to rebound from her statements. Then he asked, "Can you tell me how you feel right now, Alley? Can you tell me how you knew my name?" he continued with a quizzical look on his face.

"I... just... I know, damn it! I don't have to tell you a damn thing! I feel like being left the hell alone! Get out of my room! Get out of this house! Just get the hell out of here and take *that* man with you! *He* belongs in the damn state hospital if you want to know the truth," she yelled, pointing at Dad.

Tom leaned back out of the room and instructed the smallest of the three men to go to the truck. When he returned my eyes roamed across the white jacket with straps hanging from it. I knew this was it. A warm flush moved across my face.

"In all probability, this situation is a *little* different than what you're used to dealing with. I enlightened the doctor yesterday," he explained.

"Yes, I know, and we're well aware of the situation, Mr. Murray," Tom acknowledged.

"Good. Well then, she's all yours, and she's a mess," he said bitterly.

Dad pointed both of his index fingers at Mom signaling for them to get her.

"Alley," Tom began. "We've been instructed to take you back to the hospital for observation. Since you don't want to talk to me, I have no recourse other than to take you by force. Alley?" he began cautiously. "I'm asking you to come with us voluntarily. Will you do that for me, Alley?" Tom requested more sternly, as he tried creeping toward her one slow step at a time like a hunter.

"I'm not going anywhere! Take that bastard with you, and I'll be fine! We'll all be fine! It's him you want, not me!"

Her hysterical screams sent chills up my spine as they ricocheted off the walls and multiplied throughout the house. Dad stood in the hallway with his arms folded as Tom entered the room. The two other men guardedly followed with the straightjacket slowly moving in her direction. The horrid uproar continued. We heard heavy crashing against the walls and loud thumps on the floor as the men fought to restrain her.

"I'll kill you for this, Colin! How could you do this to me?" she cried, helplessly.

With an undisguised pleasure he explained, "See? That's one of the problems. I don't feel safe here. She's been making all sorts of threats lately. Alley, you need help," he replied in a spiteful tone. "I should have done this *years* ago." He balled up his fist and rested them on his hips.

His sadistic grin stretched from one side of his face to the other.

He triggered an emotional upset in Mom and was gaining momentum to continue.

"You don't give a damn about me! You want to get rid of me, so you can be with her! That's all it is, Colin! You want to be with your *mistress*! Did you think I didn't know who your Aunt Bronzella was? You brought that bitch into *this* house and had me cook dinner for her! Tell them about her! Go on, tell them the damn truth, Colin!" Her rage was uncontrolled while fighting with everything she had in her. "I should have poisoned the both of you then!"

The surges of ruthless words were honest and isolated. They would never have escaped her mouth toward any of us.

"Wow! That's what I'm talking about. This is standard behavior for her. Can you believe the children are routinely subjected to this insanity?" he asked biting off his words harshly.

Tom clamped down on her arm and grabbed her from behind while Bob and John struggled to trap her in the jacket. As soon as Tom and John slipped her arms into the sleeves, she kicked Bob in his groin, thrusting him into a wall. He grabbed his genitals, grunting painfully as he lost his breath before plummeting to his knees. Tom and John brought the struggle to an abrupt halt. They grabbed hold of Mom on each side and yanked the straps, immobilizing her arms, then tightly fastened them.

"Let me go! Let me go, damn it," she ordered while violently twisting and jolting to get out of the fitted straightjacket. "Did he tell you he beats the kids? Did he tell you he beats my ass to a pulp? He starves us when he's mad! He's crazy! You want him! Not me! Him, damn it! Get me out of this thing! Let me out of here! Take him! Take him, and we'll be fine! Let me go! Let me go, damn it! Help! Help me!" Her words erupted into a persuasively frightened tone. "Help me, Stanley... Somebody! Stanley," she cried passionately. "Stanley..."

For whatever reason, Mom didn't yell for the demons, and *they* didn't interfere. This was the only time in years that Mom wasn't controlled by *them*. And *they* weren't available for consultation.

The loud banging and crashes escalated as her screams intensified. Dad yelled for us to close all the windows to keep the neighbors from hearing what was going on. Stan and Colin raced up and down the stairs to shut windows only to find *groups* of neighbors assembled outside our house staring at it strangely. If they thought *this* incident was a big deal, obviously they have been missing out.

Mom was completely restrained. Dad fell back and took a stance as though he was an outsider gazing at a mere deranged stranger. He appeared slightly amused and indifferent. We gathered at the bottom of the stairs wailing as if she had died. *Mom wore an expression I'd never forget!* It was agonizing to see her like that! She displayed the same type of fear as when Dad beat her. That same look of hopelessness from all her years of abuse had returned. She looked like a captured wild animal. Echoes of vicious, painful screaming looped throughout the house bringing my brothers to the stairs.

"Mom," I called repeatedly, locking my eyes on hers. "Don't hurt her! Don't hurt her!"

Those words locked in my throat, allowing nothing else to escape. Selvin whimpered as he watched the violent display. He looked confused, and uneasy. His barren eyes never shifted away from hers. Jimmy slid his hands into his pockets and watched as his little eyes turned bloodshot and his facial expression shut down. The men in white clothes picked Mom up, carried her down the stairs, past all of her children, kicking and screaming savagely. Humiliation and cruelty don't give credence to the proper portrayal of what had transpired. Dad had defiled Mom, in the worst way, in front of the only thing she loved, us. *This* image of mom would have a permanent effect that would last a lifetime.

Once amazingly beautiful, now she looked like a wild possessed lunatic. It was painful to admit but at that moment, the straightjacket seemed appropriate.

"Can't you gag her mouth so the neighbors don't hear this crap?" Dad asked. "Boy, she's a nutcase," he added, impatiently.

"Bastard! You fucking bastard! I'll kill you for this, Colin," she threatened.

"I'm sure you would, *if* you could. But you *can't* now, can you?" he sang cheerfully.

"I hate you! Get my kids out of here! Get them away! Don't let them see me like this! Don't let them see this, Colin! *Please don't let them see this!"*

Her angry words transitioned into begging since it appeared the demons had deserted her, at least for now.

"Alley, the problem is that I've done everything I possibly could to keep from seeing you *like this*. The children didn't want to live with you *like this!* Now, all of a sudden you're begging me *not* to let them see you in the one place you belong, *a straightjacket!* What irony! What in the hell do you think you've shown them all these years? I *want* the children to see you like this! And I'd *love* for these gentlemen to see you do a little *hocus pocus* right about now! Ooops, I don't think you can. I forgot. Your hands are tied." He leaned over and said in a low voice, "One more thing, Alley. Do you know what an oxymoron is?" Her dry lips slightly parted as though she wanted to respond. Instead, her eyes rolled toward the top of her head. "I'll tell you," he said. "It's *you*, smart ass. You thought you could beat me. No one beats Colin Murray. No one!" He sneered again. *His eyes held an evil identical to Mom's when her demons were enraged.*

This was unreal! I couldn't block out the hysterical cries and screams. Every sound that escaped her lips caused me to cry harder. Dad moved closer, locking his eyes with hers; you could feel the enormous pleasure from what he had just accomplished.

Mom sucked the spit from her throat, then spit on him and kept spitting until he backed away and wiped his face with his forearm in disgust.

"Sir! Please move back," Tom said ushering Dad aside. "We need to get her out of here and away from the children! I'd prefer we do this quickly," he explained.

"I'm sorry," Dad said with fake remorse. "I have one more thing to say before you haul her out of here." He leaned over once more and warned in a scornful tone, "That's all right, Alley. I realize you're a little upset, but let's see you spit on the doctors like that. They'll give your ass a shock treatment you'll never forget, then you won't be able to pucker your damn lips together." He stepped backward and bit down on his bottom lip.

They carried my mother twisting and screaming out the front door and tossed her into the back of the white truck. Her desperate screams faded from the house but not my head… as if this were a nightmare. *I blinked my eyes and Mommy was gone.*

Dad raced upstairs, washed his face, and then brushed his hair. He changed shirts and fled past us folding a piece of gum into his mouth. He jumped into his car and followed closely behind them. *Was that the end of my mother? Was this the end of them?*

———

When Dad left, the house fell morbid. We wandered around for at least thirty minutes without a word being spoken or an expression shared. We were temporarily paralyzed at the conclusion to Mom and *them.* The house had never been that quiet while we were awake. None of us knew what to say. It would have been difficult to defend Mom. After several minutes of us staring at the closed front door, Stan finally broke the silence.

"Hey, guys, think about it logically," Stan advised bleakly. "This was probably for the best. At least now, someone can try to figure out what happened. Maybe Mom can get the help she needs. It's not like he really had a choice. How long was he supposed to let her stay like that? And to be honest, he should have done something a long time ago. We all know something bad would have happened eventually, and it could have been to one of us. Besides, we're not even sure they can help her. I know it was messed up the way he did it and all, but we already know how Dad is. We already know! I don't want Mom like that forever. I know you guys don't either. So let's just think positive for a change. Let's believe she'll get better." Stan scanned each of our faces. We remained solemn. "Not to change the subject or anything, but we know he'll be back. So I suggest we clean the house and go downstairs to read. If you don't want to read, find something constructive to keep you busy and not thinking about the situation." He looked at the apple clock and said, "Let's get started."

For the first time, without resistance, Colin agreed with Stan.

Without one word, Jimmy took Selvin's hand and headed downstairs. Before Selvin reached the bottom step, he turned and searched my face for an explanation, but I turned away.

Stan, Colin, and Clark followed me upstairs to *the room*, which was completely ripped apart. The beds were flipped over. Both mattresses along with the blankets and sheets covered the floor. Broken statues were everywhere, and the dresser was lying on its front. Clothes were randomly thrown around the room. There were thick pieces of broken glass stuck in the carpet near the door where Mom hurled the Pepsi bottle at Dad. Several wire hangers were spread throughout the room as though they were used for boomerangs. Cigarette butts and ashes were smashed into the carpet. Her books were all over the place. I couldn't go in there, but I didn't know what else to do. He had her institutionalized because of me! I told him that I was afraid of her! All of this was my fault! All of it! My conscience burned! I wanted to fall into a black hole and disappear… forever! Without warning, a crippling pain slashed through my head like a bolt of lightning, then I collapsed onto the floor.

I didn't recall how I ended up lying across Clark and Jimmy's bed covered by a yellow and white sheet with a floral pattern. It felt as though I had slept for a lifetime. The crisp wispy breeze had chilled my body enough to awaken me. It was quiet. I glanced at the small alarm clock resting on the nightstand. It was after nine-thirty. I sat up, leaned against the headboard and stretched to look out the window. Night had fallen. Scattered dark clouds raced across the moon and the crickets sang. How did I sleep that long? Was Dad home? Was Mom downstairs in her chair? The house felt serene and the pain in my head had subsided.

I slid the sheet aside, climbed out of bed, and cautiously entered the hallway. My mind was foggy. The door to *the room* was shut. I slowly turned the knob and peeked inside. It was clean. I went downstairs gripping the rail and found Colin and Clark drying dishes. Stan was cleaning the second bathroom. I stood paralyzed on the third from the bottom step and glanced around the room only moving my eyes. Mom's chair was empty. Everything was clean.

"Hey, sissy, are you okay?" Clark asked.

"Is Mommy here?" With a puzzled look on their faces, Colin and Clark looked at one another. "Is she here?" I repeated.

"Don't you remember what happened? She's gone. Dad took her to the hospital," Clark sadly explained.

"You mean the insane asylum," Colin rudely interjected laying a plate in the cabinet.

"Call it whatever you want to call it, but that's where she is, Marala. Mom's in the State Mental Hospital," Clark said compassionately.

"I wasn't dreaming," I mumbled as I stumbled downstairs rubbing my head.

"Huh?" Clark questioned.

"Nothing."

"We cleaned up your room," Clark said.

"Yeah, I saw that. Thank you, but it's *not* my room. I wish you'd quit saying that," I snapped, clinching my fist. I'd asked everyone a few years ago to stop referring to it as if it were mine.

"Yeah, that was one heck of a mess. Mom definitely put up a fight, that's for sure. I would have bet my money on Mom and the demons. I never thought they'd be able to get rid of her that easily. It would have been cool to see Mom's demons against Dad! You know, demon's wrapping around those guys from the funny farm, then jumping inside them." His cynicism strangled me. "I swear I thought something was about to happen. Especially, to Dad! Man, I thought the room was going to catch on fire. Buddy, I had my zips ready so I could get the heck out of here! Mom should have given them a show they'd never forget. I wonder why she punked out like that?" Colin asked in jest.

"Where are Jimmy and Selvin?" I asked ignoring Colin.

"They're downstairs asleep. They were worn out from all the commotion taking place. Stan laid them across his bed. Personally, I don't think they needed to see that crap! I don't think any of us did, but hey, we know how *our* father is!" Clark's tone was less sardonic as he placed the last glass in the cabinet. "Everybody's had dinner but you. We made some jelly sandwiches and chips. Want one? It's loaded with sugar. At least it'll keep you wide awake and thinking about what he did to our mother for the rest of the night. Not that we'd forget this crap anyway."

"No, I can't eat. I just wish I knew what they were doing to Mommy."

All I could think about besides Mom was Selvin and Jimmy. Dad never should have let them see Mommy carried out kicking and screaming like that. That's an awful image for anyone, let alone kids their age. They didn't know where Mom was going, or why the men took her that way. When she saw Selvin and Jimmy staring at her, it must have shattered what was left of her heart.

CHAPTER SEVEN

Cease from anger and forsake wrath; Do not
fret; it leads only to evildoing.

Psalms 37:8
New American Standard

Dad finally returned home, and it was evident that he was in a dismal state of mind. Perhaps having the unsavory task of committing his possessed wife into a mental institution is what left him in such a state. He called for us to assemble in the family room and was prepared to give us the details of what he had done and why.

"I know you're wondering where they took your mother and why."

This time, his demeanor wasn't as callous as when he taunted Mom incessantly while they hauled her out of our house. Dad's wrath was disproportionate. He had Mom committed in an insensitive, humiliating, and violent manner while pretending he did it solely for her.

"I think it was pretty obvious where they took her, Dad. They were dressed for the occasion," Clark answered despondently.

"Listen," he said putting his hand up for us to stop talking. "Each of you will have the opportunity to speak when I'm finished. As I was about to explain," he began, making heated eye contact with Clark. "I had your mother committed to the State Mental Institution. I felt institutionalizing her was the only way to help her at this point. She appears to be suffering from a multitude of things. From what I've observed, you're correct in assuming that your mother became involved with the occult. I don't know exactly what that entails, but it's not good. You kids have witnessed a lot over the past few years, and all I can say is that I should have handled this much sooner. Like I said a long time ago, those women and that crazy church messed up her mind. Hearing the voices pouring out of your mother was unnerving," he admitted. "As a parent, I can't explain everything to you kids, but what I *can* say is that your mother has always done things I didn't necessarily approve of. Unfortunately, this was one of those things. Becoming involved with that church was *her* choice, and she did it against my wishes." He folded his hands and sat quietly for a brief moment. After examining the room he studied each of our expressions. "I know it's been rough for you kids with all of this going on as long as it has." He paused and searched for a viable explanation.

"Perhaps, with a little hope, it's not too late to give her the treatment she needs. For the record, I've admitted your mother for a minimum of thirty days for observation and therapy. Most likely she'll need medication and maybe a little shock treatment, who knows. So let's pray that it works. In the meantime, I'll need a lot of cooperation from you kids." He sighed. "Marala and Stan will do the cooking and the rest of you will keep the house well organized. That means my room, the bathroom… You know what to do. We'll need to pull together so we can make it through this. If anyone asks where your mother is, simply tell them she had a death in her family and took it extremely hard. Don't say anything else," he insisted making uncompromising eye contact with Clark. "That's all anyone needs to know, especially since some of the neighbors already witnessed that shit. You know they're already talking. Enough of our business has been in the streets, so now it's time to cut it out! This household is going to run the way it used to. If any of you step out of line, I won't hesitate to tear you up. So be on top of things, and you won't have a problem with me. When I say I want something done, it means do it right the first damn time! If I say jump, you ask how high. No fighting, lying, or stealing," he said contemptuously, turning his head toward Colin. "I will not tolerate any disrespect in my house. When the time is appropriate, perhaps I'll take you to see your mother. Marala, I want you to clean up that room if you haven't already. Get rid of that shit up there! I hope now you'll be able to sleep. As for the rest of you, get with the program!"

My brothers had already cleaned the room, but I didn't want to interrupt him. After that performance, we were still filtering every scathing word. We had quite a few questions, but knew it wasn't a good time to ask everything. We'd only inquired about the specifics.

"Did they hurt Mom when they took her out of here?" Stan asked, avoiding eye contact with Dad.

"What do you think? It's not like she was willing to go peacefully. She'll have a few bumps and bruises, but that's about it. Next?"

Colin Jr. put his head up and boldly asked, "Who's going to watch us? And who's going to be responsible for Jimmy and Selvin?"

"I'm glad you asked that. First of all, it's not as if your mother has been watching them over the past few years, now has she? Since you're so concerned, I'd like you to do it, and Stan, I'd like you to help." He paused and rubbed his chin as if he were deliberating. "I have an even better solution," he said, throwing me a fleeting look. "Marala, since Selvin's attached to you, I want you to keep a close eye on him. What else?" he asked, directing his question toward Clark.

"Is she with crazy people? I mean, with people who are *really* demented?" Clark asked with a profound look on his face.

"Of course she's with crazy people, because your mother *went* crazy! Trust me, in all probability she's much worse than the nuts already in there. She's right where she should have been a *long* time ago instead of sitting around here threatening people and talking to fucking demons!"

"Is she going to come home when she gets out?" I asked.

"You mean *if* she gets out. Let's wait to see what happens with her therapy, and we'll take it from there. We shouldn't jump the gun on this," he said coldly.

Dad's thinking was methodical. I knew what his true intentions were. That aspect of his personality could never be hidden.

He concluded his question and answer session with a hard clap and said, "I think we've covered everything, so that's all I'm going to disclose for now. Simply do what needs to be done around here. I want as little hassle out of you kids as possible. Do you catch my drift?" We were silent. "Okay then. Since everyone's crystal-clear on my expectations, what I expect is no fuck-ups!"

It was too late for that! I had already messed up, and that's why Mom was gone! No one knew what I'd done. They didn't realize that I had betrayed Mom and told him what was going on from the start. Dad took the information and let it climax until he secured a solid case against her, which allowed him no opposition when he had her committed. He was the master of manipulation, and *I* had been his pawn.

With Dad in and out of our house for the past few months and his having Mom institutionalized in a timely manner, eventually he implied that she wouldn't be returning. This allowed the complete scenario to fall into place. While he spent months away from us, he was out reconstructing a new life for himself. With Mom out of the way, Dad could implement his new plan... for his new life.

We filed out of the room to get ready for bed. Again, he laid down his law, and we knew what was in store. Dad was an extremist. With him, there wasn't an in-between. It was either yes or no. There was no maybe nor shades of gray.

Although he explained what his demands were, he withheld the most pertinent information. *Were the demons still upstairs in that room? Furthermore, were they still in our house? And if they weren't in our house, where were they? Were some of them here waiting to take their next victim? On the other hand, had that already been accomplished?*

CHAPTER EIGHT

But for the cowardly and unbelieving and
abominable and murders and immoral persons
and sorcerers and idolaters and all liars, their
part will be in the lake that burns with fire in
brimstone, which is the second death.

Revelations 21:8
New American Standard

In the weeks to come, Dad was preoccupied. He'd made it clear that he didn't want us to discuss or dwell on the details of what happened. He said, "She went crazy," and that was all there was to it. He had us do a ridiculous amount of cleaning and reorganizing around the house and the yard. Dad instructed us to put all of Mom's belongings into giant garbage bags and throw them on the curb. He wanted every single item out of the house, leaving *nothing* behind.

Just as the three evil women came to our door, so did Sara. She came in the back door, twisting a razor sharp knife in Mom's spine, immobilizing her while lusting after Dad.

"Kids, get down here. I have something I want to share with you," he shouted with an artificial enthusiasm.

After colliding into one another, we positioned ourselves shoulder to shoulder, casting our eyes upon Sara, responding out of sync, "Yes, sir!"

Earlier in the week, Dad sent me to a beautician to have my hair styled. He bought me a couple of dresses, skirts, and tops with little ruffles. This morning, he instructed me to wear a blue and white dress with white stockings. I looked like I was dressing for Easter. For the first time since Mom got involved with those women, I looked somewhat like a girl. I knew there could only be one reason.

Dad stood like the captain of a cruise ship for pimps prepared to give instructions. He was wearing a burnt orange leisure suit with four pockets on the jacket. The matching flared pants were *extreme* for Dad, especially since they covered his platform shoes. He never dressed like that before. Dad's wavy hair was picked out. He changed his glasses, too. The frame was still a light gold, but instead of the business style he *was* wearing, these were larger and had a tint to them, but the lenses were still thick. Dad had a gold necklace with an anchor on it hanging slightly above his third unbuttoned blue and orange striped shirt.

The situation spoke for itself when I realized his wedding band was gone. Dad changed. He was trying to look hip and cool, but he looked nuts! This was a major transition for him. I wondered what kind of person could possibly convince him to dress like an idiot. I was certain he couldn't go to work like that. What had Sara done to him? I would have been grateful if she altered his evil personality. But I could see past the tint in his glasses, Dad's evil was still intact. His eyes gave it away. He attempted to give the appearance of the caring father who was being straightforward and concerned about us. His forehead scrunched together, and the veins in his temples were throbbing. In a matter of time, his evil would conquer Sara, too. I knew him well. He was so volatile that he couldn't contain it!

"In case you're wondering why I had Sara meet your mother, it's because I wanted her to understand the problems I was having with Alley and how it was affecting you kids."

We looked at one another knowing none of us bought that sorry excuse. He brought Sara here so he could validate why he was cheating!

"Hello," she said nervously.

We were silent.

"As you know, I've been seeing Sara for quite some time, so I've invited her to move in with us. This will allow me to be home more often instead of living between here and our apartment. I think it'll be encouraging to have a woman in the house," he said, sneering at me.

I was numb. Did he say she was moving in? My stomach turned in a nauseating fit.

"But… You said Mommy was coming back. What are we going do with *her* when Mommy gets here?" I asked, pointing at Sara with a disgusting look plastered on my face.

"What I said was, let's not jump the gun on this. If you recall correctly, I also explained to you that your mother and I haven't conducted ourselves as husband and wife for over three years." He glanced at Sara as if he were confirming what he'd previously told her. "Your mother should have been institutionalized for a long, long time. But we all know how that worked out. Her ignorant ass sisters checked her out and dropped her off at her mother's. Besides, if you want to know the truth, I ought to sue those doctors for releasing Alley before she received proper treatment. I checked your mother in for a thirty-day evaluation. I'm sure it didn't take them long to realize they couldn't fix her, as *we* very well know," he said with conviction. "Do you have anything to add, honey?" He placed his arm around Sara's wide hip and gave her a tight squeeze, then smiled smugly.

"Colin, I think we should be a little more compassionate when talking about their mother. They lost her under terrible circumstances. A nervous breakdown, wasn't it?" Dad scanned the room with a threatening look to make sure there weren't any contradictory comments. "Regardless, let's not make it any worse for them," she explained. "It's been fairly recent."

Dad's mouth broke into a sly grin and I wanted to scream. A nervous breakdown? Is that what he told her? I was curious to know exactly what he said to this woman. My stomach went through a grinder.

"Then maybe you should leave since it's been *fairly recent*," I mumbled. I rubbed my eyes like I had something in them to prevent my tears from forming. My head was pounding so hard that I wanted to go to sleep and forget about Dad and Sara.

His angry eyes seized me. He calmly sighed with arrogance and asked, "Would you like to repeat that little comment so we can all hear it?"

If I wanted everyone to hear it I would have said it louder. I hesitated for a brief moment because I knew he was setting me up. Then, the more I thought about it, the less I cared what he would do.

"All I said was, maybe she *should* leave since it's been *fairly recent*," My voice grew stronger. "Mommy didn't die; she's just gone! What if she *wants* to come back?" I asked, allowing my eyes to shift over to Sara.

"You're exactly right. Your mother isn't dead, but her mind sure the hell is! Furthermore, let me explain something to you. Your mother *isn't* coming back! And if you're so miserable, you're free to go live with her. How would you like that?"

I let my eyes fasten with his. With my heart racing, I threw my chin up and proudly replied, "I would!"

"Then I'd love to discuss that with you at a later time!" He gave an icy stare as if he wanted to power slap me down the stairs at a hundred miles per hour. "Now that you know what the situation is with Sara and me, you shouldn't have any difficulties adjusting," he said flatly.

We were smart enough not to reply. "Okay then. Stan, get her luggage out the trunk and take it into my room." He reached into his pants pocket, pulled the keys out, and tossed them to Stan. "Colin, you go with him," he ordered. "To make certain everyone's clear; Sara will be around here to help out, if you need it. It'll be good for you to finally have someone to confide in. You know, like a mother," he explained maliciously.

"What do you mean like a mother? We already have a mother! I don't care what you say about her, she's still our Mom and nobody can replace her."

I had to say something. Mom was still alive! He wasn't married to Sara, and he had the nerve to say, *like a mother!* Who'd want that thing as a mother? She was a cheater! He was a cheater! They were cheaters!

Dad knew exactly how to strike a nerve. No, dad knew how to rip me apart.

"Marala, get a grip or I'll—"

"Colin… Colin, please, let me," Sara interjected with her proper British accent. "Marala, I'm not here to become a mother to you children because I have five of my own. Your father and I are in a relationship, and that's as far as it goes. I am *not* trying to take your mother's place, and oh God, please don't think that I am," she added with an honest expression.

I could tell that Sara didn't want to be anyone's mother, which was a good thing.

I looked at Clark, standing with his head down to hide his tears. It wasn't often that I saw Clark crying unless he was beaten.

"Sir, can we go now?" Clark asked. Nervously, his hands toiled with the strings hanging from his cut-off jean shorts.

Dad flared up and blurted out crossly, "When I'm finished, I'll dismiss you! Do you catch my drift?"

"Yes, sir," he said taking two steps backwards.

Stan and Colin returned, dropping seven large flowered suitcases in front of them.

Stan handed the keys back to Dad. "Sir. We got the suitcases from the backseat, too."

"Well, now you're thinking," he said condescendingly.

Dad was incorrigible.

"Do you want all of them upstairs?"

"That's what I requested, isn't it?"

"Wait just one moment, Stanley. I need to get something out of that small suitcase. Can you hand it to me, dear?" she asked reaching for it.

"Just call me Stan, like my brothers and kid sister do."

Mom was the only one who called him Stanley.

"All right, *Stan*," Sara responded as she smiled at him.

"This one?" Stan asked, pushing the other suitcases from around it.

"Yes, that's the one. Thank you."

Sara opened the suitcase and pulled out a few toiletries, then a brown paper bag that clanked together as she held it under her arm. She placed the other items back in the suitcase and smiled excitedly at Dad.

"Does anyone have any further questions for Sara?"

"Where are *your* kids? And are you married?" Colin asked, but he already knew the answer.

"My children are with their father. And *no*, I'm not yet divorced," she replied while resting the brown paper bag on the dining room table. She opened the bag and took out a bottle of gin, then tonic. "Marala, dear, can you show me where the glasses are kept?"

Sara sounded anxious, or thirsty. I pointed at the cabinet to the right of the sink.

"Do you think you can be a little more hospitable, young lady?"

Dad was irritated, and I could care less.

I opened the cabinet and grabbed two glasses then placed them on the counter. "Is there anything else?"

"As a matter-of-fact, I'd like some ice, dear."

Sara's eyes never left the bottle as she twisted the cap off both and waited for the glasses.

I yanked the freezer door open hard enough to make it hit the wall. With a calculated movement I slammed the metal ice tray on the edge of the sink as loud as possible because I was angry. Clark smiled. I threw a couple cubes into each glass, handed them to Sara, then spitefully asked, "Is there *anything* else?"

"No, thank you, dear."

She poured herself an uneven mixture of gin and tonic. Of course, the gin was three quarters of the glass. It was evident that she was trying to tolerate us and thought a drink might make it easier. She handed the other glass to Dad.

Sara and Mom didn't have anything in common other than their choice in men. Sara wore expensive clothing, had beautifully manicured nails, and her thick curly black hair hung past her shoulders. She tried to look cheerful, but there was a hint of sadness emitting from her brown eyes. I didn't know why she was really here. Why would a woman with five children want a man with six? Although he lied and said that Mom had a nervous breakdown that alone should have made her wonder if he caused it. Something or *someone* had to make Mom that way. My eyes were fixed on Sara. She must have been desperate to leave her house. Perhaps her husband was possessed and she was trying to escape him.

"Marala, seeing as you *are* a young lady, do you have any specific questions for Sara?"

"No," I said shrugging.

"I'm sure you must have a couple," he insisted.

"No, I don't," I said casually shaking my head. "I can't think of anything I'd ask a stranger."

"You know, I've had just about enough of your impertinence," he said, slamming his glass on the table and moving toward me.

I took a deep breath and gritted my teeth. I was willing for Sara to see the *real* Dad. I welcomed the release of his razor-sharp tongue combined with his back-handed slap. And this time, I didn't mind it being at my expense.

"Colin... Colin, let's not push it," she said, fiercely clutching his elbow and pulling him away from me. "This is going to take time, especially for your daughter," she conceded.

He cut his eyes at me and confessed, "It better not take too long. That's all I have to say!"

He picked up his glass, took a sip, grinned at me scornfully, then took another sip.

"What's your last name?" Stan asked trying to change the subject.

"Cooks. Why?" she asked inquiringly.

"So we can call you *Mrs.* Cooks?" Clark chimed in.

Colin and Stan grinned at Clark's cleverness.

"I'd rather you call me Sara."

We grew silent.

Dad smiled cunningly and asked, "Is there some problem with that?"

"No, I guess we want to make sure you don't want us to call her *Mom*," Clark replied, cynically.

"Well, let's just wait and see what's next, shall we?"

"Yes, sir," Stan and Clark replied.

Dad put his glass on the table and positioned himself behind Sara. He wrapped both arms around her and locked his hands together. He kissed her neck and her makeup-stained cheek. "Do you know how much I love you?" he asked Sara while beaming irritatingly at me.

Clark and I sighed with repugnance.

One of many intrinsic characteristics Dad carried was his lack of diplomacy. Each time he made an embarrassing or inappropriate statement, he gloated in the most revolting way.

"You see, this is an example of ignorant, undisciplined, and unsophisticated children," he declared raising his glass in the air as if her were toasting. "That's why I got rid of Alley," he boasted. He released Sara, walked over to the table, and filled his glass with more gin and tonic. Then he pointed the bottle toward Sara to see if she wanted more. She shook her head, so he filled her glass with gin and picked up the bottle of tonic to cap it off. She placed her hand over her glass and stopped him.

"I'm fine, Colin."

"See? Alley couldn't teach these heathens a damn thing," he said screwing the top back on the gin. "Sara's children show respect to her at all times. That's something you all are going to learn… And soon! Make it easy on yourselves and accept Sara because she's *not* going away," he said, pointing his glass at us. "Clark, do you have any feelings about her?"

"No, sir. I don't have any yet."

"And you, Colin?"

"Sir, like Clark just said, we don't know her. Personally, I'd rather not judge her until I do."

"Smart thinking. Stan, what's your assessment of Sara? Or would you rather not critique her until you get to know her as well?"

"Yes, sir."

Manufacturing an insincere smile, he said, "Jimmy... Selvin, the two of you will be fine. Sara's fun to be around, and I think you'll like her. Besides, she's a good cook," he added, pinching her on the cheek. Sara flipped her hair off her shoulders and smiled shyly. "Marala, for the record, I don't give a damn what you think. For all I know, you might be just like Alley, given you shared a room with her," he said spitefully.

Sara glanced at Dad with a raised eyebrow. She didn't know what that meant.

At that moment, I was trying to decide if I should hate him or feel a little sorry for him. That's easy, I hate him. I recall how he initially brought Sara into our house and had Mom cook, clean, and serve this woman *before* she was possessed. At that time, Mom was just getting into the whole thing. What kind of woman would go into another woman's house like that? *What kind of woman would cheat on her own husband, break up her family, then take a man away from his family, without empathy? What kind of woman could do that without the fear of God?* It could only be someone that doesn't care about anyone other than herself. Now I knew who Sara was.

Dad grabbed Sara's hand and said, "Come on, sweetheart, we've dealt with this long enough." Sara gulped the last bit of her drink and snatched her leather purse off the table, slamming the door behind her.

"So long," Clark shouted. We laughed as Clark mocked Sara in a fake British accent, "My children are with their father. And *no*, I'm not divorced yet. I'm just a slut," he added, dancing around the kitchen. "Don't let him get to you, sissy," Clark advised. "Stay away from him. Just let them do their own thing. Maybe he'll mellow out with Sara here. Like he said, let's see what happens," he insisted. "I have an idea," he added with a bright smile. "Let's do something fun tomorrow."

"Brother here's right!" Colin put his hands on Clark's shoulders and firmly shook him. "We can do something exciting or sit around here like a bunch of fools. That's it," he said interrupting his own flow of words. "I got it! Let's build a carnival in the backyard. We can charge these kids in the neighborhood to get in, so we can make money and have pizza tomorrow," Colin proudly suggested. "They already think this place is a madhouse! Especially after what he did to Mom!"

Stan reached into the refrigerator, pulled out the plastic pitcher, and drank the last bit of cherry Kool-aid, then asked, "What do you have in mind?"

"For starters, we can put Clark in a tent with a sign on it that reads *View the Freak* since his eyebrows are connecting thanks to the blast," he joked. "And Marala, with that hairdo you can sit next to him with a sign that says, *Medusa*. Let's get started so we'll be ready for tomorrow. The devil won't be back for a while. Besides, I'm sure Sara will keep him busy," Colin added.

Clark began laughing hysterically.

Colin smiled and asked, "What do you find so funny, little buddy?"

"Why don't we… Why don't we…"

Clark couldn't stop laughing.

"What? Spit it out," Colin demanded with his smile extending.

The rest of us smiled and began to chuckle lightly with the same curiosity as Colin.

"Why don't we throw Dad in that *well* out back and put a sign on it that says *See the King of Hell!*"

"Naw, man," Stan began, laughing. "They don't need to look in the *well* to see the *King of Hell*. All they have to do is come in *this house!*"

We hit the floor cracking up.

In no time at all, Sara comfortably settled into our house. Mom had clusters of pictures, dishes, and knickknacks everywhere. Sara threw them away and replaced them with her own tasteful selection. I watched Sara eagerly discarding Mom's things by shoving them into large garbage bags. It bothered me because she did it without any consideration of the sentiment it may have had to Mom. They should have sent Mom her things.

It didn't take long for me to get over Sara and her disrespect because I was certain that she'd get what she deserved. I had little doubt that Dad would do to Sara precisely what *he* did to *Mom*, which was replacing her without forewarning. Sara would get a nice dose of her own medicine once Dad grew tired of her and went after her replacement.

I was as respectful as I could be toward Sara. In all honesty, it wasn't fair to her and it didn't help that Dad didn't tell her the truth. His explanation was a convenient lie. He didn't tell Sara how he brutally beat his wife. He didn't tell her about Mom's possession. Dad didn't say anything about *his* raging psychopathic dual personality! Sara should have backed away and given us time to adjust to Mom's absence. I found it ironic that Sara cheated her way into, of all places, *our house.*

Dad's divorce papers came, citing Mom with cruel neglect. Mom didn't contest or show up at the hearing. Shortly thereafter, Dad and Sara eloped without our knowledge until a few months later. Sara's life was destined to change to an unsolicited degree, as that of our mother's. I attempted to warn her about our father's crazed and abusive behavior. All of the physical indicators were present, and his narcissistic personality showed like a fiery comet. However, she assumed my warning was to scare her away out of aversion. *Sara would soon discover that everything we told her was true!*

CHAPTER NINE

'For I will restore you to health and I will heal
you of your wounds,' declares the LORD,
'Because they have called you an outcast,
saying: "It is Zion;
no one cares for her."'

Jeremiah 30:17
New American Standard

Regardless of Sara's presence, everything in our house continued to deteriorate. The tension exploded around us with a great deal of warning, but it was unavoidable. Colin was first. His conflicts with Dad were inevitable, and Dad's actions were predictable. As standard punishment, Dad withheld meals for a day or two at a time so Sara wouldn't observe his abuse until he was ready for her to see it. When Dad went to his room after dinner, I'd sneak food downstairs to Stan and Colin. I had to take the food from my plate by getting extra portions because he'd notice if anything was missing from the cabinets or refrigerator. Dad would have noticed a slice of cheese missing.

───────────

Colin was a junior in high school and had grown intrepid, which motivated him to become quite the thief. Dad had been so inundated with Sara that he assumed his inconspicuous ways of punishment were still effective. He was mistaken. He wasn't mindful of how significant Colin's problem had become, until it was brought to his attention.

At last, we managed to have a peaceful day carved out. Dad and Sara were relaxing in the living room listening to the *Camelot* soundtrack. Jimmy and Selvin were in the snow-covered backyard playing catch along the fence. I was in the kitchen making Dad and Sara a cup of tea, and the boys were downstairs expressing their enthusiasm about Dad taking us to the movies the following day. As soon as I placed the teabags in both cups the teapot began whistling loudly. I turned off the stove, poured the steaming water evenly into each cup allowing the tea to stain it. I folded two paper napkins, laid them on an off-white plastic tray, and searched for Sara's tea cookies or *biscuits,* as she called them.

Before I was able to serve them, someone knocked on the door. Sara answered it allowing a gust of cold air to rush in. Shivering in front of her stood two men who ran the local gym. Sara carefully lifted the tiny needle from the album and turned off the record player. Dad held open the door and invited them inside. He and Sara sat in serious conversation with the men for nearly an hour.

Colin spent most of his time working out at the gym because it was his sanctuary. The men accused Colin of going behind the counter and taking two deposit bags full of money. They discussed the particulars and asked Dad to look into it. He told them he would talk with his son and find out more about the situation, then get back to them later that day. Since they knew who Dad was, they allowed him the courtesy without involving the police, at that point.

When the men left, Dad called Colin upstairs and inquired about the accusations. Colin stood in front of him with a restrained smile and a slight trace of uneasiness.

"I'm going to give you the chance to tell me the truth. If you confess that you took the money, I won't whip your ass. That is, provided you tell me the truth and nothing but the damn truth, right now. I simply want the money returned," he said convincingly. "On the other hand, if you lie to me, and I find out that you're lying, the police will be involved, then it's out of my hands. Now tell me what happened," he demanded.

Colin cocked his head to the side and shrugged. "Sir... I didn't take it," he replied indifferently, scratching his head. "They don't know what they're talking about because I didn't take anything. I go there to work out, and that's all I do. They have to blame somebody, and they made a mistake." Colin sounded persuasive. "They don't want black kids in there. That's all it is."

"I sincerely doubt these accusations have anything to do with you being black! A crime was committed at their gym! These people have eyewitnesses placing *you* behind the counter prior to their deposit money disappearing. Now, damn it, Colin, I've given you an opportunity to tell me the truth for a change and there's nothing I hate more than a liar," he said firmly, with his eyes and nose flaring.

"I'm not lying, sir! I swear I didn't take them. I swear," he said, beginning to perspire.

"Okay, so we're back to this shit again!" He turned and glanced at Sara. "Did you hear the bullshit I have to deal with?" He bit down on his bottom lip and let his eyes evaluate Colin. "Hmmm... So you didn't take *them*. Do you know the difference between singular and plural asshole?"

"Yes, sir."

"Well now, *them*, that's *plural*, isn't it?" Colin's head hung. "Damn it… Look at me when I'm talking to you!" Instantly he returned his attention to Dad. "Those men didn't drive over here out of the random fucking blue to accuse *you* unjustly. They have *witnesses*. Do you know what a *witness* is?" Colin nodded. "I don't think you seem to understand the severity of this situation. They're accusing *you* of taking their bank deposits. So stop with your fucking little act, and let's get down to the truth! I'm asking you one last time. Did you take the money, or have anything to do with it?" His words were direct and curt as he stood over Colin, outraged.

Colin looked at Sara, who was sipping her tea and foolishly replied, "No, sir."

He quickly threw his hands up to shield his face to avoid a predicted slap, but it wasn't rendered. Dad stood in front of Colin with his hands still resting on his hips. He took a deep breath, shook his head in disbelief, then called Stan and Clark.

"Colin, maybe he didn't take the money. Let me talk to him," Sara offered.

Ignoring Sara, he lost his patience with Colin and snapped, "Sit your ass right there and don't even think about moving," he yelled pointing at the sofa.

Colin clasped his hands together and placed them on his lap. He began nervously rocking back and forth. Dad stormed into the kitchen, and Sara followed. He placed his hands on the counter, stretching away from it, then rotated his neck clockwise. "There's no need for you to get involved in this. I'll get the truth one way or another," he explained wryly.

"But I may be able to help—" she said sounding concerned.

"Honey, I know this boy better than you think. I'll talk to him, all right. But I think it's time you see exactly how I handle problems."

Cagily, Stan and Clark ran upstairs to face Dad. Since they overheard the conversation from downstairs, it was possible that he might blame one of them because they played basketball at the gym, too.

"Yes, sir," Stan replied, with Clark standing beside him.

"Okay, boys, let me net it out. Your brother in there has been *unjustly* accused of stealing money from the gym downtown. Now they claim to have seen him go behind the counter and take their deposit bags. Surprisingly, he denies it. So, I want the two of you to help me prove his innocence." He smirked. "I want you to *thoroughly* search through *all* of his belongings, starting with his dresser. Check each drawer. Pull everything out of them and look underneath as well. Pull his socks apart and check them, too. Check every damn thing inside and out!"

Dad peeked around the corner and gave Colin a brief glance, observing his nervous reaction. Colin wiped the moisture from his hands onto his pants and continued rocking.

"What are we supposed to be looking for?" Clark questioned timidly as though he didn't understand Dad.

"Money bags... Money! Anything that could be incriminating! Need I explain what incriminating means, simpleton?"

Clark shook his head *no*. He darted down the stairs to begin searching with Stan. Clark lifted Colin's mattress and looked underneath but found nothing. He carefully rummaged through his blue trunk while Stan searched inside his drawers as Dad had instructed. A few minutes later, Stan held the empty deposit bags in his hands and said, "Look! He taped them underneath the bottom drawer."

"Geez! I can't believe he hasn't learned by now! Actually, I can't believe he had the nerve. I sure hate to see Dad's reaction," Clark said climbing unsteadily to his feet.

"We have to show them to Dad; it's for his own good. Colin knows better. If we hide these bags from Dad, he'll never learn! I hate giving them to him, but we don't have a choice," Stan explained.

"I know, I know... but you've seen how Dad gets over this crap. You know what he'll do to him," Clark insisted. "I bet he stole the money to buy food. Dad's always starving somebody around here. Christ... Most of the time I don't blame him," Clark said, understandingly.

"Don't act like he doesn't starve the crap out of us and we're not *robbing* places. Besides, he's been stealing other stuff, too! When we were little, we all stole food at some time or another and I'm not saying it was right because it wasn't. The only reason we did it was to survive. This is an entirely different thing. If Colin keeps doing this crap, where's it going to lead him?"

Clark shrugged and answered, "Jail probably."

"That's right, *to jail*. I don't want to see my brother there, do you?" Stan asked sadly.

"Naw, man… but I don't want him *dead* either. I think *this* is the worst thing he's ever done. I mean, that we know of! Look, you can tell Dad because I don't want to be the cause of the crap he's about to get!"

"How are *we* the cause?" Stan asked.

"We're not," Clark snapped defensively.

"Okay then. We're not! Colin did this to himself," Stan exclaimed. "Remember that."

"Well, if Colin's lucky, maybe he won't beat him the way he used to," Clark said trying to convince himself.

"Maybe, but—"

"Well… well… well… so you've found them after all," Dad said in his distinct voice as he entered the room and leaned against the wall. "Damn that little son-of-a-bitch! What's it going to take to make you all learn?" He took off his glasses and rubbed his eyes. "Go get his sorry ass and bring him to me."

The three of them headed upstairs.

When Colin heard Dad tell Stan and Clark to get him, he knew they'd found the bags and was well aware of the penalty. He slipped on his shoes and took off out the front door without a coat, leaving Stan and Clark no choice but to race after him. It was either Colin or them. They knew that one way or the other Colin would get beaten, so there was no sense in making it worse for themselves. As Colin tore down the street, they broke into a cold sweat sprinting after him. "Colin! Come back here," Stan yelled. "Colin!"

Gaining on Colin, Stan leapt onto his back, tackling him with a firm grip. Clark wrestled to help Stan pin him down but Colin fought with everything he had to get away. The three of them struggled for a few minutes on a neighbor's front lawn in the snow covered grass until Stan locked him in a wrestling move.

"Come on… Let me go!" Colin hollered.

"It's no use. You're going to have to deal with it. Face it," Stan explained.

"It's not your problem," he yelled angrily, still struggling to get away.

Stan twisted Colin's arm behind his back and pulled Colin up with Clark's help. Dad briskly walked up behind them and announced appreciatively, "Good job, boys. Take his lying and thieving ass back to the house." Dad lowered his stern voice. Cautiously looking around to see which neighbors were watching, with brisk steps, he followed.

"Sir! Sir… Let me explain," he begged in a low panicky voice as they dragged him down the street with a forceful grip. Colin fought every step of the way ignoring the cold wind.

"You had your chance, and you blew it! Hurry up! Get him in there. Our business is all over the damn streets as it is. First, with your fucked up mother, and now this shit! Just what I need! Your ass is dead!" They shoved him inside, then Dad shut and locked the door behind them. Colin's fight knocked over a vase and broke a lamp on the end table as he tried to turn around and run again. But he wasn't escaping, not this time. Dad instructed me to bring Jimmy and Selvin inside and put them in Clark's room with the television turned up. He ordered Stan and Clark to lock the doors as Colin began screaming and begging as loud as he could.

"Please listen to me. Just listen to me, sir," Colin cried swaying back and forth drenched in fear.

Dad's seamless transformation made Sara numb as she stood in the living room helplessly watching. She raised her hand to her mouth and covered it tightly, as her eyes widened. Sara seemed as though she wanted to scream or say something, but her words were suspended.

"Don't say *sir* to me like you fucking respect my ass! You don't respect any damn body! Take your sorry ass upstairs! Get up there," he yelled, pushing his heavy hand against Colin's spine.

With boiling apprehension, Colin climbed the stairs as if he were sentenced to face death. His frantic eyes searched to find another way to escape, but the windows were fastened, and Dad was a hard breath away. Heedlessly, Dad rolled up the sleeves and unbuttoned his shirt.

As soon as Colin entered the bedroom, he spun around attempting to explain his side of the story. Before he had the chance to form a single word, Dad balled up his bare knuckles and punched him in his mouth, then beat him as if he were beating another man. I had seen the countless nosebleeds, bruises, punches, screaming, kicking, strangling, cuts, black eyes, and falling out countless times before and it was sickening that I had become immune to it.

Dad was strategic in performing his beatings as a routine. The pattern allowed him to know how long he could strangle before he killed. It allowed him to calculate how many blows and the strength of each he could render. The routine kept him beating on the edge… just like the precipice.

"Sir…" Colin cried in between his painful screams.

"This time… This time, I decided to give your ass the benefit of doubt! I tried to give you the opportunity…" He said, pausing to catch his breath. "I tried!"

"I'll tell you, sir… I'll tell you," Colin cried as loud as he could, wrapping his arms around his body to protect himself from another blow.

"Shut up! You had your chance to tell me the truth. Instead, you sat down there and lied to my fucking face! You haven't learned a damn thing after all these years, have you? You must like this shit," he insisted. Colin clamped down on his tongue spraying blood as his chin collided with Dad's uppercut. "I work my ass off every damn day making an honest living so I can support you fucking kids! Do you think I do it for *my* benefit? Hell no!"

A firm combination of repetitious jabs slammed Colin's stomach. Colin gasped, fighting for air, but there was no time. It kept raining lefts and rights until Colin dropped to the floor headfirst. He laid sprawled out spitting up blood after a hefty gurgle. For a three-minute intermission Dad struggled to catch his breath and shake the pain off his hand from the violent blows.

Dad took a heavy step closer, positioning himself in front of Colin demanding that he get up. With exhausted strength, Colin reached for the dresser and sloppily pulled himself to a standing position. Dad's ranting continued where he left off as Colin swayed unsteadily.

"I do it because of my own stupidity since I had your asses!" The vicious circles in his eyes swirled as he squinted. The brief moment of contemplation flashed a warning that he wasn't finished. He removed his shirt, tossed it on the bed, and took another step closer. "Do you think I want to work all day and have this shit to come home to? I come home to a damn lying ass son-of-a-bitch!" He paused for a moment while his face morphed into something different. With dark expressionless eyes he locked his thick fingers together and cracked his knuckles.

Colin begged him to stop.

"No... No... Sir." His speech was scarcely coherent.

When dad drew his right arm back he tried to protect his stomach with his arms, but he was too weak.

Dad started swinging. His fist launched random right and left hooks as blood splattered on his drenched t-shirt leaving red droplets on the carpet. Colin was soaked in foul sweat. Dad beat Colin so horribly that his own breath became short, causing him to gasp for air. Colin's screams hit an invisible wall and no longer made it out of his mouth! The brutal thumping and crashing finally gave Sara enough concern to rush into the room. When Sara reached the doorway, for a brief moment, she couldn't move.

"Colin! Stop it! This isn't the proper way to reprimand a child! There are more civilized ways to do it! Please, stop this!"

Dad's eyes vaguely hit her face. Tugging on his arm, she begged him to stop, but with a heavy hand to her face, he sent her plunging to the floor. Her mouth fell open.

Again, Colin tried to catch his breath in between the brutal blows, but couldn't. Nothing except short wheezes escaped his beaten body. He swung aimlessly from side to side taking the abuse. He had to take it. He'd never fight back because, one way or another, his life would end.

"Colin, stop it! He's had enough already," Sara's yelling sounded like a passive plea.

He ignored her as a supreme look of pleasure briskly swept across his face.

Traumatized, Sara watched a man who had now become a stranger beat his own son with an inherent hatred. *His soul was in pain because it needed to release the hate. His eyes hungered for more fear. His nose flared for the smell of blood and his mouth watered for the taste of death. But Dad's hands... His hands needed to feel the power of abuse. The evil power of an abuser took over and dad was no longer in control... the abuse was!*

He rammed his fist wherever Colin couldn't shield. It didn't matter where his potent blows landed. It never mattered!

"How dare you lie to me? Who the hell do you think you are lying to me! After all I've done for your... your... sorry ass," he panted before gathering more hatred for adrenaline, hurling it into Colin.

"Nobody. I'm nobody, sir," he whispered faintly with a raw hoarseness scraping his throat like broken glass after every word.

After taking a deep breath, he threw a sedating jab to Colin's head. The force hurled him into a wall and he plunged to the floor! "Look what you've done to my hand. Look at this shit," he screamed shaking it.

"Colin, that's enough," Sara cried. "Please!"

Still shocked over his viciousness she pulled herself up by the side of the bed and tried to wedge herself in between them. She grabbed Dad's arm holding it as firmly as she could trying to pull him back. He pried her clinging hands off him and thrust her onto the bed in one swift movement.

"Don't tell me how to discipline this sorry ass little thief!"

The deadening expression in Colin's eyes continued to progress even as Dad yanked the extension cord from the lamp and whipped it with as much force as he could gather. The cord ripped through Colin's shirt shredding off pieces of flesh. The pain no longer existed, but the *reality* of death did. Dad swung the cord so violently that Sara couldn't move to protect Colin. He didn't care where or who it struck.

"This is uncalled for! There's no need to beat him like this!"

"No shit! Maybe I'll kill him instead! Then..." he threatened, "I won't have to waste my fucking energy beating him *like this*!"

He dropped the extension cord and pulled Colin's lethargic body upright and pinned his neck against the wall, lifting him off the floor.

"You'll break his neck! He's a child! Let him go. Please, Colin. Look at him," she said in a soothing, pleading tone. "You're choking him to death. Please."

Sara's face was swathed with terror. She was now tasting the abusive cocktail that Mom was forced to drink until she was so intoxicated she couldn't fight back. Colin's glassy-eyed lifeless stare vanished when his eyes shut. His arms and legs were flaccid.

"Oh, you want to play for sympathy *again*? Well, this is your lesson in lying… You don't!" He released Colin and let him drop to the floor like a brick. With a lingering evil, he kicked his head against the wall, watching as blood pooled from it.

"Colin, I'm calling the authorities! That's it! I've seen enough of this outrageous display!"

"Go ahead… Be my guest fat ass!"

Sara snatched the phone from the nightstand and with trembling fingers dialed for operator assistance. He reached over and ripped the phone from her hand, yanked it from the wall, and threw it at her. Sara jumped back against the door, floored by her own discharge of terror. Her eyes broadened, and her mouth quivered. She didn't know whether to help Colin or run for help!

He feasted his eyes on her and announced crazily, "Look, bitch! Let's get something straight right now! These are *my* fucking kids so I discipline them the way *I* see fit! Neither you nor anyone else will *ever* dictate how *I* handle them! Do I make myself clear?" His cold-blooded words chilled her from the inside out.

For the first time, Sara's self-righteous look was torn off her face. She was stunned by her husband's actions. When her eyes shifted to Colin, on the floor, she replied in a stronger voice, "Can't you see what you're doing? You're going to *kill* him! Let the proper authorities handle him! Let them do it," she yelled, appealing for any sense of compassion he might have roaming in the depths of his consciousness but it wasn't there.

He turned to face her and inhaled, absorbing her fear he announced, "You're a little slow on the uptake, aren't you? *I am* the proper authority around here! The fact that I pay all the bills proves it!"

He returned his attention to Colin and began his sadistic demand for him to get up for more. Colin didn't move. He tried pulling Colin up by his arms, but inanimately Colin dropped back to the floor.

"Wake up! Wake your sorry ass up, you damn faker!" Colin didn't budge.

Sara pushed him away and tried to protect Colin's body with her own by wrapping her heavy arms around him.

"Come on, Colin. I'll help you. Come on." Sara cried. She pulled him closer for what little protection she could offer.

"Help his sorry ass all you want! I hope he's dead! I should have let all of them live with that crazy ass mother of theirs! I should have dropped them off to rot in the same miserable environment she's in! But no! I thought it was cheaper to keep their asses! I didn't know they were going to be this much trouble! They're not worth it," he shouted only a foot away from Colin's face. "None of them are worth it! They're all a fucking waste, just like Alley! Your crazy ass mother didn't want any of you! So guess who got stuck with the burden? Me! I'm stuck with your asses!"

Dad was merciless. Unfortunately, his continuum of verbal hatred would never cease because it was too powerful for him to end on his own. Eroding the self-esteem of others was among the many arts he learned to master. He could do it at will. Sara lucked out because she was in the degenerating stages of his abuse, and didn't know it. For now, he was still congested with evil.

"Colin, shut up! He's not breathing!"

"Who the hell cares? I don't, that's for sure!"

His impervious demeanor was astonishing. Dad had no trace of mortification. He stomped around the room ranting as if Colin could hear him.

"Colin," Sara cried shaking him.

"I thought I told you to stay out of this!"

"He's *not* breathing," she yelled hysterically.

Sara knelt over Colin's motionless body searching for a response. Any response.

He leaned over and shouted in Colin's ear, "I knew you were a liar... but a lying thief! That's worse! I'm sick of your shit! I'm sick of everyone's shit! They're ungrateful bastards!"

He paced the floor as if no one understood the cause of his rage.

No one could.

"Stan, call an ambulance! Call for help," she screamed, waving her hands around like a lunatic.

Stan was in the hallway, but he didn't attempt to call anyone. He backed away from the door because there was nothing he could do. He'd never cross that line with dad.

"I'm sick of this shit," Dad bellowed.

Once more, he leaned down and jabbed Colin in the stomach to arouse him. He couldn't stop because Colin was the means to temporarily work the anger out of his system. Every conjured piece of hate within him was steadily mounting, like an anxious storm on its way to being unrestricted.

"So you want to steal? I hope it was worth it! What the hell did you think you were going to get away with?" His voice was erratic. He paced the floor several times before stopping. "Move it, fat ass! Don't try to save him! Let him die," he shouted giving Sara a vigorous shove with his foot.

Sara didn't leave. She flipped her hair off her face, tilted Colin's head back, then pinched his nose.

"Look at your sorry ass trying to save him! You're just like Alley! I can see the fucking similarities!"

She gave a heavy exhalation into Colin's mouth but no response was returned.

"Alley wasn't as bad as you've made her seem if she had to go through this," she said without making eye contact with Dad.

She forced another breath of air into Colin's lungs.

"Do you know how easily I could go through you? Damn it! Don't piss me off even more," he said clenching his thirsty fists. "Move it!"

Sara didn't acknowledge him. Instead, at the count of five, she kept sending a mouthful of air, into Colin.

"He's faking it! He always does."

"Clark! Call a bloody ambulance," she yelled, before forcing more air into Colin's lungs.

Clark reached the doorway and met Dad's evil gaze, then returned to his room.

"Call an ambulance and you'll be the one in it, bitch! Don't test me! You only get one warning in this house! What I did to him is nothing compared to what I'll do to *you* if you run your damn mouth! What goes on in our house stays in our house! Got it?"

Sara didn't respond. He twisted his hand around her thick hair and jerked her head back, then repeated, "Got it?"

"Yes. I get it," she agreed absently.

"Keep it that way and you won't end up like Alley."

His eyes shimmered with satisfaction.

Dad left the room savoring Sara's fear. The pretense he had to display while courting, then marrying Sara, was over. No longer did he have to hide his evil behind a mask. Now that Sara had become one of us it was time that she saw Dad the way we did.

"Colin," Sara called as a slight trace of air returned from his mouth. "Colin. Say something if you can hear me," she said with a hint of optimism escaping.

"*Something*," Dad joked, returning with a beer in his hand and an immense look of pleasure. He was crazy.

"Make a sound. Move! Move anything," she said in a hushed tone.

"You couldn't be a damn doctor, that's for sure! Can't you see his chest *is* moving again? You're little kissing game worked. I know your kind. If you wanted to kiss my son, you should have said so. Yuck! Revolting. That's why I had to leave."

"You're sick!"

"Yeah. And you're fat."

"If you're not going to help this child then—"

"Don't get me started! This time it'll be your fucking fault," he said, pointing the can at her. "And for the record," he began with a nauseating laughter, "I've never hit a fat ass bitch before, just a crazy ass bitch."

"Please, Colin. Help him," she said noticing his faint breathing.

Dad cocked his head to the side and smiled weakly. He let his eyes singe Sara as he slowly wet his lips.

"Stan! Get in here! Let's show this bitch he's faking! Get *all* the ice from the freezer and throw it in the tub, then fill it with cold water. Ice-cold water! You know the routine."

"Yes, sir," Stan replied, running into the bathroom.

"Take his clothes off," he instructed Sara while sipping his beer.

"Colin, how could you do this to your son? How could you?" Sara's plump face reddened with her sobbing.

"When all I have to do is look at him and see a lying, thieving, and no good son-of-a-crazy-bitch... It's easy!"

"This is child abuse! You're nothing but a bloody monster!"

"Call it whatever you want, but I call it discipline! Good old-fashioned discipline! Incidentally, you cheated on your husband and did whatever it took to get me. You loved the *perception* of who you thought I was! This is the *reality*, baby! This is what happens *in our house* when these bastards don't listen!"

The heavy stream of water hitting the bathtub played in the background like a familiar song. The sound of ice being dropped into the tub added musical notes that gave it a critical meaning. Sara stroked Colin's brow and spoke to him in an authoritative tone, trying to make him open his eyes.

"Colin, honey it's me, Sara! Wake up! Come on, you can do it!" She gently shook him again, trying to get more of a response until his breathing returned to a normal pace. She realized her husband had done this several times before, especially when he said *routine*.

Stan timidly came out of the bathroom and said, "Sir, the water's ready."

"Don't just stand there, throw him in it! Did you add enough ice?"

"Yes, sir." He quickly helped Sara strip Colin down to his underwear. Sara and Stan carried him to the bathtub and gently laid him in it. Dad strolled effortlessly into the hallway and shoved his beer can into my hand then asked, "Hey, honey, can you get Daddy another beer please? I'm trying to deal with these idiots in here."

The ice cubes floated in the tub while the water immediately gave the appearance of a red water-colored paint. Cupping her hands together, Sara trickled water down Colin's face and chest. When Dad entered the bathroom, he detected a slight but noticeable response and showed greater aversion.

"Move, fat ass! This is how you do it!" He shoved Sara aside and grabbed Colin's head, holding it up with one hand while briskly slapping his face with the other. "Wake up! That's enough of your damn acting! Wake up or I'll give your ass more when you do... fucking son-of-a-bitch!" Colin's head slid along the tile. "I told you he's faking it! Didn't you just learn he's a *bloody* liar? I guarantee that's all it is. I should have poured a box of *salt* in the damn water. He would have *jumped* his ass out of the tub."

"Colin, call this boy an ambulance or take him to the hospital. He could have brain damage or be hemorrhaging internally! Please, Colin," she begged.

"Dry him off and toss him on the bed. He'll eventually wake up. Learn not to panic so damn much!" Dad met me in the hallway and took the beer from my hand. He noticed the blood spots on his shirt, pulled it off, and went downstairs mumbling, "Fucking bastard messed up my good t-shirt!" The lines in his forehead relaxed, and his temper slipped back inside. He turned the news on, then comfortably stretched out on the sofa as though that incident never happened.

Sara stayed with Colin and held his hand. She was waiting for him to become more alert. Dad had disconnected the phones and thrown them into the backyard to make sure she didn't call for help. He told her if she called the police or tried to leave she'd be an accessory to child endangerment. She bought it and now, he owned her. He branded Sara with fear using his invisible red-hot iron.

Oddly enough, I watched this incident transpire without tears and little emotion. *I wanted Colin to be free of the obligatory relationship he had with Dad so I thought he'd be better off dead! I hated seeing him tread water in the cryptic Devil's Triangle.*

It felt as though days had passed, but it was only a matter of hours. That morning Colin didn't say anything when he grabbed his ribcage and turned to find Sara sitting on the edge of the bed beside him smoothing the blanket. He couldn't open his swollen eyes more than a sliver. Some of the swelling remained red and puffy, but the swelling that circled both eyes were turning black and blue. The gashes in his flesh were everywhere. He had deep bruising and scratches around his stiff neck.

"Colin, honey, how do you feel?" she asked, choking up. Although

Sara tried icing his bruises to minimize the swelling, it didn't help. Colin carefully turned his swollen face away from her and stared at the wall. "Colin, explain something to me. *Why* on earth would you lie to your father like that? Why did you steal that money to begin with? Help me understand. What would make you do such a thing?" she asked.

He gave no response. His jaw and mouth were too swollen to speak. Although Sara had gently tried to wash the blood off his face, blood remained hardened in the cuts on his mouth and forehead. "Come on, Colin, I'm the one who stopped him from possibly killing you. In fact, if I hadn't given you mouth-to-mouth, you wouldn't be here right now! I think it's time you tell me what's going on with you. How do you think I felt watching him beat you like that?" she asked, trying to turn his head back toward her. He lightly resisted, so she let go. He was in too much pain. "Is he always that bad?" Colin was silent. "Make no mistake, what you did was wrong. There's no excuse for stealing, and the way your father handled the situation was wrong. It was totally unnecessary. He asked you to tell him the truth from the start. Why didn't you tell him the bloody truth?" she asked, tearing up. "You could have avoided all of this. Do you understand that man almost killed you? I thought you were dead!"

That day passed with Sara afraid of leaving Colin in the room alone.

Dad spent most of his day in the family room watching football games. After one game, he'd turn on another. None of us favored walking past him, so we stayed out of his sight as much as possible.

When he saw me walk out of the laundry room that afternoon, he smiled and said, "Hey, sweetheart, can you make Daddy a liverwurst sandwich? Make that two sandwiches, and grab me an ice-cold beer to go with it," he requested pleasantly.

He was schizoid! Dad actually acted as though nothing had occurred in our house! Late that evening he took a shower and comfortably fell to sleep in the family room watching a game.

The following morning I got dressed for school and went across the hall. I pressed my right ear against the door. I was hoping Dad wasn't in the room so I could see my brother. I didn't hear his voice so I turned the knob and entered. Sara and Colin were in the middle of a soft conversation since he had difficulty talking and breathing. Colin's sore movements and deep gasp at the slightest motion made it probable that Dad broke a rib or so.

Sara was sitting on the side of the bed as though she had never left Colin. But her hair was pinned up in a neat French twist and her makeup was fresh.

"Oh, rubbish," Sara exclaimed.

Colin was trying to explain why he stole the money, but Sara didn't believe his explanation. What she didn't know was that Colin had an excuse for practically everything, but whatever he told her about Dad wasn't a lie.

"Trust me. You don't have a clue what he's like. What you saw was nothing," he said, with mounting irritation. "You don't understand what's been going on in this house. So don't sit here and try to figure me out. You can't. Go find Dad and analyze him," he said, holding his right jaw as he spoke.

Stan came in a few minutes later, followed by Clark. Both sat on the floor alongside the bed.

"Are you feeling better?" I asked, afraid to touch him.

"No," he replied angrily. "I keep having these flashback episodes of Dad trying to kill me. And your brothers, *the rescue squad*, handed me over to him." He began coughing violently gasping for air in between his bitter words. He pressed on his ribs as though he were trying to hold them in place. "Does that ring a bell to you, Stan?" He grunted. "What about you, Clark? Did that happen or what?"

"Man, you know that's not fair," Stan argued.

"Sure it is! If you guys stayed… out of it…" He took in a slow breath of air, then carefully exhaled. He used his fingers to check the damage on both of his swollen and bruised jaws, then continued. "I would have been out of this place, and no one would have found me. All you had to do was let me go. What do you think the money was for?"

Sara placed another pillow behind Colin's head to make him more comfortable.

"So now you want to flip it," Clark responded boldly. "So it's our fault? It's all *our* fault! Did you get that, Stan? What a prick!"

Colin started coughing and scrunched his face each time. "Yeah, it is. You guys knew he was going to do this."

"I've had enough of your blaming us crap! Who put a gun to your head and made you go out and steal money from the gym? We're not going to sit here and cover up for your butt or let you run away so we can get beaten for it! You're not worth it. You brought this on yourself out of your own greed and selfishness. You have no one else to blame, so don't go pointing the finger at us! As far as I'm concerned, yeah, you're right, we knew what he was going to do. And so did you," Clark argued.

"Wrong! You knew he was going to beat me to death. Get it right," Colin said straining to talk.

"Whatever, man. *You* of all people knew what you'd be facing if you got caught. You took that risk! As much as I hate to see you suffering the consequences, you gambled, and you lost, brother. We're smart enough not to suffer along with you. What good is that going to do?" Clark questioned.

"Just get out of here," he mumbled angrily, coughing up specks of blood.

Sara leaned over and pulled a tissue from its box, then handed it to Colin.

"That's enough. Let your brother rest. He's asking that you leave, and I think that's probably a good idea so that he doesn't get upset. It's not good for him."

Sara picked up the glass of water on the nightstand and helped Colin drink it. He cringed with every swallow.

"Sara, it's not like we enjoy seeing him like this, but he knew what would happen. He knew," Stan explained with genuine remorse.

"Yeah, well this is asinine! We're sitting here defending ourselves to *him*! Can you believe this crap?" Clark asked angrily.

"Sorry, brother," I replied sympathetically. I didn't want to upset him further, so I kissed my finger, then laid it on the top of his sweaty forehead.

Suddenly, the door swung open, hitting the wall.

"Look who finally woke up, sleeping fucking beauty! Boy, aren't you a sight for sore eyes," Dad said. He set his cup on the dresser and announced, "I want everyone to clear out of here so I can deal with Robin Hood!"

"Colin, this boy doesn't need—"

He pointed his finger at her then dragged it toward the door advising her to shut her mouth and get out. Without another word, she grabbed her cigarettes and left.

Dad refused to resign any level of his abuse. His objective was to drive us to that invisible precipice and let whomever was being tormented suspend from it by their fingertips. At the instant where he achieves the most gratification attainable from our affliction, he must visibly identify our level of mental incapacity. He seeks to determine if he can insert one more infliction. Upon his realization that we're incapable of such, he casually offers his hand, but only at the point we've let go and begun to fall.

A week later, Colin was finally up and beginning to move around. The swelling in his eyes was gone, but the discoloration and purple patches underneath his skin remained. The large knots on his forehead were still visible. His ribs pitched a deep aching at every breath. With gathered composure Dad called Colin into his room. His tone was normal and his eyes appeared more relaxed but the hostility hid behind his pupils. He looked satisfied.

"I've tried to help you all I can. When you make the conscious decision to lie to me, you only display your ability to handle the consequences. I've decided to let those people prosecute you however they deem necessary. You think you're a man now, so handle your punishment like one. And just for the record, I decided to disown you, because you're nothing to me… nothing but a fucking inconvenience. So let's see how much of a man you are now. I hope they lock your ass up for good!"

That was the end of their conversation. Colin left the room with a sullen expression draped over his face and went downstairs. Dad followed a few minutes later and went into the living room.

"Sara? Where the hell are you?" he asked, calling out to her.

She entered the living room in a classy yellow and black dress with a pair of tasteful black boots cutting just below her knee. Her hair was hanging off her shoulders with the shape of the rollers still intact. Her light rose-colored lipstick, blue Estee Lauder eye shadow, and blush softly painted over her smooth foundation were the final touch.

"What now?" she asked offhandedly.

"Put on a pot of coffee," he ordered with his back to her as he looked out the front door allowing the sunlight to glisten through the glass. A draft of cold air slid underneath the door forcing him to close it.

"Is there anything else I can get you, your majesty?"

He spun around to address her clever remark, then abruptly changed the subject as his inquiring eyes met hers.

"Where are you going, dressed like that?"

"I'm going to visit my children."

"When were you going to tell me about it?"

"I didn't know it was necessary. You handle your children the way you choose, and I shall handle mine the way I choose fit. Today, I choose to spend time with them and my grandchildren," she said, using her fingers to separate her curls.

"Is that so?"

"Yes, that's so."

"Since you didn't care to ask my permission, you're not using my damn cars. How do you like that?"

"That's fine. Anna's picking me up shortly."

"I don't want your kids in this house!"

"And they don't want to come in here. Anna will blow the horn and that's all there is to it."

"Hmm. Well, what's for dinner?"

"I hadn't really thought about it. However, there's a pork roast in the refrigerator. I'm sure Marala can put it on the cooker. She knows very well what to do."

"The reason I have your ass around here is so you can help take care of these children. If Marala has to do the damn cooking, then what do I need you for?"

"Good question. I've been trying to figure that one out."

"Cut the cynicism."

"Let me explain something to you, Colin. I'm not one of your children."

"No shit. You're too damn old and too fucking fat!"

"I don't appreciate you ordering me around as though I'm supposed to be afraid of speaking *my* mind. The way you handled little Colin was deplorable, and I can't deal with you right now. I've never seen such atrocious abuse toward a child in all my life," she said, completely flushed.

"And it's been a long one, hasn't it?"

"Colin," she said raising her hand to stop him from talking. "Let me finish! For once, I empathize with Alley. If this behavior is what she had to contend with for all those years, no wonder she had a psychotic break from reality! Maybe it was more than that! Only God knows what you did to that woman! And if it *was* a breakdown, I would have had one too dealing with this abuse!"

"You don't know what caused Alley's mind to collapse, so don't ever fucking speculate!"

"That's right. I only know what you've told me. Obviously you left out the truth!"

"Look, bitch, if you don't—"

"Don't forget who you're talking to. I don't think you understand that I won't tolerate your uncouth attitude toward me! I'm not a *bitch*, nor have I *ever* been called one by anyone other than you! Don't use that word with me! I don't know what your problem is, but I don't like what I see in you! Something is terribly wrong with the picture *you* painted," she said, raising her voice and shaking her head. She locked eyes with him for a brief moment.

"If you don't like the way I paint, then leave! Just for the record, I'll call you a *bitch* whenever I opt! This is my house, I pay the bills—"

"*And these are my kids, so I'll beat them any way I see fit!* Is that it? Did I get it right?" she asked, mocking his standard retort. "You're nothing but a bloody child abuser!"

"If you're so damn concerned, why don't you be their fucking mother? Then you can analyze them all you want!"

"I'm not their mother, and I've told you before I have no intention of ever being a mother to these children. They have one, or shall I say *had* one thanks to you."

"Isn't that fucking ironic! You have the audacity to criticize how I discipline my kids, but you don't want to help do it! And to top it off, you didn't want to take care of your own! That's why you left them and shacked up with me," he said proudly.

He stuck his chest out and took a few steps around the living room with a pompous grimace. Sara vaguely acknowledged him visually.

"You're sick! You're nothing but an ill-mannered—"

"*Bastard*! Is that all you can come up with? Yeah, I've heard that before," he said, dusting off his new mustache with his finger. "Sara, don't you know there's nothing you can say to me that will make a difference? This is who I am," he said, thumping on his chest with his index finger, "If you don't like it... get the hell out! Leave!"

"You abuse these children! You beat little Colin with an extension cord; you're dead wrong!"

"Oh, you think so?" he asked extending his grimace.

"Wait and see. God will punish you for this one day," she added shaking her head with aversion. "You are really going to suffer."

"Well then, you've been ill-advised because it's *you* he'll get for committing adultery! That's one of his commandments. Or don't you care."

"And didn't you break that same commandment? I would never have imagined in a million years that you could be so callous! The next time you raise a hand toward any of these children, I'll call the authorities! This abuse is simply uncalled for!"

"I'll tell you what, since you obviously don't like the way I run my household... Take your fucking fat, uneducated ass on out of here," he said. "Oh! I forgot, you can't because you don't have anywhere to go!"

"Don't threaten me, damn it! If I were—"

The blaring sound of a horn interrupted their fueling dialogue. Sara snatched her coat and purse from the dining room table and picked up her bags. Dad firmly gripped her elbow as she started to leave.

"Hold on a second. I need to know what time you plan on getting back here. And what's that about?" he asked, nodding toward her small overnight bag and makeup case.

Sara jerked her arm away and nonchalantly responded, "Quite frankly, I don't know if I'm coming back."

———

The day after Sara left, the police took Colin and sent him to a detention center. Dad told us he'd be gone *indefinitely*. None of us had the chance to say goodbye. I envied him. I was mindful that it wasn't a place without its own problems. Nevertheless, the only comfort was thinking that if he were to have a physical confrontation, it wouldn't have the same unyielding impact as with Dad. Despite everything, Colin endured over the years, I felt sorry for anyone who gave my brother so much as a provoking twitch! The inherent aggression brewing inside him would erupt in the worst way!

———

Sara didn't come back that weekend. In fact, she stayed gone for a few weeks. One morning the phone rang and it was Sara. When Dad finished the conversation, he stormed into the kitchen, threw his hand back like a golfer, and slapped me without warning. Blood ran across my quivering lips as confusion corrupted my thoughts. I tasted the blood and listened to the sound of my pounding heart.

I swore to myself that I'd never say a word to Sara about Dad. But after what happened to Colin, she asked. I tried to warn her, but she couldn't wrap her mind around all of the horrible things that occur in our house. It was just too inconceivable for her to believe. Besides, she didn't want to because she was married to him.

When he asked why she hadn't called or returned home, she told Dad that I concocted a story about Mom's possession by demons and Dad beating her to that point. She told him that I advised her to leave before the same thing happened to her. She acknowledged that as crazy as it sounded, she believed most of what I had said. Dad lost it! He snatched a blanket and a pillow from my bed and pushed me down the stairs, causing me to land on my back. He explained that since I betrayed him, he was going to treat me like a traitor, once caught.

He grabbed my arm, shoved me into the laundry room, and said,

"This is your little prison cell for being disloyal to me. You'll live down here from this point on. Incidentally, you're not permitted to leave this laundry room unless it's necessary for you to shit or piss, in which case you have three minutes to do so. Should I catch you outside of this room, I will beat you and keep beating your ass until you drop dead! Is that clear?"

"Yes, sir," I replied.

"I strongly recommend that you get used to the spiders and water bugs down here because they'll be your damn roommates for quite some time!" He unbuttoned his heavily starched shirt and neatly folded the sleeves back. I knew what that meant. I caught a glimpse of his deceptive mesmeric veneer. Dad was such a handsome man that it would be unthinkable for anyone to ascertain his vile conversion when he was in the confines of his house. It was purely unimaginable! "Your ugly ass is about to be reminded of who's in command around here! As I've said all along, your crazy ass mother rubbed off on you," he alleged. Dad had so much hatred burning inside of him that it spilled over onto the cement floor. I inched away as if the hot liquid would set me ablaze. "Didn't she?" I didn't respond and before I saw it coming, he slapped me against the washing machine and stared at me with flaring malevolence. I thought he had half of my face in his hand. "I said… didn't… she?" he asked, pounding his fist on top of the dryer like a mallet with those four words.

I staggered to my feet, holding the right side of my burning face, and said, "Sir… I… I…"

"You had to go running your damn trap and tell Sara something she *didn't* need to know! I didn't ask you to talk about my marriage to your mother with *Sara*! Did I?" With one measured step at a time, his evil spirit guided him closer to me. He thumped his index finger on my forehead, forcing my head to jolt back each time. I knew better than to shun away. "That's *my* business! I don't give a damn how you feel about the situation because your little opinion doesn't matter! You don't matter! Who the hell do you think you are to undermine my authority?" He waited for me to answer but I was too afraid to open my mouth. "Say it! Say that you're like your crazy ass pathetic mother, and you're going to learn *not* to tell anyone what goes on in *my* house! Say it!"

I didn't say it, so he slid off his thin black belt and beat me until I curled into a ball, screaming as though I'd lost my mind.

"Say it! Say it," he shouted, striking my body anywhere the belt landed, including my head. He was certain he'd get those words to fly out my mouth and when they didn't, he turned the strap to the other end and began using the buckle. The pain was unbearable. I begged and screamed for him to stop! Yet I didn't give in. I couldn't allow him the satisfaction of *boasting* about my mother being crazy nor was I going to concede to the fact that I was either. I screamed and screamed until I didn't remember anything else.

———

I awakened and found myself lying on a white blanket stained with blood. I was unaware of the time or day. The welts slashed open my flesh and were beginning to form a yellow film over them. I tasted blood. The bruises to my face from the belt were swollen and sore to the touch. My right eye was swollen. I couldn't move because every part of me was in pain. I laid there observing a large black spider biting my bruised leg, but I didn't care. I couldn't feel it anyway.

At some point, the door flew open, and I heard a hateful compilation of words exploding from his mouth. When he entered the room, I was hoping he was nothing more than a mirage.

"Get up, bitch!"

I didn't move. I could barely see him.

"I can't, sir," I mumbled. I tried to look at him but I couldn't lift my head.

The door slammed shut and he was gone.

A few hours later he returned. "Your break is up," he announced. "I want you to clean this house from top to bottom without saying *one* fucking word to anyone! You'll clean until I tell you to stop! I don't want you eating one fucking crumb unless I tell you to! You got that, you crazy little bitch?" He turned and began to walk away when he remembered he wasn't finished. "I find it amusing that you want to defend your mother, and she's not here to save your sorry ass! By the way, you'll be missing school again today because you look a fucking mess! Go take a shower. Clean yourself up, and make sure you wipe the damn blood off your ugly ass face! Now get to it!"

The door slammed shut behind him.

I'd been used to hearing Stan and Colin's hollering enough to know that the pressure from the shower would sting the gashes on my body. Gently, I washed myself from the sink, being careful not to touch any of my wounds. I ran the shower to make Dad think I had obeyed his orders. Before I began my chores, I looked out the window and saw the beautiful silhouette of Mom through the light dusting of snow-covered trees. I saw her the way she was before the madness. It took my mind off my pain.

Dad corrupted my initial love for him into the most anomalous relationship. The untainted love I had for him was obligatory because he was my father and provided for me. Strangely enough, at times I saw his love slowly escape like air from a balloon with a tiny hole. His personality randomly exposed what love he was capable of offering. Oddly enough, I knew when those instances were.

Dad's rage was much like Mom's demons. Regretfully, it owned him. We were the outlets that he plugged himself into. We gave him that explosive charge he needed. We were how he released his coils of pain. I was afraid of him because of the physical and emotional abuse. I hated him for what he did to Mom. He helped Mom find her demons or caused them to find her. I loved him because he was all I ever knew. I saw the many things he tried to do for us, but he was never free from his generational curse. I realized that Dad was all Sara had, too. *Love-hate is what I call this type of relationship..*

Although Sara eventually came back, it wasn't out of love for Dad, but because she had abandoned her children for him. They loved her, but didn't want her back, not after she had her whirlwind affair with Dad and destroyed her own family. Her impression of Dad changed significantly. She tried to get us to talk more about what happened to Mom, but that was now a closed subject. She didn't listen when I tried to caution her. The fact that she remained with him was validation of her stupidity and desperation. Sadly, Sara needed more gin and tonics to cope with *her monster.*

With Colin away, our unity with one another was breaking down. Stan couldn't wait to get out of the house and into the Navy. Everyone knew he was buying his time. As predicted, *all* of the physical abuse went to Stan and intensified whenever Dad was warm enough to ignite. His beatings were unremitting. Stan attended school with the identical signs of severe beatings as before. This time, there was no *brother* to blame. Clark didn't fight with Stan. Besides, he wasn't in high school. As predicted, even after years of abuse, no one cited the issue.

Stan was quiet around Dad and Sara, yet remained compassionate and protective toward us. He made sure we had whatever we needed before he had it, including food. In general, Stan showed us the kindness that Dad was incapable of producing. His time was winding down in our house and he had been deprived of a normal childhood. We all were. He wrestled in his spare time to avoid Dad whenever feasible. He took a job that kept him busy the balance of his sentence. Stan was gifted in several areas, but never had the encouragement to succeed, other than from Mom, who was no longer a part of our lives.

Clark began to make friends and stay away from home. His grades were average because he didn't put forth a great deal of effort in school. He was intelligent and expressive. He became a little withdrawn because he learned that a mild incident in our house could cause problems. He enjoyed watching the news and was able to discuss political and world topics like he was an anchorman.

Jimmy never took to Sara. At times, it seemed as though he didn't exist. He stayed pensive. He had a progressive stream of anger that everyone overlooked but the scent of it mirrored Dad's. His handsome face rarely let a smile climb upon it. He didn't interact with us much, but occasionally he'd play football or baseball with Selvin because he was extremely competitive and loved sports. He played almost everything.

I took Selvin everywhere I could. Selvin was happy as long as our house wasn't filled with screaming. He was used to the arguing because it was anticipated. In appearance, he gave the impression that he had adjusted to the aberrant environment. Unfortunately, I was convinced it had some effect on him. I prayed he wouldn't lock away the traumatic experiences in our house, and save them to come out and ruin his life later.

At this point, the role of a mother was completely passed down to me, so I continued taking care of my brothers. It wasn't much different from when Mom was there. Sara spent her time shopping when she went into the city with Dad, so I had no choice in the matter. I never had a choice in any matter.

Even with Mom gone, I hated the room. I believed that there could be something lingering. Oddly enough, Dad had Selvin share a room with me again. I was scared out of my mind, but refused to scare Selvin out of his. I tried to talk Selvin into sleeping with Jimmy and Clark as much as possible. When he didn't, without an option, insomnia seemed to kick in for the duration of the night. I wanted to protect him.

CHAPTER TEN

Jesus answered, "It was neither that this man
sinned, nor his parents; but it was so that the
works of God might be displayed in him.

John 9:3
New American Standard

Three months later, Colin returned home. Reminiscent of Mom, he, too, had changed. He was antagonistic, irresponsible, and rebellious. Colin persistently initiated fights with Stan and taunted the rest of us. He had more problems than before. While Colin was in the detention home he lifted weights. He was bigger, stronger, and more muscular than before he left. The last beating Dad gave Colin was the last one he took. He had random bouts of disrespect but Dad was preoccupied and didn't appear concerned with Colin's behavior. Dad spent the majority of time traveling, and although they were mainly business trips, he took Sara with him.

Given that Dad's paychecks came to the house, Colin decided to intercept them. One day he went to the bank, signed Dad's signature, and handed it to the teller. He showed an identification card and waited for the teller to give him the money, which almost touched his fingertips. The bank manager caught him and called Dad. Colin was sent back to the detention center for a few more months. When he came home again, he got into more trouble. He tried to rob a store, but the police caught him before he got away. It took some time for us to realize that Colin deliberately misbehaved so he would be sent away from Dad and our house.

Nearly a year after Mom was gone, Dad took us to see her. Fortunately, Colin returned after a four-month stay at the detention center. Dad dropped us off in front of the little house with white aluminum siding and stone around the bottom half of the porch. Dad told us he'd return in a few hours, and we weren't to mention anything about Sara. He went back to his mother's house where Sara was waiting for him.

Clark knocked on the screened door, but there was no answer. With a playful grin on his face, Colin shoved him aside and began pounding so hard that it looked like the door was about to cave in. When Grandma answered the door, she looked at us with the warmest smile, then began fussing.

"Well ain't it about time you children came to see about your mama." Her eyes flickered with delight. "Why did it take so long for you all to come? I suppose your daddy doesn't want you near her. He doesn't want you all to have anything to do with Alley. Anyways, you all look good! Look at Selvin. Your mama's going to be happy to see you children. How old are you now, nine or ten?"

"I'm seven, but I'll be eight soon," he answered beaming with pride.

"What a big boy," she said, half listening before she scooted him inside. "Come on in," she said hugging us one at a time before ushering us through the door. "Have a seat. Don't stand around like a bunch of strangers. Do you all want something to drink?" she asked in between calling out for Mom. "Alley... Alley, get down here!"

"No thanks, Grandma," I replied.

"I don't know where your mama went. Hold on a minute; let me yell in the basement. Sometimes she goes down there to sit in her daddy's barber chair. I think she still misses him. Your mama wasn't here when he got sick before he passed. I think that tore her up something terrible!" Grandma went to the basement stairs and called for Mom. Colin was sliding his butt back and forth across the heavy plastic covering on the sofa to makes sounds like he was farting. Grandma kept looking back at him and finally asked, "Baby, do you have to use the bathroom or something? It's right down there." She pointed down the hallway.

"Thanks, Grandma, but that's Stan over here breaking wind," he joked.

We smiled.

Grandma entered the living room and waited for Mom to come in. The television was blasting with Billy Graham. She turned it down so she could hear herself talk. I glanced around and noticed the crosses hanging all over the place. There were big ones and little ones. Crosses were everywhere. She had a big black Bible resting in the reclining rocking chair where Grandpa always sat before he died two years prior.

"I don't know if my Alley's ever going to be right again. After what your father did to my child," she said shaking her head in disbelief. "She just stays to herself. The demons sure got a hold on her. When she comes in here talking to those things, I just go in my room and lock the door. That's all I can do. Those demons ain't going anywhere until God says it's time. They sure do scare me, though," she said admittedly.

"Has anyone tried to do anything for her? I mean, Aunt Danielle took her out of the institution, but has she tried to help Mom?" Colin asked brazen with his words.

"Sure did. Danielle had that pastor from the church put holy water on Alley. They prayed over my poor child and she went even crazier! She went wild!"

I tapped Selvin and Jimmy and said, "Go sit on the porch." Selvin got up, but Jimmy stayed in his seat until Stan pulled him from the sofa and sent him with Selvin. They didn't need to hear this commentary.

Grandma continued, "It took about twelve people to try and hold Alley down! That holy water made her so mad, *the* demons came right on out and started saying all kinds of evil things. Nobody could help her," she said picking up a stack of newspapers. "They ain't trying the right way or something. Maybe the demons are just too strong. The *Lord* has to fix Alley." She peeked at the ceiling as if she were secretly talking to God. "I can't say I've ever seen anything like that," she added before wandering into the kitchen.

Grandma took a large glass pitcher from the cabinet and a paring knife from the kitchen drawer, then set them on the table.

"Words like what?" Clark asked with a serious expression.

"Who knows what those words were. I can't repeat them because I don't want anything those things have to say in my head. I just shut *them* out of my mind and pray. I sit and pray all the time. God ain't going to let anything happen to me."

"I believe that, too, Grandma, because God didn't let anything happen to me," I said with a grateful smile. "So what else happened?" I asked, scooting to the edge of my seat.

"I ain't seen anything like that! Never," she repeated. "Sometimes you can feel demons walking around here with her. *They* live in her, around here, and *they're* probably in this room right now," she said suspiciously. "That's why I keep that religious channel on," she admitted nodding at the television. "I don't play anything but that.

When one goes off, I turn on another. That stays on all night."

"Did the pastor help her?" Stan asked.

"Go see for yourself."

"Where is she?" I asked, noticing Mom hadn't come down yet.

"Try out back in the garden," she advised pointing the paring knife toward the door while holding a plump lemon in the other hand.

No one moved, so I got up, went out the side door and around back through the worn metal gate. There she sat in a green and white lawn chair with her back to me. The garden was exactly the way it had always been. The pear and apple trees were abundant with fruit, while her cabbage, greens, lettuce, and green beans were plentiful. Mom always loved her mother's garden. Grandma did a lot of canning and gave some to Mom whenever she saw her.

I moved closer to Mom and heard *them*! *They* were there, just like *they'd* always been. *They* were still there! Just as I could hear her, I heard *them*! I stepped back, went outside the gate, and waited until they stopped. Then I went back inside the yard.

"Mom?" I whispered. She didn't respond, so I inched a little closer as if I was playing *What time is it, Mr. Fox?* I was anxious to talk to her but afraid of being rejected since it had been so long. I wondered if she wanted to see us. I didn't know if she was creepier than before. She went through shock treatment, so I wasn't sure what I might find. Especially after what Grandma explained.

"Mom?" I called out softly, tapping her on the shoulder. Her whispers stopped, she uncrossed her legs, then slowly rotated in my direction. Her eyes softened then welled. She stared at me without saying a word while tears streamed down her face. "Mom, we've missed you."

I moved closer with reservation, then wrapped my arms around her as firmly as possible. Gently, she pushed me back, placed her hands on my face, and gazed into my eyes.

"Where… How… How did you get here?" she asked stumbling over her words.

"Dad dropped us off."

She looked confused.

"Colin? Is he in there?" she asked, looking toward the house.

"No. Dad went to his mom's."

"Good. That's good." She sighed with relief as she dropped her head. There was no lingering anger in her shaky voice.

"How've you been? I have a lot to tell you, and we miss you so much. It's hard not having you with us," I said, choking up. The lump in my throat got heavier after every word, then traveled to my heart and rested. My eyes watered.

"I don't know about you, but I never thought that man would ever bring you all to see me," she said patting my butt.

"If he didn't, you know we'd find a way to see you. Remember the time Stan ran away?" I asked.

She forced a smile.

"Stanley was always running away, or was that little Colin? Maybe it was the both of them." She tilted her head to the side fighting to remember. Her face displayed a familiar sheer confusion.

"You're right, they both ran away all the time, but I'm talking about when Stan made it here by himself. Don't underestimate us. It's just a matter of time before we can visit when we want. I'll be out of there in a few years."

"You can't afford to do anything stupid to see me. As much as I'd love to have you all with me, I'm not worth it," she said shaking her head.

She turned her drawn face away. Mom appeared to have significantly aged. Her frail body appeared sickly. The skin on her hands was thin, like tissue. Her half-gray hair was cut into an even shorter afro than before, and her yellow teeth were nearly rotted. Those things were destroying Mom.

"Let's not talk about Dad anymore. All that matters is that we're finally here, with you," I said, hugging her tightly.

She picked up a glass of melting ice, put a chunk in her mouth, and crunched on it like a child.

"That's a good idea," she said, forcing a smile. I gazed into Mom's eyes. They were sad, confused, and mystical.

"Are you happy here? Do you need anything?"

"Yeah, I need that annoying sister of mine to leave me the hell alone! She's always meddling in my business! I can't stand her," she snapped angrily. Then there was silence for a moment. She crossed her legs and began rocking them.

"Mom, why don't you write me? I keep writing, but I never hear from you. Do you love me anymore?"

"Of course I do, but it's hard for me. You know, with everything that man has put me through. It's just that I can't stand to even think about that place anymore," she said with an angry frown.

She stopped rocking and uncrossed her legs, then quickly crossed them again and continued rocking. She grabbed a cigarette from the pack in her shirt pocket, tapped it on the arm of the chair, and lit it. She inhaled as hard as she could, then released a haze of smoke that drifted through her parched lips and nostrils. Her hand was shaking and her legs rocked faster. I wanted to change the subject, then realized that I'd forgotten my brothers were inside.

"Selvin and the boys are here, too."

"My boys! Where are my boys? How are Selvin and Jimmy?" she asked with bubbling enthusiasm.

"Come on, they're inside with Grandma. She sent me out here to find you."

I tried pulling her up by her arm, but she resisted.

"Wait a minute," she said, dropping a light shower of cigarette ashes on the thick grass.

"Yes?"

"How are they? How's your father treating them?"

"I'll just say you're not missing anything."

"He's still that bad, huh?"

I shrugged. "Yeah, he's still that bad."

"You poor kids," she said, getting up from the lawn chair, leaving it to topple over. She walked toward the house with me. Her steps were short and quick, not slow and at ease the way she used to walk.

"It's all right, Mom. Remember, we're used to him. At least he finally did something nice for a change."

"And what could that possibly be?" She stopped and looked at me inquisitively, then tapped a few more ashes on the grass.

"He brought us to see you." She wrapped her thin arms around me again and squeezed tightly. I planted a kiss on her cheek and she smiled.

She took a long drag on her cigarette, turned her back to me, and began talking with her demons in an angry tone. She threw her cigarette on the ground and stomped it out with her foot as though it was a small fire. Before another word came out of her mouth, I went inside and let the door slam shut behind me.

"Did you find your mama?" Grandma asked.

"Yes, ma'am. She said she'd be right in."

Clark jumped up and suggested, "Let's go out back."

"Wait. She'll be in," I said, standing in front of him to block his path.

"Does Mommy want to see us?" Selvin asked with an air of disappointment.

"Yes, she does, but she was doing something in the garden. Don't worry; Mommy can't wait to see you."

Colin stood and disrespectfully announced, "She's probably out there talking to those demons instead of us! What's that all about? We came all this way to see her and *now* we have to wait!"

"Man, just shut up for a change and think for a minute. She had to wait nearly a year to see us," Stan argued defensively. Before he could finish, Mom walked up behind him.

"It has been a while," she said sadly. "The last time I saw you all I was looking out the window through the bars… when I… when I was in the institution. I remember you all standing outside the car waving up at me. That must have been you all… They said it was."

Her eyes and words drifted. It was us. She was on the fourth floor. We couldn't go inside because we were too young so dad let us wave to her in the parking lot. She was in a white gown. I couldn't see her face, just a person despondently waving at us.

"Mom, how've you been? You look good," Clark lied, kissing her in a reserved manner.

She rubbed his hand, then pulled him closer, touching his hair and face as she had mine. She gave him the most heartfelt look and opened her arms for Stan and Colin to join in.

"Mom, Clark's right. You look beautiful! Just the way we remember you," Colin added, attempting to redeem himself from his earlier sarcasm.

"No, I don't! I look a mess," she replied tightening her blue and white bandana. She licked her chapped lips to add moisture then plopped down on the sofa. Stan sat next to her.

"He's right, you do look beautiful. You haven't changed a bit." The sincerity in Stan's voice rejuvenated her smile. She knew Stan saw her the way an artist would. If he said it, then she'd believe him. She created an appreciative smile and ran her hand down his back.

"It must be all Mama's cooking," she said proudly. Jimmy and Selvin entered the room from the porch and leaned against the wall, immediately catching her attention. "Look at you, Jimmy! Come here and sit on Mommy's lap. You, too, Selvin! My babies are so handsome!" Her desperate eyes searched for a glimmer of happiness while she covered their faces with hard kisses and locked her arms around the both of them. She closed her eyes as if she were reminiscing. "Oh, just look at you boys! I love the little outfits you have on. You're growing up too fast. It seems like just yesterday I…"

Mom's distraction was abrupt. Her facial expression changed from cheerful to sinister. Without saying a word, she slid Jimmy and Selvin off her lap onto the sofa and did a speed walk out of the room. She was trying to hide the demons from us, but they were already evident. They were talking before she reached the hallway.

"What's wrong, Mommy?" Jimmy asked, calling after her.

"Can I go?" Selvin asked, getting up to follow, but I grabbed his hand and told him to sit down.

He tried pulling away so I calmly explained, "Mommy will be right back. She has to take care of something."

"Yeah, but what's wrong with her? She looked mad. Did we do something? Or is it those things?" Jimmy asked with serious eyes. He got up like he wanted to follow her but didn't.

"It's not us she wants to get away from. It's you. And those things, as you call them, are helping her," Colin joked.

Jimmy sank into his seat and frowned without uttering a word.

"See, there you go again. That's inappropriate. Don't say crap like that to our little brother. You're making things worse. Try acting your age for a change or at least watch what you say around them. It's been a while since they've seen her, so don't spoil it," Stan explained.

Grandma came out of the kitchen drying her hands on a dishtowel.

"Alley's as thin as a twig. I've been trying to fatten her up some but she just doesn't eat like she used to. Caroline, can you cook?"

"Yes ma'am. I can cook, Grandma."

"Good. Girls should know how to cook. These little girls around here don't want to do nothing but chase boys and eat. They don't like to cook nowadays," she explained.

As far back as I can recall she always called me Caroline. Dad wanted to name me Carol, but Mom chose Marala. I guess Grandma's mind was set on Caroline and stayed there.

"I made some fresh lemonade," Grandma said holding up a tall glass jingling the ice-cubes. She took a sip then asked enticingly, "Are you sure you don't want something to drink?"

"Can I have some, Grandma?" Selvin asked, fidgeting with the buttons on his olive shirt.

"Sure, baby, sit right there and I'll get it."

"Me, too, Grandma," Jimmy asked, with a somber expression.

Grandma walked into the kitchen to pour the lemonade, still talking. Colin and Clark pointed at the crosses, laughing uncontrollably. Colin leaned over and quickly turned the channel to see what Grandma would say, then gave Clark a high-five. Jimmy, Selvin, and I smiled. Even Stan broke into a slight grin. Grandma returned with two canning jars filled with plenty of ice and freshly squeezed lemonade, then handed them to Jimmy and Selvin. Without hesitation, she turned the channel back to Billy Graham and finished talking where she left off.

"It's true. Those things run Alley something terrible. The people in this neighborhood are afraid to mess with her. They don't know what to think. Some people say she's crazy, but then others say she's the devil. Nobody knows what's wrong with that child except her family, and God. Oh yeah, don't forget the devil. But God's going to fix my child, one way or another. Your daddy knows what he did. God will surely punish him for what he did to her. You can best believe God will deal with that evil man because she wasn't like that when he married her."

Grandma turned the corner wiping her eyes with the corner of her apron. It was disheartening to see Grandma cry because I'd never seen her before. The room was quiet because there was nothing to say.

Within minutes, Mom rushed back in the room wearing the same ominous look, whispering in rapid conversations with an unlit cigarette hanging from her mouth. In between her exchange with *them*, she spoke to us sporadically. At this point, we couldn't hear the demons, only Mom. I still found it strange how they turned themselves on and off.

"Mama, *God's* going to deal with *you* if you keep telling my business to everybody. There's nothing wrong with me, and you know it! So don't go telling my kids anything about me! You don't know me!" She struck the match in her hand, lit the cigarette, then blew a stream of smoke upwards into the air. She tossed the match into the ashtray on the table, turned her head to whisper something then began talking to us again. "Don't you see why I stay in the garden most of the time? Somebody's always talking, talking, talking all the damn time about your father and how he messed me up!" Becoming even more agitated, she turned to her mother and snapped bitterly, "Nobody's crazy around here but their father... and sometimes you, Mama!"

Mom blew out a gust of smoke as her mind sailed away for a few seconds before she rubbed Selvin's hair and kissed him. "My damn sister gets on my last nerve, too!" Hastily, she turned her head to the side, inhaled again, and blew out more smoke. She tapped the tip of the cigarette into the ashtray and continued her whispers. Thirty seconds later she stopped. "Don't pay any attention to Mama; she's just *old* and doesn't know what she's talking about half the damn time. She sits around listening to that television and won't let anybody change the channel. She keeps it on all night and all day like that's going to protect her from something." Grandma appeared uncomfortable when Mom whipped her eyes at her. Within seconds, she disappeared through the side door without saying another word. "I think Mama's the one who's crazy. Don't you? She thinks that damn Billy somebody's really going to protect her! Shoot! Protect her from what? She can listen to that man all she wants, but it won't make a bit of difference. Not one bit. I know!" Her tone changed and she smiled like an innocent child and said with elation, "Okay, now tell me one at a time what's been going on with you. Clark, you start." She blew out a long line of smoke and smiled.

"Umm, well not much. Things really haven't changed," he answered while fanning the smoke away. "Come on, you of all people know exactly how Dad is. He's still the same old *Dad*." Clark caught himself when he saw Mom's face sadden by his comment. She knew what we had to deal with. "Sorry, Mom. It's just that I don't want you to think he's gotten better because you're gone. It wasn't you is all I'm saying. It was him. It's always been him."

"You're such a handsome boy," she said admiringly. "I love that pretty smile of yours, and look at those freckles." She smashed her cigarette into the ashtray, then blew the last puff of smoke away from Clark. Although she attempted to act like the mother we used to know, she couldn't. Her eyes were full of confusion. The only thing left was that same mystical stare I'd seen for years.

"Come on, Mom, I look just like you. What'd you expect?" he said, flattering her.

"Boy, you've always had a way with words," she said brushing off his comments.

Colin chuckled and said, "Yeah, until he tries to talk to girls."

She playfully rolled her eyes at Colin ignoring him, then continued, "You're a young man now. Let's see," she said, counting out loud. "Fifth, sixth, seventh." Her eyebrows scrunched together and arched. The wrinkles on her forehead disappeared as her memory returned. "That's it," she said, flashing a gorgeous smile. Her eyes lit up and she proudly announced, "You're in the eighth grade!"

"Yeah, he's going to be there for a while, too," Colin continued.

"Wait a minute, Einstein; I don't recall you being in school last semester," Clark retorted.

"What do you mean, he wasn't in school last semester? Boy, have you been cutting class? Or have you gotten into trouble with… Well, you know what I'm talking about. Don't you?"

Colin dropped his head.

"He's fine, Mom," Stan lied.

"Then that's good, Colin. Finally, I don't have to tell you to behave then." She leaned over and whispered to Stanley, "I don't want you lying to me, boy. I can tell when you are, but we'll let it go for now." She pinched him on his arm, sat back up and asked, "How are you doing in school?"

"I'm doing okay," he sighed. "Except art isn't the same without you helping me with some of the projects. The one with the tree and its shadow with the beautiful background was one of my favorites. We did that together. Remember?"

She smiled and said, "You know you've never needed my help. You're a natural born artist. You made the most beautiful pictures for me. Do you still paint?"

"To tell you the truth, Mom, it's been a while. I've been working at a garage so I can buy the supplies I need. By the time I get home, I'm too tired to draw, and Dad takes most of my money for rent." He shrugged.

"That's a shame," she said, shaking her head. "Don't ever let go of your passion for drawing."

"I won't."

"So, tell me, when's the last time you won a contest? Are you still competing in those science fairs? The last time I recall, you came in third place. No! I think it was second. Do you remember?"

Stan's face lit up and his voice carried a wave of disbelief. "Wow. I can't believe *you* do."

She hugged Stan again. "Boy, you'd be surprised how much I remember."

She got up and went into the hallway talking with *them*. They were angry. She returned about four minutes later. "Now where was I?" Before she could begin, she got up and left again for ten minutes while we sat in silence listening to *Billy* preach on television. When she came back, her expression was different. It seemed as if she were desperately trying to hold back the demons so she could spend time with us. At least she was trying. She pulled a blue turtleneck over her head, then patted her hair back into shape. It was hot outside and even warmer in the small living room. But that didn't matter to Mom.

"Remember we used to play jacks on the kitchen floor, Marala?" she asked winking at me. "You sure loved to play jacks. Then we'd jump rope and play hopscotch. We had a lot of fun, didn't we?"

She sat down, folded her arms, and erratically rocked her legs while looking around. Her eyes moved slowly, from one corner to the other, as though they were following something pacing the room. Even though she was asking questions, her mind continued to wander in and out.

"How could I forget? Remember how you'd carve pumpkins and bake the seeds for us on Halloween. Oh, and what about the Easter egg hunts?" I asked.

"Oh, my goodness!" She giggled as her smile and eyes widened. "Clark and Colin used to get up early in the morning and cheat like the dickens! The both of you would find all the eggs ahead of time, then go back to bed. You two were always *greedy*," she teased, shaking her finger at Colin and Clark. They both laughed.

"It would be nice if we could do those things again."

I was waiting for her to agree, but she didn't.

She turned away for a moment and said something to *them*. Acting as if she was sneaking away from something she walked over to me, took my hand, then whispered, "These things are always distracting me. They're greedy, you know. Like Colin and Clark," she said with a slight grin. "They don't want me talking to you all, but I remember a whole lot," she said in a hushed tone. "I remember more than what people think. I sure do. Then those doctors tried to take away what's left. All that shock treatment couldn't take it away. But they tried like the dickens." Tears fell. She wiped the corners of her eyes with her sleeve and forced a smile, then grew silent for a few minutes. "I'm sorry you were in that room. I'm sorry I put you through that." I hugged her as tightly as I could. I didn't want to let go. I couldn't speak! My tears dropped. A moment later she pulled away and continued. "Stanley. You'd take everything you could get your little hands on apart and put it back together some kind of way. Then it never worked the same. You were always the creative one. Yes, that's who you are! The creative one!" Her eyes found a temporary spark. "Selvin, baby, you wouldn't go to sleep unless I laid down with you." She moved to the sofa and sat down. She glanced over at Selvin and patted her lap for him to sit on it. "And you always wanted my spaghetti, but you couldn't pronounce it." She kissed him again and squeezed him tightly. "Jimmy, don't you remember that little red *Close and Play* thing I bought for your birthday?" Jimmy smiled. She had his full attention. "Your sister had one, so you had to have one too. You used to sit and play with that little thing for hours, and hours singing along with the records. And boy, you never took a picture without scrunching up your little face," she added touching the tip of his nose. "You never liked being bothered much, but you used to bother the heck out of me to get some of my sugar cookies. You sure loved my sugar cookies," she said, giving him a quick tickle. "And you followed me everywhere! You always wanted to stay with me, right?" she asked, rushing her words. She knew she didn't have much time to say everything before *they'd* return.

Surprisingly, Jimmy smiled again and nodded his head in agreement. She ran her fingers through his curls, then plastered soft kisses all over his face.

Colin finally stopped joking long enough to ask, "How are things here with you? Are you eating right? Are they treating you good? Are you happy? Do you need anything?"

"Boy, you sure have a zillion questions. Let me ask you some." She leaned over and pinched his cheek. "Have you been good? Do you have a girlfriend? I see your muscles are getting bigger!" She poked her finger into his triceps.

"Come on, Mom, I'm asking about you," he replied, displaying a warm and genuine smile. His hidden concern surfaced.

"And I'm asking about you… My big, strong baby! Can't I do that for a change? I miss you so much! And I want to find out all about what you're doing now! Is that okay?"

"Yeah, but I was…"

"Boy, you've always been stubborn… and a clown, too! You and Clark got into trouble almost every single day. You two were a mess. You made a joke out of every little thing. And don't forget how you damn near blew off Clark's face!" We started laughing. "But Colin, I've always loved your…"

We were silent while Colin scooted to the edge of his seat starving for the memories she had of him.

"Mom... Mom," Colin snapped.

She pulled another cigarette from a fresh pack inside her brown Indian-style purse resting on the side of the sofa. She struck a match lighting her cigarette as she left the room with the demons roaring louder and louder. Her attention faded, and all we heard were quick, heavy footsteps heading up the stairs.

"Geez! So much for our visit, huh?" Colin asked. He walked over to the screen door and leaned his head back. That meant he was trying to stop his tears from falling.

"Man, cut her a break. She's trying! Remember, it's been a little while since we've seen her. She's had a lot to deal with, and we knew not to expect much of a change," Stan explained. "Actually, according to Dad, because of the shock treatment and all, she should be a heck of a lot worse. Like he said, we're lucky she's talking at all." I added, cringing at the thought.

Jimmy got up, squeezed his way past Colin, and went on the porch while Selvin let his head hang.

"Yeah, well, regardless, she should want to focus on us for a change instead of talking to those... those... things," Clark sulked, squirming in his seat.

"For the last time, shut up! So what? She *can't* focus on us, but we haven't exactly taken into account her feelings either, now have we? Don't you think it's hard for her to handle us waltzing in here unexpectedly, especially when she knows we're going to leave her again? Yeah, you're right, she might be distracted, but she's not stupid. So take it easy on her. It's hard for all of us to deal with this situation, but think about Jimmy and Selvin. They're not complaining, so why should we? Who's really suffering here, us or Mom?" I shouted crossly.

"Well somebody needs to go get her... because Dad will be here soon," Clark said tightening his jaws.

Grandma returned from the backyard with her apron turned up and full of sweet fragrant peaches. She went in the kitchen and rolled them out of her apron into the sink.

While running cold water over them, she asked, "Do you want

to take some peaches or pears home? Go on. Help yourself. There's plenty out there. And tell your mama to pick you some of the greens and cabbage if you want. I have plenty of peppers and... Oh, just go out back and see! Caroline, get a paper bag from under the sink to put them in. Take two if you want."

"Thank you," I said.

"Don't go throwing my tomatoes." She looked at Colin in a mischievous way and warned, "I mean it! I know how you are. You're always acting silly," she said with a loving smile.

I got a paper bag and walked over to the screen door and said to Jimmy, "Are you coming?" He didn't respond. Instead, he folded his arms and followed me out the side door along with Selvin and Stan.

The air was fresher outside. I could smell the potpourri of floral scents when the wind blew past my face. Jimmy and Selvin skipped around the yard picking fruit while Stan picked the vegetables. I picked up the lawn chair, facing it toward the garden, then sat down. I closed my eyes and stretched out my legs letting the sun heat my face. I wondered what Mom thought about when she was out here. More specifically, I wondered if she thought of us.

Twenty minutes later we went back inside with a full bag of fruit and vegetables from the garden.

"Did Mom come back yet?" I asked.

"Do you see her?" Clark questioned with his usual wave of cynicism.

I walked over to the narrow stairway that led to her room and called her with a slight degree of annoyance in my voice. There was no reply. I called again. Still, there was no reply, so I began to tiptoe upstairs. I reached the top of the steps and cautiously turned the corner. I smelled her cigarette and heard the conversations between her and *them*.

I covered my nose and mouth but the stench in the congested room was nauseating and the heat made it worse. I felt sick. The clothes were piled so high that they hit the low ceiling. There were dusty books, statues, candles, jewelry, and several other items in the dark, cluttered room. In a corner was a twin bed with piles of clothing covering it. The window over the bed was parallel to a window on the next house. It was only a broomstick away. I wondered what they saw.

Several candles were carelessly lit on a beautiful but old wooden vanity. Piles of tangled jewelry covered its top. There was an oval-shaped mirror over the vanity that captured her reflection as she stared into it. When I peeked around the piles of clothing, there she sat. She spoke angrily with the demons, and they sounded hostile with her! The difficulty with approaching Mom was that it took me back into the scenario I prayed desperately to be released from. I tapped her on the shoulder and stepped back. She didn't sound this scary in the backyard.

"Mom," I said catching her off guard.

She quickly spun around and startled me. I jumped.

"Who told you to come up here? Get out of here now! Now," she yelled pointing at the stairs.

I didn't waste time backing out of the room, bumping into her junk and then a wall. I was too afraid to turn my back to *them!*

"We… we… Mom, we were just wondering if you're coming back down. We wanted to spend more time with you before Dad gets here," I explained while trying to feel my way out of the room.

"I don't care! Go… Go now! This is my room! It's mine, and you're not welcome in it! *They* don't want you here!"

"Okay, okay, Mom! I'm sorry," I explained apologetically. I was beginning to lose it. "I'm sorry!"

I made my way out of the room without turning around until I reached the stairs.

Her ranting continued as she yelled viciously, "Don't come up here again! Can't you see we're busy? Go on! You're making *them* angry! *They* don't like you all being here! Get out of here! Get out, now!"

She turned away and stormed back into her room. Her angry voice intertwined with the voices of the wrathful demons overlapping one another in wretched, chilling conversations. I fled down the stairs slipping on the last four. Clark was standing at the foot of the stairs. He appeared alarmed.

"Where's Mom, and what's all that yelling about?" he asked.

I rushed past him and sat next to Stan. He studied my face, then held my hand. He knew what happened because she hadn't changed. Clark began to climb the stairs.

"Clark, don't bother her! You know how she gets when you interrupt her. Just wait until she comes down," Stan suggested.

"You mean *if* she comes down," Clark said in an irate tone. He plopped down on the sofa and shoved his hands in his pockets.

"Crap! It's insane to see her talking with those things! And that shock treatment messed her up even more! Look at her. She can't hold a conversation if you put it in a bucket. Where are her sisters? They couldn't wait to sign her out of the institution. She may have had a chance if they left her alone," Colin complained with his eyes watering.

None of us uttered a word.

Grandma came back into the living room and saw the full bag next to Colin, then smiled.

"Where's your mama?"

"Upstairs with *them*," Colin snapped before anyone else had a chance to reply.

"Sometimes Alley doesn't like being around anybody. She mostly stays in her room or keeps to herself in the garden. She sure doesn't act like she's from this world anymore. Your daddy started this mess, and the devil's trying to finish it. Maybe he is the devil, who knows." Grandma threw her hands in the air. "The demons stay with her. They tell her what to do most of the time."

"They tell *Dad* what to do, too," Colin said in a serious tone while surveying our faces to see if any of us disagreed.

Again, no one said a word. Grandma continued with her random conversation.

"Your daddy probably already has another woman up in that house with you all," she said raising her eyebrow suspiciously. "Alley doesn't need him. I think she might need one of those exorcisms though. She needs something powerful to cast those demons out. They need to be casting them out your daddy, too! The Lord's letting this thing with Alley go on for some reason or another. Maybe we'll find out and maybe we won't. But he could fix Alley anytime *He's* ready! I suppose

He has a reason for why that happened to her. You ain't supposed to question the Lord. So whatever it is, I surely don't know, but I have to let it run its course," she said sadly.

She got up and wandered back into the kitchen. "Stan?" she called.

"Yes, ma'am."

"Come help me see if you can find what I'm looking for in here!"

"What is it, Grandma?" he asked, heading into the kitchen.

"Boy, if I knew what it was, I wouldn't need you to help me find it. Just look around and see if there's something that looks like I might need it."

He flashed a silly grin as he turned the corner. "Yes, ma'am."

Minute's later Dad was outside pounding on his horn. Sara wasn't with him. Grandma called Mommy down to say good-bye and surprisingly, after a few minutes, she came. Mom kissed and hugged each of us. Her eyes held confusion, and tears. It was agonizing to leave her in that enslaved state of mind. She said that she couldn't stand to watch us leave, so she backed away from the door then turned and walked away. She said she didn't want Dad to see her either.

"You kids be good! And come back to see me, but don't wait so long," she yelled with her words sounding rattled.

My heart was broken, *again*.

The fallacy of Mom improving no longer existed. It was notably apparent that she was worse. Her physical deterioration was observable. Perhaps Dad was right. If they had left Mom in the institution she may have been better by now. At least, she may have been able to hold a conversation with us for the duration of our visit.

I wondered if Mom would have separation anxiety if the tormenting demons were cast out of her by an exorcism. They'd been with her for so long, I couldn't imagine her not missing or needing them.

There didn't seem to be much hope that things would change for her. Her family took her back there, then left her to merely exist. She wasn't receiving counseling or therapy. They thought taking her away from us and Dad would make a difference. Mom needed a lot of everything—health care, love, therapy, and for the most part *God*. She didn't need to be dropped off at her mother's to be disregarded.

After visiting with Mom, I knew that her removal from the institution ended the possibility of her getting help. She went right back to the way she was in our house. Obviously, they didn't care. It was a financial issue. Her family kept the money she received. They kept Mom imprisoned *in that house* with demons feasting away on her soul. *What a way to exist.*

———————

Although I wrote Mom quite often, I never received a letter from her. I continued to write, telling her how Dad hadn't changed but I didn't tell her about the abuse. I communicated our progress in school and told her of the silly things my brothers did. I never mentioned Sara. I kept the letters positive.

It didn't matter that we'd been running the house for years by ourselves. The difficulty I had was doing it without Mom. Her rocking chair remained empty until Sara sat in it, which bothered me greatly. Mom was an amazing mother, before those women forced their way into her life. Clark and I often sat and compared notes about our best memories of Mom because it almost seemed as though she had died. We agreed that when Mom was normal, everything she did was special and done with pure love.

One occasion in particular, Dad was in one of his moods and didn't leave food in the refrigerator. There wasn't anything to take for lunch. Clark and I went to school wondering what we were going to do. When the bell rang for lunch, we met in the hallway and stared at one another, when Mom came sneaking up behind us. She held two shopping bags full of the best things we could possibly imagine. We peeked inside our bags to find a bag of Cheetos, Susie Qs, thick ham and cheese sandwiches with lettuce *and* tomatoes on it, a big Sunkist orange, an ice-cold can of red pop, and a pack of Chicklets. Mom was so thoughtful that she even placed a napkin in our bags.

"Mom, where'd you—" Clark began.

"Never mind that for now. You didn't think I'd forget about my babies, did you? Enjoy your lunches, and don't get a stomachache from all that good stuff in there." She flashed a gorgeous smile and waved good-bye.

The mom I remember didn't forget about us. That was just one of the many times she proved it. She did countless things that were sentimental to each of us. Now, she was out of our lives. For her not to write or call any of us, I knew it was something beyond her control. Because of what happened in our house, I was invisible to Mom.

The fact that I missed Mom caused me to suffer greatly. I didn't suffer because I was desperate for her to come back in any form. It was that I missed her prior to the demons. I needed my mother. Most of the girls I knew had nice things to say about their mothers. They had a mother to do things with or just talk to. The only resource I had was Dad, and his was Sara. He tried to loan her to me when he thought I required a woman's point of view. Nevertheless, her view was narrow and aimed right into the gin bottle. Her favorite repetitive phrase was, "You mean to tell me your mother didn't teach you that?"

My standard reply was, "No, she didn't teach me that because she was busy being beaten beyond recognition, then possessed by a bunch of demons that refused to relinquish her while Dad was out with *you*. So tell me, Sara, when do you think my mother had time to teach me things?" I said in an even tone. "I'm not asking you to teach me anything. Dad is. I'm good," I'd snap and walk away.

For the most part, I tried to learn as much as I could on my own. By the time I finished middle school, I was prepared to take on anything life threw at me. I couldn't imagine anything worse than what I'd already experienced. *My life was surreal.*

Because of everything I'd been through, I was still a nervous wreck, skinny, and ugly. As for self-esteem, I had none. Nothing about me ever flourished, and I didn't care if it had or not. Although I'd lost nearly all of my strength a long time ago and the light of my soul was smothered by pain, my sanity was the only aspect worth fighting for. Mercifully *God* fought my battle, and I knew it. *He carried me.*

CHAPTER ELEVEN

But I say to you, love your enemies and pray for those who persecute you, so that you may be sons of your Father who is in heaven; for He causes His sun to rise on the evil and the good, and sends rain on the righteous and the unrighteous.

Matthew 5:44, 45

New American Standard

Stan couldn't wait to break away from the pre-eminence and claws of dad and his insane measures of discipline. Dad had endless variations to inflict hate and display evil. Stan's beatings were perpetual and his psychological abuse intrinsic. It could only have been through God's grace and mercy that he managed to survive. His scars were for life and his contempt for Dad had reached its peak. Stan couldn't take another breath in our house or he would asphyxiate to his death. This was his escape! Two days prior to his graduation, he left for the Navy trying to get as far from our house as possible. His elation over his unpredicted freedom was visibly upsetting to Dad because Stan made it out alive *and* with his sanity. He physically escaped Dad, but not the horrific memories created in our house. Stan's accounts of his life would never allow him to be free of *Dad* or the memories of *them*.

Stan always promised he wouldn't endure one day more than necessary, and he kept his word. "Today is the day," he announced proudly tossing a few of his belongings into a green duffle bag.

"We know," Clark said. "You've been bragging about leaving this place for months."

"You could at least pretend that you'll miss it here," I added while biting my nails.

"Pretend? Come on, kiddo. Get real," he said slapping my hand away from my mouth. "Pretend to tolerate this place is what I've had to do all my life. I'm sorry, but there's no way I can fake it, especially after the crap I've dealt with because of him. You couldn't pay me a million bucks to spend another day here."

Colin grabbed Stan giving him a bear hug and said, "I'm happy for you, brother. To be honest, I wish it were *me* leaving instead of you." His bloodshot eyes were wet with tears.

"You can't imagine how I feel. You have no idea, man! *Freedom! I finally made it!*" He threw his hands in the air as if he finished a victory lap. His smile wasn't so convincing.

"What do you mean, *I* can't imagine? I sure as heck can, buddy boy! I'm just sorry it has to be like this. Don't get me wrong, brother.

Of course we're happy that you survived this place. Instead of being sad, thank *God* that he didn't forsake *you* or else you'd be screwed. Anyway you slice it, the fact that we're not going to be together is hard to swallow," Colin admitted.

"There were times we never thought we'd get this far. A lot of bad stuff happened in this place," Stan said, glancing around the room.

"I'll second that," Colin added.

"Man, it seemed like it just *kept* coming. Ours is the never ending story," Stan said sluggishly.

"You're right about that. And don't forget that story's still going on for the rest of us," Clark reminded while rubbing the sleep from his eyes.

"Yeah, I know," Stan said, dropping his head to hide the tears, but it was too late, they hit the floor. Without raising his head, he added, "You don't have a clue how many times I wanted him to get it over with and just kill me. I didn't want to work this hard to survive, but I'm glad I hung in there. The Bible says that God would save those who believed in Him. Remember to keep the faith. I had to, because I had nothing else but you guys. I'm not leaving you guys... it's him I'm leaving," he said, pointing upstairs. "And a whole lot of sleepless nights," he added with a grimace.

"But look. You made it! And that's inspiration for the rest of us. Just don't forget about us little people back here suffering in hell," Colin said lightheartedly. He patted Stan on the back, then fell back on his bed. He reached over and picked up one of Stan's shirts, then asked, "Can I keep this?"

"Sure," Stan replied with a smile.

"Hey, buddy, we're going to miss you. Things definitely won't be the same. But like Colin said, try to keep in touch with us. I know you won't want to think about what went on in this place, but hey, you're a reason for us to be optimistic," Clark admitted. "The fact of the matter is, *we're* still screwed, and *you're* done with it. Be proud of yourself. You should be doing cartwheels," he said with a big grin. "Man, just think. You should be messed up leaving this place. The funny thing is, who knows, maybe we all are and don't know it," he said. "I wonder what your life will be like away from this place. Do you think you'll ever come back?"

He shrugged. "I guess I would," he said unconvincingly.

"What for?" Clark asked raising his eyebrow with a look of confusion.

Stan removed his last pair of white socks from his bottom drawer and slid it shut. It seemed as though he was trying to come up with a valid reason.

"To see you guys again." He tossed the socks in his bag and continued. "I can't just leave my brothers and kid sister behind and not care anymore. Come on, you know we've been through too much for me to make it out of here and keep going. Right? You'll always know where I am in case you ever need me," he said with sincerity.

"We need you now," I mumbled.

"What?" Stan asked.

"I didn't say anything," I lied.

"Sure you did. What? Do you think I'm stupid? Come on, kiddo, get it off your chest and just say it."

"Never mind. It's no big deal," I insisted.

"If it's no big deal, you wouldn't be crying," he explained rubbing my hair.

"All I said was… we need you now."

"Listen. As soon as I can, I'm going to try and get set up so if any of you want to come live with me, you can. Remember one thing, Colin; you don't have much longer before you're out of here. Finish up with summer school and don't push your luck around him."

"What luck? When have I ever had any luck around our father?" Colin asked.

"Come on, you know what I mean. Try and take care of these guys as best as you can," he said, glancing at each of us.

"Did you tell Mom about this? I mean, does she know you've already enlisted and that you leave today?" Clark asked.

"Brother, of course I told Mom. We talked about it the last time we went to see her. That was about three months ago. Remember when Dad left Sara here and we went with him? That's when I told her," he looked away.

Clark plunked down on the bed and continued with his

questioning.

"What did *she* have to say? Or should I ask, what did *they* have to say?"

"She seemed okay with it, because she didn't say anything," he replied sadly.

"Why not? Was she talking to her buddies?" Clark asked, annoyingly.

"Yeah, she was preoccupied with *them*. To be honest, I don't know if she understood what I was saying. I wanted to tell her, so I did. I thought she had the right to know before I left. She kind of smiled, then asked if I wanted a slice of strawberry pie." He started laughing.

"You know, we love Mom and all, but I wish this crap would have ended differently," Clark said.

"Yeah, I second that," Colin added.

"It would be nice if she listened to us sometimes. I don't think she hears a word we say. I mean, I do think she hears us, but I don't think it fazes her because she doesn't really answer. That's why I don't get into lengthy conversations with her," Clark explained.

"She hears us just fine," Jimmy grumbled, folding his little arms across his chest, pouting.

"Are you going to visit her anymore?" Clark asked.

"Sure, I'll go see Mom, but unfortunately it won't be for a long time. To tell you the truth, I won't be visiting anyone any time soon," he admitted.

"I'm going to miss you," Jimmy said, inching closer to Stan.

Stan put his arm around him and replied, "I'm going to miss you, too, little brother. Keep your grades up. You'll be fine. You've always been a good kid."

"Am *I* going to see you anymore?" he asked tugging at Stan's shirt.

"Jimmy, I'm not going away forever. I'll come back. I won't come back *here* to live, but I'll come to see you."

Jimmy pulled away from Stan. "You promise?"

"Of course I do."

"Then say it. Say you promise that you'll come back to see *me*." Jimmy frowned. He started to walk away, but Stan grabbed his arm and yanked him back. He put both hands on his shoulders and looked him in the eyes. "Jimmy, *I promise* I'll come back to see *you*."

"Do you have time for breakfast?" Sara asked kindly, entering the room. "Your sister can make it for you if—"

"No! He doesn't," Dad interrupted. "Let the Navy feed him now!"

Dad had on a blue v-neck sweater with a pair of gray slacks with black slippers. His hair was neatly combed and his evil grin was sincere. He couldn't bring his antagonism with Stan to an end and let him to leave in peace.

Sara gave Stan a hug and whispered, "I'm going to miss you around here. Take care of yourself." She quickly left the room.

"Good morning, sir," Stan said trying to ignore Dad's unconstructive comments.

Dad cleared his throat. "So you're off to the Navy to see the world and all that good stuff," he said condescendingly, then let out a fake sigh.

"Yes, sir. I can't wait." Without making eye contact he closed the blue trunk resting at the end of his twin bed.

"Before you go, let me give you a piece of advice," he said, stretching as he let out a long yawn. "For starters, I never wanted you to enlist to begin with because you should have taken your sorry ass to college. Nevertheless, it was your choice, and you couldn't wait to sign the papers without my permission, I might add. So now you're on your own. And quite frankly, the reason I didn't want you to enlist is that you *aren't* Navy material. So my advice to you is to toughen up real quick and be prepared for some bona fide discipline."

"Sir, that's the reason I'm going in the Navy. When I said I was going to college, you told me I wasn't college material. You always had some unforgettable discouraging words for us. Thanks, I'll make sure I take them with me, in case I need them and all. Regardless of anything any of us wanted to do, you always let us know we *wouldn't* succeed. We could never be you. Sir, you've never supported anything I tried to do. And you've always reminded me that none of us can accomplish what you have. Just for the record, I'd never want to accomplish the things you have," he said calmly. "Now I don't have to worry about being told what I can and cannot do."

"Well, let me be clear on this. The Navy's all about being told what to do! Expect to be in for a rude awakening," he huffed. "You're exactly like that mother of yours. She didn't want to be told what to do either and look what happened because she didn't listen! Well, damn it, mister, from this point on, you're going to have a whole hell of a lot of people telling your sorry ass what to do, what to think, when to shit, when to sleep, and how to do every fucking thing else. After one week of the shit they'll dish out this place is going to look like a fucking summer camp. So all I have to say is good fucking luck! Good-bye and good riddance," he said, giving Stan an informal Navy salute. "You're going to need all the luck you can get!"

"Sir, I disagree."

"What do you mean, you disagree? Do you know what the damn Navy is all about? I was there! Don't you think I'd know?"

"That's right, Sir, you *were* there, and that's how *you* perceived it to be. Don't forget, like you've reminded me my whole life… I'm not *you*!"

"Thanks for the fucking reminder! Nevertheless, you'll surely wish you were a fraction of the man I am once they get a hold of your little squirrel ass. In case you didn't know, the Navy hates blacks!"

"Can't you be happy for me, just once?"

"Happy? What the hell for? You haven't made me happy over the past eighteen fucking years!"

"At least that's one less mouth you have to feed. For as long as I can remember, you always let us know that you couldn't wait until we were *grown* and *gone*. Now I will be, and you still aren't happy. I don't think there's anything any of us can do to make you happy."

"You know what? You're probably right!"

"Well then, I don't think there's anything else we need to say to one another."

"You listen to me good, you little asshole! I'm glad your ass is finally out of here! I'm fucking ecstatic, in case you can't tell," he said, forming a huge, but angry, grin. "I've had enough of your sorry ass to last me a lifetime! Furthermore, I don't care if I ever see the likes of you again!"

Stan continued placing his neatly folded clothes into his green duffle bag. Dad stormed out of the room. We heard him upstairs complaining to Sara. It didn't matter this time, because at least Stan defeated Dad before he caused complete death to Stan's soul!

"And what was his point?" Stan asked with a silly grin.

"Man, bro, we did some crazy things over the years because we had to find things to keep us occupied or we would have cracked up. I'm glad that we have a few good memories," Clark said.

"Yeah," Stan replied with a partial grin.

Clark picked up a *Mad* comic book from the dresser and asked, "What do you want us to do with your stuff? You know, your artwork, train set, comic books, clothes—"

"Keep them," he replied. "But take care of my train set and comic books. They'll be worth money one day. Those are collectibles." He turned to Colin and said firmly, "Don't go selling them. I already know how you think."

Colin smiled back and said, "Good thing you said that, because they were goners!"

"Man, you guys," he said tearing up again. "I'm going to miss you. And I know if *I* can make it out of here, so can you. Just believe that. I did. I had to. Try not to think about what happened to Mom. We couldn't do anything to help her. And regardless of what Dad says, it wasn't *our* fault. You're next, Colin! You'll make it, and so will the rest of you. I can't say it enough, but 907 will be history for all of us, in no time at all!"

There was loud knocking on the front door. The room grew silent. Stan picked up his duffle bag and headed upstairs. Jimmy, Selvin, Clark, and I cried as hard as we could. Stan dropped his bag, ran back down the steps, gave Clark a big hug, picked Jimmy up and kissed him on the forehead, then Selvin, and me last. Colin didn't come out of the room, but we heard his loud sobbing. He went back upstairs, turned around, and blew us a kiss, taking one last look, and like a melting snowdrop… our brother was gone. *Our bond was broken.*

The Navy only allowed their recruits to leave with one bag of luggage; however, Stan left our house with two. He would never be able to let go of it, nor could he open it again. If he did, he would be cursed for the remainder of his life. The invisible tag on his luggage read, *This is a bag full of Demons, Discouragement and Hatred. Return to Owner, Stanley Murray, if lost.*

———

Upon Stan's departure, our life was altered yet again. Our laughter was diminishing and so was our close relationship with one another. Unfortunately, this was the first sign of our preparation for the division among us. Colin walked a thin line, but after watching Stan escape the confines of our house, it seemed to give him an incentive to straighten up and concentrate on doing the same. He needed to survive through the upcoming summer. Outside of Dad inquiring about Colin's chores or behavior, their interaction was rare. He wanted to make certain Colin achieved passing grades so he could shove him out of his house.

When Colin graduated, he fled a few days after graduation and entered the Navy. He took off like a bat out of hell! Like Stan, Colin was emotional about leaving us behind. But his sentiment quickly vanished. He said, regardless of where he went, he'd never be able to rid himself of his experiences in our house. Colin warned us that he'd *never* return because he wanted to get as far away from Dad and the memories as he possibly could.

Much like Mom, the essence of Colin died in our house. He'd remain incapable of starting over or forgetting his past unless he reached out for God's loving hand. Every single detail of his life would follow him because it was chained to his soul. Dad and the memory of Mom slashed Colin open with a razor-sharp knife. Pain and horror was thrust into him, then he was sewn up and left that way for all eternity. Whatever wasn't inside, he wore outside. Now that his cover of laughter and cynicism had been removed, how would he deal with reality, assuming he could decipher what it was? Colin's pain was beyond description. Had our house destroyed him forever? His eyes were hollow, and his heart turned to stone.

Surely hate and evil shall follow him all the days of his life. And he shall dwell in the flames of hell… forever and ever.

CHAPTER TWELVE

**On the day I called, You answered; You made
me bold with strength in my soul.**

Psalms 138:3

Shortly after Colin managed to escape, we moved again, only ten miles away from the pits of hell. Before we left, I buried my *Flying Nun* lunch box in the backyard on the edge of the house so I wouldn't forget where it was. I made a time capsule and wrapped it in a black plastic garbage bag, then taped it up. I filled it with several items, such as my diary, a piece of Mom's jewelry, and a bracelet with my name on it that Dad had given me as a birthday present. I had an item or two from each of my brothers. I placed a letter inside for the person who found it, and another letter to myself that reminded me of what transpired in that house, not that I'd ever forget! I left it behind, hoping to retrieve it one day; however, it may turn out to be *Pandora's Box*. This lunch box could possibly release the ills that may plague others!

Sara decorated the house with beautiful furniture before we moved in. The oversized sofa and loveseat in the great room had soft specks of yellow on a turquoise and white floral pattern. Off-white carpeting ran throughout the upstairs and rested beneath the marble tables in the living room. The considerably large eat-in kitchen held an abundance of counter space and cabinets. The large picture window above the sink overlooked a large shaded yard with tall trees along its edge. On display in the dining room was an expensive and exquisite dark wooden table. A detailed champagne gold pattern was etched underneath the high gloss. The chairs featured intricate carvings and inviting white seats, which we weren't allowed to sit on. The sliding glass doors in the dining room led to an upper deck with stairs leading to the lower patio and yard.

There were three spacious bedrooms upstairs. Dad and Sara's room had an adjoining bathroom. It had been furnished like an elegant showroom. Astonishingly, Dad laced my room with beautiful new white furniture inclusive of a desk and bookshelf. Selvin and Jimmy shared a room next to mine. Clark had his own comfortable bedroom off the extremely large family room and bathroom downstairs. The laundry room was to the left of the door, which led to the two-car garage. The front porch had four tall imposing columns. With the exception of the marble coffee and end tables, every piece of furniture was new. Sara had impeccable taste and thought Mom had none. This was 954, and Dad took the helm to stir this house into hell, too.

I reached the point of complete exhaustion from my standard routine. There had to be more to my days other than coming home from school, cooking, cleaning, and taking care of my younger brothers as I'd done for years. Early in the spring, one of my classmates dragged me to tryouts for the track team, and I ran fairly well. However, I knew I needed Dad's permission to run in the upcoming time trials to make the team, especially since I wouldn't get home until six o'clock in the evening. I was certain Dad wouldn't allow it, but on the other hand, there were many dimensions to his logic. I had to ask. I rotated my mood ring around my finger. I thought it would be perfect if it were big enough to slip on Dad's head to see what mood he was in before I asked my question. Since his bedroom door was shut, I was hesitant to knock. But I did.

"What? What is it?" he asked in a stern voice.

"Can I to talk to you? I need to ask you something."

"Can't you ask it through the door? Sound travels you know."

"Not really."

"This had better be good."

A few seconds later, he unlocked the door. I opened it and went inside. Sara was lying in bed, facing the large picture window as if she were asleep. It was a cool and overcast day, which set the stage for a miserable conversation. When Dad turned to face me, it was obvious that he was slightly disturbed. I had a feeling this wasn't going to be easy.

"They had the first round of tryouts for track during gym today, and I participated to see how I'd do. The coach said he was impressed and that he thought I could have a good future on the team if I stayed disciplined and trained properly. He said if I was state material, I could get a scholarship for college as long as I ran throughout high school."

"And after school you have *what to do*?" He slammed his wallet on the top of his dresser, casting an intense visual fixation on me. "The answer is, no! You need to have your little ass right here, taking care of this house! This *is* your after school practice to prepare you for adulthood!"

He walked inside his large closet to decide which sweater to wear over his white t-shirt. After a moment of deliberation, he reached for a charcoal crewneck sweater on his top shelf. He removed the white tissue paper from inside it and pulled the sweater over his head, trying not to touch his hair.

"If I'm good enough, it's possible that I can get a scholarship to go to college. Dad, you should have seen me run," I said excitedly. "I didn't think that—"

"Are you fucking deaf or just plain stupid? Perhaps you need me to clean out your damn ears! I just explained that you have too many chores that require your immediate attention around here after school! Furthermore, you're too damn dumb to get a scholarship! All your little ass is good for is making babies like your mother! You're not running track, and that's final! Make yourself useful and make me a cup of tea!"

He was trying to provoke further conflict so he could erupt.

"Yes, sir," I replied, still standing in the same spot with my heart aching.

"Yes, sir. Yes, sir," he mocked. "Quit biting your damn fingernails. You look fucking neurotic. When people see your nails bitten down to your fucking skin, they probably wonder what the hell your damn problem is. To top it off, your fucking hair's shedding like a damn snake. Boy, oh, boy, if someone asked me what's wrong with you, I wouldn't know where to begin. Learn how to contain yourself!"

I put my hands behind my back and tried to curl my fingers into my sweaty palms so the bitten nails would stop stinging. I leaned over and peeked into Dad's mirror as he ran the Chap Stick across his lips. He was right. I looked terrible.

I was used to taking care of everyone but myself. I already knew I was ugly, but until then, I didn't realize that I was growing uglier each day. I was in high school and usually wore my clothes in layers to hide my undeveloped breasts and boyish figure.

"Can I ask you something?"

"What? What is it? Speak!"

"Are you going to pay for me to go to college if I keep my grades up?"

"*If* you keep your grades up? You've got to be kidding me," he huffed. "You're not equipped with the intellectual capacity to attend college! No university in the country would accept you! Besides, I wouldn't waste a dime sending a little bitch to college."

Sara sat up and slid out of bed. She slipped into her pink satin robe and tied it around her thick waist, then put on her pink satin slippers. She took a deep breath and boldly spoke up.

"Colin, perhaps you should let the child run. I'm sure practice isn't that long, is it, Marala?"

"I don't think so, but I can find out tomorrow," I replied with a glimmer of hope in my voice.

He shook his head and angrily blurted, "You don't need to find out *shit* tomorrow! Who's going to keep this house the way *I* like it?" He turned and scornfully addressed Sara, "*You*?" Sara didn't answer his question. "Then cut out the sob story. I've heard enough."

"Colin, Marala will continue doing her chores, I have no doubt about that. Let the girl get involved in a sport. It will be healthy for her to get away from here sometimes. When I was a young girl in England, Colin, I participated in track. I used to high jump," she said, reminiscent of her own childhood.

"Yeah, well, by the looks of it, I doubt you ever got off the ground," he said with a nasty grin.

"Now, Colin, is that necessary?" she asked sounding irritated.

"Yes, it's necessary, because I like to speak my mind."

Dad took his watch out of the tray on his dresser and strapped it on his wrist.

"If you don't want to hear what I have to say, then I'll leave so I don't have to hear anymore of your nonsense!" Sara picked up an empty wine glass on her nightstand and went to the other side of the bed, removed two empty beer bottles on Dad's nightstand, and headed for the door.

He sat on the edge of the bed and hesitantly said, "Fine, continue. Go on. Let's hear it. Let's hear what you have to say about the matter. Spit it out before I change my damn mind!"

Sara went to the kitchen and quickly returned empty handed. She began pacing as though she were in a courtroom defending me. She locked her fingers together and began to present my case.

"Marala handles everything around here just fine. She doesn't miss anything, in case you haven't noticed," she said winking at me. "Regardless of what we ask her to do, she gets it done. Now this child is asking to participate in a sport. Let her do it. She'll be home in time to cook dinner and maintain her chores. Jimmy and Selvin are old enough to manage their own schedules. Additionally, those boys are old enough to help out. Clark can start doing more around here, too. That should free up some of her time. Besides, she loves to cook. So that won't change."

That was a nice speech and all, but why do *I* have to cook almost every night? I thought. This isn't my house. I'm stuck doing everything around here as if it's my sole responsibility. Does she hear herself?

"No disrespect, sir, but it's not fair that I can't play a sport, but Jimmy and Selvin play any sport they want. Clark does his photography thing. And I've never asked to do anything because I don't have time. But Sara's right. If the boys do their own chores, I'll have time to run. My grades are good—"

"Your grades are fair."

"I don't bother anyone, and I do everything you ask me to. I've never participated in school activities. I don't have a life outside of this place. The majority of my time is spent cooking and cleaning."

"That's bullshit! You have your friends down the street, so don't act as if you're so fucking isolated!" He grabbed his keys from his dresser and slid them into his front pocket.

This man is nuts! Friends? Everybody knows I can't to do anything but go straight home after school.

"Dad, I see them after school because Ms. Talon brings me home. You act like I have all the time in the world to spend with *friends*. Think about the schedule I have. I'm sorry if I appear to have fifteen minutes of my day, out of a thousand—"

"You just made my point! You can't even fucking add! For your information, there are one thousand four hundred and forty minutes in a damn day!"

"But if all I have to spend with classmates is fifteen minutes out of one thousand four hundred and forty... Come on, Dad, that's worse. It's already impossible for me to find time to make friends."

"I thought you relished cooking? Besides, you're so good at it," Sara commented, returning from a daze.

After everything I just explained, all she picked up was my statement about doing everything inclusive of *cooking*!

"Sara, you're right, I'm good at it because I've had years of practice. What do you mean, like it? I like it as much as you do. I'm not trying to be disrespectful, but I *have* to do it. I've always *had* to do it."

"Look, smart ass, I want you here... In this house... After school... And nowhere else! Don't ever bring your simple, no-good ass in here talking about a scholarship! Do you hear me? You're just taking up space on this earth like that no good ex-wife of mine! The two of you are identical! She wasted her life, didn't accomplish shit, and neither will you! You're a pathetic little bitch and I don't want to hear you mention college again! Look at yourself! You're skinny, ugly, stupid, and crazy, like your mother!"

"Colin!"

"Shut up, fat ass!"

"Colin, that's enough—"

"Shut your damn trap! If you don't like this little discussion, then go make yourself a cup of tea!" He pointed at his watch and said, "It is tea-time, isn't it?"

"You're right, Colin, it is! So why don't *you* go have a cup your bloody self!"

He ignored Sara as if she'd left the room. He observed me for a few minutes, and I observed the floor. I tried to look at something other than his abrasive stare, so I searched for a piece of lint, paper, thread, or something on his floor to focus on. His room was spotless. There was nothing on the floor but our feet.

"Since you do so much damn work around here, maybe you should be concerned with getting more rest instead of running track. Then you'll have more energy to get your chores done faster. Do you know you fucking sleepwalk almost every damn night? Perhaps you should get a damn third shift job since you like walking around so fucking much! Hmmm... Or maybe I should just open the damn door and let your ass keep walking!" He grabbed my chin and jerked my head upward. "Look at me when I'm speaking to you, damn it!"

Dad tried studying my reaction as I tried unsuccessfully not to give him one. Before Colin left, he mastered the art of withholding his fear and pain as long as possible. It infuriated Dad when he had to work harder to break us down. Nevertheless, he never rejected the challenge.

"Colin, must you go through this sadistic name calling every time you attempt to make a point? Is it necessary? This child simply asked to join the bloody track team. I think it's healthy for her to set goals for herself. Track will help her do that. Marala, go make your father and me a cup of tea, please."

I thought I was getting away from them. Instead, they followed me into the kitchen, still debating. I pulled out two Lipton teabags and laid them on the counter. Dad wanted cream and sugar in his tea, and Sara wanted hers plain. I filled the teapot with cold water and removed two heavy brown coffee mugs from the cabinet. Sara glanced over and shook her head, then said, "No, dear, those cups are too large. I prefer the cute little Blue Willow teacups on the top shelf."

I hopped on the countertop and began shuffling the cups and glasses around as though I couldn't find them. Then Sara stood and pointed at the very top shelf. "Sweetheart, look behind those cups. I'm quite certain you'll find them. I don't know who keeps placing them up that high, behind all the other cups. I'm not very tall, so I have difficulty reaching them by myself. Harry's mother used to have one just like it. The set is lovely, especially when you place it on a white tablecloth and set a vase of fresh flowers in the center. It brightens up the entire room."

These were Mom's favorite set of teacups, and Sara knew it! Why would she want to drink from them? I set the two cups and saucers on the counter beside me, then closed the cabinet. As I turned to jump down, I knocked a cup to the floor and watched it shatter. I stared at the broken pieces with my eyes displaying panic. I wanted to scream, but I knew I couldn't. Mom loved that set.

"I should make you pay for that! Sweep it up," he ordered

belligerently, as if I were going to leave the broken pieces on the floor. "Wash those damn dishes while you're at it! See, just like I said, she's neurotic... biting her nails, hair falling out, sleepwalking, legs shaking every time she sits down, and now she's dropping things! Shit, what's next? She's fucking useless!"

"Colin!"

"Alley had goals! She ran track, and it didn't do her a damn bit of good. It was a fucking waste of time because she won everything she ran but didn't want to go to college. She was extremely talented when it came to dancing. Alley was accepted into dance school in New York, but guess what happened? She didn't want to go because she let me knock her ass up. She never had any real ambitions. She wasn't even good at making babies, to say the least, because she didn't know when to stop. She was like a fucking rabbit."

"Perhaps it was *you* who didn't know when to stop. Colin, you need to stop putting Alley down in front of her children like that. Alley's not here to defend herself, so let it go, for Christ sake."

"Let it go? In case you hadn't noticed, I did let her go... straight to the loony bin! That's why you're here, remember?" Sara took a nervous, fleeting glace in my direction while Dad smiled proudly. "Sara, let me explain something to you. I *want* these kids to know how crazy their mother is. I want them to understand how she fucked up my life with her shit! It's all in the genes, you know, mental illness," he said, twirling his finger around in the air. "She was coo-coo! Since these bastards are part of their loony mother, it's in their genes, too! Guess who's next in line to crack up the way Alley did?" He nodded in my direction. "You best believe it. She is! It's destined to happen... Completely unavoidable! She's next to have a nice psychotic break from reality."

"That's ludicrous, and you know it! You're always trying to put labels on people and figure them out. Marala, don't believe a word he says!"

"That's precisely why I've achieved what I have now. I determine what my obstacles are, and then get rid of them." Once more, he cut his eyes at me with a scathing beam. "That's what I do, I get rid of them! Does that sound familiar to you, Marala?"

"Yes, sir," I said as I squeezed the yellow dish liquid into the sink under the running hot water. I pulled a fresh handy-wipe from the drawer and began washing dishes, pressing harder and harder on each plate. I clenched my teeth because I wanted to scream. Actually, I wanted to jump through the window to get away from Dad, but it was only one floor up.

"Her mother couldn't be fixed, and take a good look at her. Shit, I'll tell you one thing… I sure have some weak ass kids. What did I do to deserve them? Watch her snap any minute, just watch. She's going to be crazy like her mother. She's just about there."

"Leave this child alone. Stan and Colin are gone, so now you want to redirect your hostility. You have a tremendous amount of animosity for your children. I've always wondered what your parents did to screw you up so damn bad. You are unbelievably cruel!"

"Animosity. That's putting it mildly."

I reached for another teacup from the cabinet and carefully poured the hot water over the tea bags. They had to be just right, or both of them would complain, making this situation even worse. I placed the teacups in front of them, spilling half of Dad's piping hot tea on his lap. He jumped out of his chair, trying to wipe it off, but it had already soaked into his pants and part of his sweater.

"Damn it! You stupid little bitch! Spill another damn thing on me, and your ass will be in deep shit! Get me a fucking towel or something! Hurry the fuck up! Hurry up, you fucking idiot," he yelled.

"Here, Colin, take this," Sara insisted, handing him a paper towel.

"I'm sorry, Dad. It was an accident," I acknowledged quickly.

"Accident, my ass. *You* were a fucking accident! Get me another paper towel!"

I pulled two paper towels from the holder and handed them to him.

"I'll make you another cup," I offered.

"Not with those shaky ass hands of yours. Can you manage to get me a beer? Or will the bottle be too cold and slip out your damn hands?"

Without responding, I grabbed a Budweiser from the refrigerator, opened the cap, and placed it in front of him.

"You dismantle these children until you find their weakness," Sara explained.

"I already know their damn weaknesses!"

"Then you use it against them in the most destructive manner. You must always play the bloody psychologist, right, Colin?"

"That's right; I must. Are you jealous because I'm so damn good at it? You're simply too fucking dense to figure anything out."

"Colin, must you be so bloody condescending? Is this really necessary? Look at Marala. Look at the poor thing over there. She's afraid to move around you. You cram hatred into them like you have stock in hell!"

"Maybe I do bitch!"

"Damn it! You haven't provided these children with an inkling of self-worth, and you want to boast that they're useless! That's the most absurd thing I've ever heard. All this nonsense started over a question about her running track."

Sara took another sip of her tea and looked away from him.

"Shit, that little bitch is a worthless nut like her worthless nut of a mother! You know what they say. If the shoe fits." He crumpled his paper towel and threw it, hitting the back of my head. "The shoe fits you, doesn't it, nut? Hell, in fact, you're wearing the whole damn outfit. Keep it up and I'll get you a nice white jacket, just like your mother's! You've got to be a damn nut to think you can run track and win anything," he said starting to laugh. "To top it off, I need to go get you a damn straitjacket just for you thinking you could get a scholarship to college!"

Sara placed her empty teacup in the sink and left the room without so much as a glance at me. Dad finished sipping his beer.

I put the dishes away and timidly left the kitchen and went into my room. I sat on the end of my bed rocking back and forth. I didn't want to hear anymore of his dialogue nor look at him. I covered my ears. My body was taut. I knew exactly what this was. Dad was taking me through a destabilization process, and I was trying to prevent it. His words raced in and out of my mind. I was trying to push the pain out, but it didn't work. He forced it in.

"Why... Why... Why?" I cried. "Why is he doing this to me?

Why? Why?"

I'd taken his verbal abuse for so many years that the surge of his hate dominated me. I had to remove him from my head. I had to find a way to fight back against this man. He was sent from hell to destroy me, and he had the ability to do it!

I tried to grip my sanity so I began to pray in whispers, "Father. Help me, please. Don't let this happen. Don't let this happen to me, too! Father… How does it go?" I said as I hit my head, hoping the words would become clear. They weren't, so I tried punching the side of my head, but it didn't help. My head was filled with echoes of Dad's words. They flowed smoothly. Crazy, ugly, neurotic, pathetic, stupid, mental illness, idiot, useless, bitch, worthless, possessed, straitjacket, I hate you… His words were staunch. Before I realized it, Dad was in front of me with his hands on his hip.

"I can see that I'm going to have to lock your ass up, too. Say something, damn it. Say something, you ugly little bitch."

He continued his rampant emotional attack on me. I couldn't reply because my mouth couldn't move. I couldn't move. I couldn't do anything but take it. My rocking stopped, and I snapped like a rubber band stretched too far. Dad supplied me with negative reinforcement for the majority of my life. He achieved his goal that resulted in my mental degeneration, allowing me to deem myself as worthless and unstable. Finally, Dad triumphed! He had driven me *over* that invisible precipice. This time, he couldn't grab hold of my hand because I had fallen. He accomplished his goal of destroying me. Dad calculated his chess moves, and it worked. He beat my brothers into a lifeless and dysfunctional state, then merrily sent them into the world to fend for themselves carrying our generational curse! He battered, then ripped the love, hope, strength, trust, sanity, and life out of my mother, and smiled proudly. As though that weren't enough, he tormented her into a fiery realm of demonic possession! Kindly, he shared his cruelty, allowing Jimmy and Selvin to digest the hatred and bury it into their subconscious's, only for it to explode at another stage in their life.

I sat completely relaxed, Indian-style, on my bed. I could hear what he said, but couldn't respond. My eyes were fixated on the evil man in front of me. I wondered why he kept yelling at me. He knocked on my forehead, but it didn't bother me. I thought, maybe this is good. I do feel better like this. He can't hurt me. He can't reach my mind because there's a barrier surrounding it. *Ha! Ha! You can't get in.* I smiled. *Stan and Colin should have let this happen to them years ago. Sticks and stones may break my bones but words will never hurt me again. I wonder if Mom is this happy. Hmm? I can sit like this for hours and hours, maybe days. I'll have to wear the white jacket and go away like Mommy. Mommy isn't wearing the jacket anymore, is she?* I flashed a quick smile at every complete thought. My body felt like a broken rubber band instead of a stretched one.

I don't know exactly how long I was in that state. I don't know if it was a day or two. It may have been longer. It may have been less. But reality wasn't mine, because sometimes he was there and sometimes he vanished. It didn't matter because I didn't care.

At some point, things changed. *What's happening? What's going on? My hands and legs are unthawing. Oh no, hypothermia is setting in. I'm cold! It's unusually cold… My legs are trembling again. I don't want to go back there! How do I prevent it? Please let me stay here! I want to stay here!*

I don't know how long it took, but it was unavoidable. I was back. I felt it. Dad was right. I was going to be crazy, like Mom, but for years I tried not to claim it. Although I was cold, every nerve in my body was dancing on hot flames trying to do its own thing. His abuse owned me once again.

"You're no damn good, and you're exactly like your mother. Demons are all inside you just waiting to take over! I bet you hear them talking to you already! Don't you? Answer me, damn it! Don't you? Look at you sitting there as if you've lost your damn mind. You're crazy… like your mother! They got you, too! That's why you're sitting there like that, rocking back and forth… *back and forth*," he sang sweetly. "Don't cover your ears, damn it," he yelled as he slapped my hands off them. My hands had to keep moving. Either I was going to cover my frozen ears again or hit my head to get him out of it. "Oh, I see. Now you want to punch yourself in the head. Would you like me to do it for you?" he asked. Then he did. I held my head and started screaming from the pain. "Let's see. Where was I? Oh, I was telling you how crazy you are. Now, I'd like you to repeat it for me. Say it *nice* and *slow* so you understand what you're saying, and what you are. Okay, let's hear you give it a try."

I studied every minute detail of his face. Each tiny bead of perspiration had a number. I examined the lines, wrinkles, and shaped moles that were part of his iniquitous composition. The core of his hazel eyes held lurid flames. I couldn't think straight. I didn't know what to say. I stopped breathing for a moment and stared at his fire. He was smiling at me; therefore, I, too, began to smile. I thought if I were compliant, he'd stop destroying me and let me go back inside, where I was safe and sound.

My quivering lips were forming words, "I'm crazy."

"Yes, you are." He had an extraordinary look of accomplishment upon his face. "Very good. Now let me hear you say it again."

"I'm crazy," I said in a frail whisper.

"Again, but louder this time. I want you to hear yourself."

"I'm crazy," I said slightly elevating my voice.

"Come on, more," he said, pulling the words out of me.

"I'm crazy, crazy…" The words surged out effortlessly. I rocked faster and faster. I was finally making Dad happy, and this was alleviating my stress. I thought that must be a good thing.

"I'm crazy… I'm crazy… I'm crazy! Crazy, crazy…"

The words flowed naturally, like a stream.

A portly woman wearing an expression of utter shock entered the room. She held a glass in her hand with a clear substance inside. She hurled the glass at the evil man, but he kept talking to me.

"You're one little nut on your way to the nuthouse, aren't you?"

I rubbed my sweaty hair and recited, "Nut. Right?"

The woman began banging on his back as if she were playing a drum. She was angry. The evil man took hold of her hands and pinned her against the wall. Was he going to put an end to her as he'd done me? The portly woman kept fighting him off. He slapped her. Then… he slapped her again. She fell to the floor and angry words flew out her mouth! I wanted her to run. She didn't need to fight him now; it was too late because he already conquered me. Man, my brothers would be sad, I thought. Maybe they'd be happy that *I* got away from him, too. Colin, now he'd be angry with me! I was one hundred percent certifiably nuts! Yeah, that's right. Colin would be angry!

Something began to happen. Was he doing something to make me worse? No, no… This was far more powerful than the evil man. This feels like… I should know what it is. I'm safe! This is my *Father!* *This is God! He heard me!* "In my distress, I called upon the Lord, and cried unto my God. He heard my voice out of his temple, and my cry came before him, even unto his ears." Psalms 18:6.

At the instant where I believed I'd lost my battle with Dad… *God's loving hand reached out to me and pulled me away from Satan. He removed me from his evil and merciless clutches! God saved me! Serenity overcame the destruction that Satan tried to implant deep within me. My shackles were destroyed, and I was free!*

———

Sara continued her fight with Dad while pushing him away from me as hard as she could. He stumbled backwards, laughing. This incident amused him. He tried to drive his daughter insane, and all he could do was laugh!

"Colin, I've had it! That's enough, you sick bloody bastard! Is this what you did to Alley? Marala was right about you! This *is* how you've treated your children all these years? Isn't it? Isn't it, Colin? Get out of here! Get out before I call the bloody authorities and have you locked up!" Sara knelt in front of me. "Marala," she yelled. "Marala, listen to me!"

"She can't. She's in a fucking trance or some shit like that, in case you hadn't noticed." He stumbled out of the room, not intoxicated, but laughing hysterically.

"Marala!" She shook me as hard as she could.

I was already back, but my body hadn't finished thawing yet. I needed a powerful shaking, and God gave it to me. *I was back!*

Sara sat with her arms around me as she'd done many times with Colin after Dad's triumphant abuse. The funny thing about all of this was that Dad actually believed he could defeat *God.* The saddest part of all was that for a moment, I thought he was going to achieve his goal. Although I was greatly comforted that *God my Father* didn't forsake me, Dad's intent was weighing heavily on my mind. I called on *Him*, and *He* came. That's what faith in *Him* will do. I went into the bathroom and splashed cold water on my tear-stained face. I looked in the mirror, and strangely enough, it appeared as if I had aged ten years. Inside, there was a lingering emptiness.

———————

After the incident, Sara convinced Dad to let me join the track team. I didn't ask Dad for anything, not even a pair of spikes. I ran in my tennis shoes for the first year and didn't need them anyway.

The year before Clark left for college, Dad took us to upstate New York to go camping along with Sara's son. During the trip I reflected upon my life. I realized that I could breathe outside of that house, even more so outside of that city!

Dad traveled on business trips, often for a week or two at a time, and was too busy to care how well I was doing in track, but I didn't care. I had grown older, not defiant, but pragmatic. I knew I had one option to get out of our house. I believed this could be my solution; I wasn't going into the Navy if I could help it. I didn't have a boyfriend because I wasn't allowed to date. My grades were good. I kept up with my chores and became more creative with cooking. I believed this would help make Dad realize that I hadn't neglected anything at home. In my spare time, I worked out as hard as possible. My discipline was without comparison. I finally found something that I did well. It gave me a distraction from my pain.

As Dad grew older, his success at work mounted. Whenever he made salesperson of the year, or reached an unprecedented quota, he was awarded trips to Florida, California, Mexico, and other places. Sara, Jimmy, and Selvin traveled with him leaving me behind to watch the house. Dad said it was because I went on my eighth grade fieldtrip to DC for three days. I didn't have the benefit of enjoying that trip because I was mindful that I had to return home. It didn't bother me when he left me behind because I was better off with him gone. I called Mom nearly every day! She didn't converse much because I heard the distraction of her demons. Even so, I was certain she heard some of what I had to say because she seldom hung up on me. If her demons had overtaken her, Grandma would tell me that Mom wasn't coming to the phone.

Since Clark was a year ahead of me, I still had him to confide in. He didn't make it to my track meets often, but he always wished me luck. Somehow, Clark always found me in between classes to see if I had money for lunch. I learned not to ask Dad for anything so most of the time I didn't.

"What's up, bonehead? How was social studies?" Clark asked.

"It was good. I like Mr. Holton. Believe it or not, he's the best teacher in this place. He actually makes learning that stuff fun. The funny thing is he always talks about you," I said, tossing my books into my locker. "He mentioned *something* about you always being a comedian… I don't know. It was something like that," I teased.

"Yeah, well, we all know you're the smart one… except when it comes to math," he teased back.

"Brother, that's a snazzy jacket," I said, looking inside for the label.

It was chocolate corduroy with oval tan patches on the sleeves. He wore a cream cashmere mock turtleneck underneath. His pants matched the sleeves on his jacket, and he wore a pair of argyle socks with his dark brown penny loafers. He had a preppy look. Because he liked wearing cashmere and dressed so well, everyone called him *Cashmere Murray*.

Clark was funny, and the girls loved him. He was charismatic and began his conversations with a compliment. He had thick black eyebrows over his soft, gentle eyes. With the exception of Dad's thick lenses, his gold-framed eyeglasses were identical to Dad's. His soft hair was picked into a perfectly shaped and tapered three-inch afro. His smile displayed beautiful white teeth with one middle tooth slightly overlapping the other.

"Thanks," he said, admiring his own good taste. "I bought it Saturday when I got paid. Where are *you* headed?" He waited for an answer, but I didn't say anything. "Could it be lunch?" I smiled as I slammed my locker shut and leaned against it. "Did he give you lunch money this morning?" Clark studied my expression.

"No, but I don't ask him anymore. If there's nothing to make I don't bother. It's okay."

"He's a scumbag!" Clark reached into his back pocket, took out his brown leather wallet, and handed me two crisp dollar bills. "Will this do the trick?"

I took the money and said in a soft voice, "That's more than enough. Thanks, brother."

"I don't know why you don't ask me before we leave for school in the morning or the night before. I don't want you shitting bricks when it's lunchtime! Just tell me when you need money! How do you think I'd feel come lunchtime when I'm eating a big sub and my little sister doesn't have anything?"

"Full," I joked.

He grabbed my shoulders and whispered in my ear, "Naw. That would suck."

"I don't ask because you're not my father, and I'm not your liability. Brother, you work hard for your little money, and you've been trying to save for college," I said looking at his jacket again.

"Why does my money have to be *little*?" he asked jokingly.

"You know what I mean," I said, giving him a hefty shove.

"Giving my sister lunch money isn't going to break me. What kind of brother would I be if I didn't look out for you? It's not as if you don't want to work. It's just that you don't have an option. Don't worry, it's no big deal."

"Thanks, brother, I owe you," I said, kissing him on the cheek.

"Not now you don't. What are you going to pay me with, rocks?"

"I'll pay you back one day."

"Get a track scholarship, then your degree, so you can get a good job and never have to look back! When you're making the big bucks, then you can give me my two dollars back! Deal?"

"Deal!"

He looked at his *Swatch* watch and said, "The bell's about to ring, and I have to get going."

"See you later," I shouted, jogging toward the lunchroom with a smile.

"Marala?" Clark shouted as two girls tugged at him.

"Huh?"

"I love you, knucklehead!"

"I love you, too!"

Clark made sure I had money for lunch throughout that year even though our schedules were conflicting. We didn't spend much time together, yet we remained close. I knew I'd miss him when he left for college. His last year at home, Clark attempted to avoid Dad by working overnight and filling his schedule with various activities daily. His primary focus was his girlfriend, then college. Clark had high aspirations for himself although his grades weren't the best. He created a plan, and worked it, in order to achieve his goals. Clark grew out of his pranks and into his weird disco music and *Playboy* magazines, while occasionally smoking weed.

Following graduation, Clark seized his opportunity to subsist outside of our house. Utilizing his intellect, he elected a path that avoided Dad and kept him from enlisting. Dad still had his incensed moments, but Clark just took it, then went to smoke his weed. There was never a real comfort level until he left home but hopefully he'd find one in college.

Clark didn't carry any luggage with him. He was smart enough to leave it in our house. Unfortunately, what he did have was a long fishing pole that caught painful flashbacks and reeled them in from time to time. When he tried to release them, the hook caught his hand, reminding him that he'd never completely be able to let go of the horror. With Clark gone, I was abandoned. Clark did call and write me, but it wasn't the same. Now, Clark was on his own to pick up the shattered pieces of his life and try to glue them back together. *It was possible, but the cracks would always show.*

My older brothers left me all alone. I felt worthless, but tried to remember the advice that each of them gave me. Clark's suggestion to get a track scholarship was all I focused on. I did well my first two years of track, placing in the state meet each year. Although my father was opposed to my participation, in time he came around and watched me run twice in three years. Jimmy and Selvin faithfully came to almost every home meet. I was constantly in the newspaper and even sparked a headline here and there. Now that I had proven Dad wrong, he realized I was good enough to get a scholarship, but never came to see me run in the state meet. No one did.

Without Dad's awareness, my senior year I followed in the footsteps of Clark, securing a job at a fast food restaurant. Since Dad was in California for three weeks, training on new systems, I thought he wouldn't mind. I continued to run track and prayed that I'd earn a scholarship. Still, I needed a backup plan for additional security. Dad reiterated I had to leave upon graduation. If I didn't go into the Navy or college, it didn't matter. I had to get out. I knew he meant it. Besides, why would I want to stay?

I enjoyed my little job at the restaurant. It didn't take long before they made me a supervisor. It meant I had to work later hours, but it kept me away from home, which I didn't mind. Jimmy and Selvin were well into their routines and way beneath Dad's radar. The problems that my older brothers and I encountered diminished with Jimmy and Selvin. With three out of six children gone, there was substantially less housework and cooking that I had to maintain. My schedule permitted time for me to complete my chores, so working was never an obstacle. Sara was thrilled that I still had time to cook dinner and have it ready before I went to work.

I worked after school during the year from five in the evening until one in the morning. During track season, my days off were on the days I had a meet. My work schedule changed from six in the evening until midnight. The inconvenience with working was when I had school or a track meet the next morning and walked home. Dad drove in from Cleveland on Rt. 301 late at night and sometimes passed me walking home. If he were in a good mood, he'd stop and give me a ride. If not, he'd pick up speed and drive right past me, blowing his horn so I knew it was him.

When I got paid, Dad was shrewd. He took my paychecks. Clark didn't save as much as he thought he could, and it left him in a small bind when he went to college. Surprisingly, dad helped pay for his first semester. I signed my checks over to Dad or cashed them and gave him the money, and he put it in his account so I would have savings for college. I made close to two hundred dollars a week.

Upon qualifying for the regional meet in three events my senior year, I quit the team subsequent to realizing my new coach wasn't presenting me as a prospect for a scholarship to the scouts who appeared at the meets. I was exhausted from being on a team that didn't nourish my ambition. Given that track wasn't going to *literally* help me run away from home, it was senseless to waste time running with my workload. Dad was furious when I told him the news. I knew that was the end of what little tolerance he had for me. I finally gathered the nerve to address it. Once I quit the track team, his hatred for me mounted again.

After cooking dinner one evening, I asked, "Dad, what have I done to deserve you treating me the way you do? Do you really hate me that much? Is it because I remind you of Mommy? Is that it? I feel like you have me playing the resident maid, out of resentment. Every time you look at me, I'm a constant reminder of Mom. You look at me with so much hostility, it's incredible, and I've had to deal with it for the majority of my life. You have no idea what it feels like knowing the degree of hate you have for me. You do *hate* me, don't you?" He mimicked playing the violin. "Admit it so I won't have to wonder if I'm right or wrong anymore. You've done a great job in making me feel it. But without you being angry about something that causes you to blurt it out, do you feel like that now? Do you hate me? Do I disgust you that much?"

"You got me! You know what, you're right. I've always hated your sorry ass! And yes! You disgust me as much as your crazy ass mother," he announced coldly with unyielding eye contact.

The phone rang in the background, and a lethal dose of tension began to spread through the air. A few seconds later, Sara interrupted, "Colin, it's for you."

"What? What's for me?" he snapped.

"The phone! You have a phone call."

"Well, don't you know how to take a damn message, or can't you spell? Shit, can't you see I'm in the middle of a conversation here with this little bitch?"

"Don't start your shit with me," Sara responded with a relaxed tone because she was drunk. "Keep talking, and I'll tell him you're too ignorant to come to the phone because you're too busy chastising your little bitch of a daughter. How's that sound, huh, Colin? This is the call you've been waiting for! Now what shall I—"

"Well, why didn't you say so in the first damn place! Get my briefcase!"

When Dad knew I was winning my events, he was proud of what I had achieved as his child, especially since he ran track in high school. However, he wasn't proud of *me*, and didn't love me anymore. It was that, for once, and for just a little while, he saw some of his own strength, and discipline in me.

CHAPTER THIRTEEN

By wisdom a house is built, and by
understanding it is established;
And by knowledge the rooms are filled with all
precious and pleasant riches.

Proverbs 24:3-4
New American Standard

When I graduated high school I left a week later to run in a summer track camp without Dad's encouragement. The legendary head track coach at a college in Michigan took me under his wing, because he knew my mom since high school. He exposed me to more than what he was aware of during my transition out of our house. He provided me with the opportunity to take a path to begin my life. He didn't know what he was giving me, and he unselfishly provided it. He heard rumors of what happened to mom but was unclear of the rest. He never asked. He didn't judge. He said if I wanted to talk he'd listen, but I never spoke a word of what happened.

He invited me to stay with him and his wife in their home and introduced me to everyone as his niece. It was this man who treated me as family and had me trained by a young lady that was among the best hurdlers in the country. He surrounded me by people that had passion and knew their purpose. It was because of him that I met his son's close friend, who played in the NBA. He had no idea of the imprint he had on me because of his encouragement. *To put it simply, he believed in me.*

At the end of that summer, contrary to Dad's conviction, I *did* receive a *full* scholarship to college. My uncle was proud of me! God put this man in my path, because I'd only met him briefly, while visiting mom, after I quit the track team. God knew my heart. I wanted to go to school in Michigan only to be near mom.

Dad appeared to be proud of me for obtaining the scholarship and beating the odds and time. Unfortunately, his perception didn't matter. A few weeks prior to my leaving, I asked Dad for my money since he'd been saving it for me. I was floored when he said, "I kept it as *rent* for raising your ass! Besides you got your scholarship so you won't be needing it!" He always said he wouldn't give me a dime for college, *not even my own!*

My condemnation to hell was over and I was free to leave. I didn't react as I had imagined. I thought I'd be overjoyed, but I was scared and apprehensive. Although I prevailed against my enemies, I was dead inside, and no one knew it. I had been sentenced for seventeen grueling years. I had escaped my enemy, beaten the odds, and made it out without a straitjacket. My sanity was still intact... Or was it?

I left hell with a permanent concrete psyche jam-packed with demons of my own, which was the evil that ran through 319... 16... 907 and 954. The verbal and physical abuse, crowned with an overabundance of worthlessness, now belonged to me. The evil that existed in our house planned to follow each of us! *I was afraid that it could, so I prayed for God to recreate me and purge my soul of my private torment.*

I spent several years fighting to survive in our house that I was unprepared for anything else. The thought of life on my own produced great anxiety. I didn't have encouraging experiences to take with me. I missed my brothers. The only true emotion I mastered was anger. I carried nothing other than pain, fear, and a great sense of loss. *Physically, I made it out of our house, but the house hadn't made it out of me.*

Mom's unrelenting deterioration was horrible. After four years of living in Detroit, she was worse than before. She couldn't hold a conversation longer than thirty seconds before her demons ended her conversation with me. Mom walked around the neighborhood with a black hooded cape and demons. She preferred seclusion.

I knew Mom had a fascination with jewelry, so if I had a piece on when I visited, I'd give it to her. Each time I saw Mom, she was wearing my jewelry, until I replaced it with another piece. We didn't talk much, but we developed our own way of communicating. She didn't ask how anyone was doing. Sometimes, she just stared at me as I spoke to her until her time was up.

Ironically, my freshman year of college brought a small beam of encouragement. Living in Michigan allowed me to visit Mom more often. I was able to spend time with her. The pain didn't diminish, nor did the memories grow fainter, but I wanted to gather strength to move forward with my life. Although it was extremely difficult, I was becoming a part of the mainstream of society. Being in a college environment appeared to facilitate my development to function somewhat normally. Quite honestly, I wasn't sure if that was normal either, because I didn't know what normal was. I only knew what I'd perceived normal to be, any dissimilarity to occurrences in our house.

I met new associates in college, but had great difficulty relating to them. People wanted to be around me, only I despised being around people. I had to hide that glitch in my personality. I didn't trust anyone; I was disinclined. For the most part, I preferred solitude. I planned to become a psychologist; however, I acknowledged that I needed to come to terms with the events my life plagued me with before I could venture into the psyche of others.

Tragically, the mystery that captured my mother remained. Sister Cyprus and the church were filed in my memory. I wanted to burn their file and let it dissolve into the ashes of hell. I wanted nothing more than to eradicate the women who brought the evil, which eradicated my mother. The evil of Sister Cyprus and the devil's workers, Sister Lewis and Sypher (Lew-Sypher or Lucifer), would continue their mission and destroy the lives of others. *God will handle them.*

The one thing that Mom's family did accomplish was to get her away from Dad's abuse, the church, and the mental institution. Mom's family resorted to having her physically restrained by several men as an exorcism was preformed! It didn't work. They tried again. And that didn't work. *They* were still feasting on her soul! Satan displayed his power to them because they allowed it. *Faith... You must have unconditional faith! None of us truly had it!*

━━━━━━━━━

I met Cole in college. Both of us were on the track team. Cole ran with fervor, and I had lost mine. I began to dislike track because it was my way out of that house. Regrettably, that's all it was. The onset of our relationship was challenging because I had been isolated from reality whether I was inside or outside of that house. Prior to our relationship becoming serious, I thought it was ethical to caution him of my childhood, what I was capable of becoming from the aftermath, and the psychological damage I held. I told Cole the truth... *The whole truth.* I gave him ample opportunity to back away, or shall I say, *run away,* but he never left.

Cole had an abundance of inquiries regarding my complicated life. I decided to take him to meet Mom. Until that point, I didn't trust he conceived everything I conveyed as valid. Most of it seemed doubtful.

When Cole met Mom, she immediately liked him. *They* didn't. He was afraid at first, then he accepted the fact that if Mom hadn't hurt any of us, after all these years, she wouldn't hurt him. He was quiet when he was around Mom and appeared nervous here and there, but still he was curious and a little strange! Mom called him Darren because she didn't like Cole.

Once I corrected her and said, "Mom, his name is Cole."

She examined him closely and replied, "I know. But Darren fits him better. Yeah, that's right; he looks like a Darren. Doesn't he?"

Cole or *Darren* smiled, and never corrected her.

Cole and I ventured on the path to a serious relationship. My sleepwalking and nightmares were always difficult for him to handle, but he never gave up. The screams and night terrors were part of our life. I had developed acrophobia because of the precipice that Dad dropped me from. My astraphobia came from the lightning that frightened me when I lived in that room with Mom. I remembered the night I fled into Dad's room with the lightning crashing as Mom wandered the house, with *them*. As a child, those fears, among others, followed me out of that house. Initially when Cole met Dad, he didn't see the evil because he wasn't around him much. At that stage in Dad's life, it wasn't going away, but he was able to conceal it from outsiders.

When Dad called, Cole heard his intense verbal abuse. He knew every way to manipulate me. Dad was like a highly addictive drug. I had to go through the agonizing withdrawals after a simple conversation with him. When he felt the need to expend his evil, he hurled hateful blows in the subtlest of ways, causing terrible setbacks in my progress. It didn't take more than five minutes before he'd upset me. Each time, Cole took the phone and calmly hung it up without saying a word. Dad kept calling. But after his third or forth attempt, Cole would unplug the phone. After a few years of reducing my association with Dad, I developed a degree of resistance to his hatred toward me.

The more I began to distance myself from Dad, and the tragedy of

Mom, the more I began to love myself! I was letting go of the pain.

CHAPTER FOURTEEN

Do not be wise in your own eyes; Fear the LORD
and turn away from evil. It will be healing to
your body and refreshment to your bones.

Proverbs 3:7, 8
New American Standard

Time had beaten away at Grandma. Her age crept up on her and signs of her frailty were evident. Her face had become haggard and somber. Her beautiful eyes that had witnessed so much abnormality were tired. The cheerful smile had worn away.

"Hello, Caroline," she said unlocking the screen door.

"Hi Grandma. How have you been?" I asked kissing her withered cheek.

"I'm still going. But, your mama ain't looking too good. She's a little under the weather with a toothache or something. Danielle was going to take her to the doctor but I don't know if she has an appointment yet. Come in and see about her. Is that you Cole?" She lifted her eyeglasses with heavily smeared lenses, squinted and peeked beneath them. She turned to walk away and a heavy limp rocked her unsteadily from side to side.

"Yes, ma'am," he replied.

"I can barely see anymore. Maybe these glasses are dirty or something," she said taking them off as she fell back onto the sofa. She licked the lenses and wiped them on her apron. She put them back on and grunted. "That is you. Now I guess I can see," she said mindlessly.

"Where's mom?" I asked.

Grandma pointed down the hall as she turned her attention to the pastor on television.

I looked into Grandma's modest bedroom and found my mother crouched on the dirty floor by the side of the bed. It brought back the image of her hiding underneath the stairs. There were books and dirty dishes scattered on the floor. It appeared as though mom had been there for a while. Mom had great difficulty communicating. Her look was despondent and her eyes hardly met mine. She made an effort to smile, but couldn't manage it. Her teeth were so badly abscessed that the draining was visible. She carefully held her jaw while trying to slip three aspirin into her mouth. Her shaking, weak hands could barely hold them.

"Mom, what's wrong?" She didn't say anything. "You look sick." She turned her head away from me. "Cole, help me pick her up. We have to take her to the hospital; I can't let her sit here like this. Look at her." Mom resisted when we tried to touch her.

Her moaning clearly indicated that she was in a great deal of pain. As Mom protected her stomach with one hand and her jaw with the other, all she could manage was choppy, painful dialogue.

"Teeth… it's teeth… I need a… a dentist. I'm okay. Okay," she said, trying to fan me away from her. "Dan… Danni… sister take me."

"No, Mom, *we'll* take you!" I was exhausted at the thought of Danielle doing anything for Mom. All of them were liars, even Jeanie. Where was she?

"Just teeth hurt. Aspirin… ain't helping," she said, grunting. She opened her mouth slowly trying to show me her teeth, most of which were missing. What was left had decayed terribly.

"Mom, please. Just come back with us. We'll take you to the doctor. We'll fix your teeth and anything else. Just come home with us," I said, looking at her with a great deal of regret. I had abandoned her, too. My visits, letters, money… None of it mattered. It wasn't enough. There had to be something I could do. "You don't need any of this stuff," I said looking around. "Come on, let's get you out of this place!"

I began sobbing as I rubbed her hand. She tried to hold back her tears, but couldn't.

"No cry, baby. Mommy… fine. I can't leave… Can't go…"

"Why not? Why can't you go? You don't need anything. You already know that. Mommy… if you come with us…" I said, sobbing, "Cole and I will take care of you. I promise."

Cole's concern for my mother mounted as his sorrow appeared to overwhelm him. He'd seen Mom many times, but never like this.

"A little… house. Little house… me?" She spewed random thoughts while forcing a smile.

"If you want a house Cole and I will buy one for you. We'll get one right across the street from us. How's that?"

Again she tried to smile, but couldn't manage it. It was difficult to stand there and beg Mom to come with me. It was even more difficult to see her neglected like this, and in pain. If I didn't take Mom with us, I wouldn't have another chance. I was certain of that. I had to keep trying.

"Mom, Marala's right," Cole began. "We'll get you any house you want if you come home with us. Then you can play with your grandson all you want," he said, delicately rubbing her thinning hair. "It would be good for Aaron to grow up with his grandmother around."

Her eyes turned upward toward Cole. She tried to squeeze his hand to acknowledge him. But she barely had strength to move her fingers.

"Little… house… that's so… so… sweet," she said softly, as if she were drifting off to sleep. Her eyes gently shut. She looked peaceful, but she wasn't. She was in pain.

"Mom, are you okay?" I tapped her lightly on her shoulder as not to hurt her. She half opened her eyes and pointed to a glass of room temperature water on the floor next to her. "Let me get you some fresh water. I'll be right back."

"No, no…" She tried to reach for the glass before I stood. "I fine. Just… give it."

"No, I'll be back." I insisted.

I went into the dirty kitchen, got a clean glass from the cabinet, and washed it out again. I ran the water in the sink so that it was as cold as possible. I opened the freezer to get ice, but there was only one piece in the tray, with hair in it. I closed the freezer, returned to Mom, and helped her drink.

Mom was still fighting to communicate. Every word was forced, as if she were on a respirator. I helped her take another drink, but she couldn't swallow well. I knew she kept trying to force a smile so we wouldn't worry, but it was too late. Mom was always like that. I sent Cole to get Grandma, or call Aunt Danielle but before he had a chance to turn around, Danielle walked up behind him.

Danielle was two inches shorter than Mom and thick. She had the same complexion and freckles, but there was nothing beautiful about her. Her bushy eyebrows matched her hairy legs and her legs matched her jet-black wig. Danielle was built like a short linebacker and always seemed to be in a rush, so were her words.

"So, I see you came to visit Alley. Ain't your momma doing so good?" she said cheerfully.

Malevolence spit out of Danielle's ugly mouth. She leaned over and grabbed Mom's aching jaw smiling as Mom grunted. Mom looked like she wanted to scream or slap the mess out of Danielle. Instead, her eyes filled with tears. Her sister was lacking concern. Mom was sick and Danielle brushed it off like she was used to seeing her this way.

"No, she doesn't! Can't you see that?" I removed her hand from Mom's jaw, trying not to add any more pressure.

"Naw, ain't nothing wrong with Alley. She has an abscessed tooth, that's all." She yanked open Mommy's mouth again, causing her to groan louder, and said, "Show them, Alley." Danielle put her face down toward Mom's mouth and looked in. "My goodness, we need to get that done." She stood there sucking her teeth and announced, "Oh, I forgot. I made a doctor appointment for your momma on Wednesday. Yes, I sure did. She'll be fine. So how long are you all staying here this time? Alley sure is glad to see you. Ain't you, Alley?" She didn't wait for a response; she just kept running her mouth. "It's too bad those bad boys don't come around. They ain't been here in years to see about their momma. You two are the only kids that come around. She looks forward to your visits. Oh, well. I always knew those boys didn't give a damn. They learned that from their daddy!"

"Danielle. I'd like to take Mom to live with us. We don't need any of her things. We just want to take her with us so—"

"Oh, I'm afraid that's not possible. You see, Momma here has custody of Alley. That means nobody can take her without *our* consent. Marala, you don't want to do that with your son and all. You know your momma ain't right. Especially with those demons and all," she whispered. "Alley likes it here, don't you, Alley?"

Sadness overtook Mom's face. She didn't mumble a word; instead, she let her head drop and stared at the floor despondently.

"Look at her. She's popping aspirin for the pain. She looks worse than I've ever seen her. I can't leave my mother like this." I explained.

"Baby, I'm afraid you'll have to. Alley ain't going anywhere. All her welfare money, Medicare, and everything else goes through us. It would take too long to get it in… Pennsylvania or wherever you are."

"Pennsylvania."

Mom mouthed the words, "It's fine… fine… don't worry about

me. I'll … be fine." She nodded for me to let it go. She didn't want this arguing. She was right. Now wasn't the time.

"But Mom…"

"Let your momma rest now," Danielle insisted.

I pulled back the blankets on Grandma's bed and said, "Cole, help me get her on the bed." With a lot of grunting and groaning, we laid her down. "Don't take anymore of this aspirin; it'll give you an ulcer," I said putting the bottle on the dresser.

I opened the two small windows, allowing fresh air to flow through. Mom slept for a little while, intermittently squirming in pain. When she woke up, we spent more time together. Not once did I hear the demons. In fact, I didn't hear *them* at all. I suppose because I was so accustomed to hearing *them*, I expected *they* were there. This time, I didn't know where *they* were.

When Cole and I got up to leave, I kissed Mom on her cheeks and forehead. I tried to give her a frail hug. When my hand touched her stomach, it was as hard as a brick. Something was protruding from her stomach, something awful!

"What the heck is that?" I tried to lift her shirt, but she put her hands over her stomach to stop me. "Mom, please, show me what that is!" She shook her head no.

Cole asked, "Mom, can we take a look and see what that is? We won't hurt you."

She looked into his eyes as though she were about to concede, then shook her head no again. I moved her hands aside and lifted her shirt. Cole's eyes widened as he stumbled backwards. It frightened me, too!

"Oh, my God. What the heck is that thing?"

Pitifully, mom waved her hand to send us away. Cole's eyes turned to shock! Protruding from Mom's stomach was a mass the size of a large phone book!

"How long has this been here? How long?" I asked snapping at Danielle.

Danielle shrugged and said, "Oh, that little bump, it ain't nothing. I think Alley fell and hit something. Didn't you, Alley?"

Mom didn't acknowledge.

"We need to take her to the hospital, now! Right now," I insisted. "This is ridiculous! Just take a look at my mother and tell me that came from a damn fall! Come on, Danielle… a fall?" I tightened my fist to contain my boiling anger. I couldn't explode in front of Mom because it would only upset her.

"I said your momma ain't going anywhere! Now Alley's fine! She just needs some rest."

"Mom, come with us. Please!"

She looked at me, then Cole. I was certain she wanted to come with us, but for whatever reason, she seemed afraid to respond. Her eyes were sad, as though she wanted to say *yes*, but she was afraid to say so.

"Now, Marala, I ain't going to stand here and watch you take my sister out of this house!"

Her jet-black wig tilted sideways because of the way she was flopping her head around. The dark wig helped reveal every ugly line and wrinkle on her face. Danielle's entire face looked like crow's feet!

"Look at her! Look how well you've treated Mom… or *your sister*! You were screaming and hollering about what Dad did to *your sister*, but look what you guys are doing! Clearly nothing! This is absurd! You said you wanted your sister back. For what? This?" I said, pointing angrily at Mom.

I didn't mean to hurt her feelings, but I couldn't help but address the issue. Cole grabbed my arm and pulled me out of the room.

"Marala, listen! Listen to me for a minute," he said.

"Listen to what?" I shouted with annoyance.

"Calm down. We can't do anything for your mother right now. Let's leave and call Social Services, and send them out here to see that she's not being taken care of properly. Look at your mother over there. This is making things worse for her. Is that what you want to do?"

"No. But Cole—"

"Let's not make this worse for your mother. Besides, you're probably hurting her feelings reminding her that nobody's taking care of her. She's taking all this in. I guarantee it."

"But—"

"But nothing. I know you're upset, but legally your aunt's right.

343

There's nothing *we* can do at this point. Let it go... *for now.*"

After holding Mom's hands for a while longer under Danielle's watchful eye, we left. *We abandoned my mother just like everyone else.*

When I returned home, I called my brother Clark and told him what happened. He and I decided to contact Social Services in Detroit, as Cole had suggested. After explaining what we observed, they sent a social worker out to Mom's house a few days later. They said Mom answered the door, and appeared sickly but competent enough to send them away. She refused to go with them, so legally there was nothing they could do.

———————————

A few months later, I received a call from Dad. His mother told him that Danielle called her and said Mom was in the hospital. The large mass that Cole and I had seen was a tumor causing a heavy strain on her heart. Eventually, it rendered her unconscious. The doctors had to remove it immediately or they thought she *would* die! Once they stabilized Mom, they would perform an emergency surgery. I left for Detroit.

I called Selvin and met him at the house. We went together, however, by the time we got there, Mom's surgery was over. When we reached her floor, we walked down the dimly lit and cold corridor looking for mom. Selvin looked at each patient in the first, second, then third room and kept walking. I paused in front of the second door.

"Selvin, where are you going? That's Mom, right there," I whispered as I pointed into her room.

"You're kidding, right? That can't be... That's—"

"Yeah, that's Mommy. It's been a long time since you've seen her."

It had been years since anyone had visited Mom other than Stan, Cole, and I. Mom looked like a skeleton lying in the hospital bed. Her hair had receded and turned entirely gray. Deep wrinkles and lines defined her face. Her weary eyes were sunken in. I saw nothing in them but pain, sadness, and fear. Mom was afraid.

Upon our entering the room, Mom's eyes filled with tears. Selvin immediately choked up.

"Mom, how are you feeling?" I asked softly. She tried to look up, but her movement was slow and restricted by pain. "Mom, guess who's here with me? Selvin. He's here." Her eyes lifted and searched for her son. "Mom, this is Selvin, right here." I reached for Selvin's hand and pulled him in front of her. The nervousness in his face showed. Her tears hit the pillowcase as she slowly reached for his hand.

Selvin was six feet, lean, but cut and had a preppy style of dress as well as a neatly tapered haircut. Mom had trouble recognizing her youngest son. Selvin was gorgeous and had changed quite a bit since she last saw him.

Her dry lips were sealed together by a white film. She tried to run her tongue across them but it too, was dry. The tube in her mouth rendered her speechless. Her eyebrows slowly arched together, as she used her eyes to motion toward the water pitcher. I took a piece of ice from the pitcher on her nightstand and rubbed it across her mouth but she tried to suck the ice in. A middle-aged nurse entered the room preparing to take Mom's blood pressure.

"She can't swallow that ice," she scolded. "You can run it across her lips, but she can't swallow it, not yet. Our Ms. Murray here's been through a lot," she said, smiling at Mom. "But we're expecting a full recovery, aren't we?" Without looking up she asked, "And who might you be?"

"I'm her daughter Marala, and this is her youngest son, Selvin."

"Really. That's interesting. Her sister signed her in and on the form we asked if she had any immediate family. She put *none*. Hold on a second; let me get her doctor in here. He's making the rounds now."

She drew the curtain three quarters of the way around Mom's bed, not to disturb the woman that was groaning painfully on the other side of the room.

A few minutes later, the doctor came in. He explained to us that Mom went into a coma because of the tremendous strain on her heart. What they removed was a massive fifteen-pound tumor. They didn't expect Mom to live because they thought it was cancerous, and once they cut it open, she'd die. They were wrong! It wasn't cancerous. *I believe that tumor housed the turmoil of the demons that infested Mom for all those years!*

I remembered how much Mom loved my jewelry. Every time I saw her I gave her a piece that I was wearing. She'd wear it until I replaced it with something else. This time I had on two diamond rings. I slid them off my fingers and carefully onto hers. She shook her head no, but I insisted.

"Mom, you know what we've always done. These are for you. They'll remind you of me. In case you forget, you'll know I was here when you look at your finger. You'll know I didn't forget." I kissed her finger with the rings and placed her hand gently on her bed. Her tears fell in heavy streams. I pulled back the white sheet and looked at her stomach, mom was sewn up like a rag doll. The stitches were at least a foot long. A hard chill shook my body.

"I don't have anything to give her," Selvin whispered in my ear.

"Sure you do," I said, tapping his watch.

Without a word he loosened the clasp and showed Mom the watch. She smiled weakly.

"Hey, this is for you. I want you to have something from me, too. Just like Marala said, when you look at it, I want you to think of me. I want you to remember that I love you. I love you, Mom. Do you hear me?" he whispered, kissing her on the cheek.

She closed her eyes.

———

That year, due to Cole's job relocating him, it took me farther from Mom. She refused our help, and I was unable to see her as often as I wanted. I found what little comfort I could in hearing her voice, so I continued to call. I asked her to call me collect if she needed anything; she never did. She never called any of us.

Dad continued with his life, never assuming responsibility for his actions. He had his own miserable existence in the hateful environment that he created. Regardless of how much they despised one another, they had grown accustomed to and absorbed by their insufferable rage. They appeared to need it. That environment fueled both of them.

After nearly fifteen years with Mom, and seventeen years with Sara, once again, Dad continued his predatory pattern of seeking out yet another soul to raze. He spent his nights in the arms of another victim. Sara's dependency to alcohol didn't conceal her misery. The alcohol became an ineffective comfort. Her anger randomly exploded. Sara was without a solution to end her pain.

Sara tried to understand our suffering and the pain her *monster* caused, but that was something she would never accomplish. It would remain a mystery to her, just as it had us. *What Sara had done to my mother was finally being reciprocated!*

CHAPTER FIFTEEN

And He will wipe away every tear from their
eyes; and there will no longer be any death;
there will no longer be any mourning, or crying,
or pain; the first things have passed away.

Revelation 21:4
New American Standard

Cole, Aaron, and I had been living in Pennsylvania for slightly over a year. A friend of mine, Sheryl, came to visit. Sheryl and I were never at a loss for words. Our straightforward conversations about her family caused thoughts of mom to roam in my head.

"Hey you. Are you okay?" she asked.

"Of course. Why?"

"What's the last thing I said?"

I smiled.

"Sorry."

"Yeah, well, that's what I thought. What's going on? Should I be worried?"

"No! Oh No," I said looking down. "It's just that this conversation is making me think about Mom. Maybe I should call her. Do you mind holding that thought a moment?"

"Of course not. Do you want me to leave the room?" she asked.

"No. You're fine."

Sheryl was five feet nine, had long blond hair and vibrant blue eyes. She was striking enough to be a model. Her passion was working in real estate and she did extremely well. Since she lived next door, when she wasn't working she was hanging out with me.

"No, you're fine." I got up and headed into the kitchen. "Sheryl?"

"Yeah?" she replied. She reached into her Fendi purse and pulled out a compact mirror and red lipstick.

"Do you ever get the feeling that something's wrong? Like someone's—"

"Going to die or something weird is going to happen. Yeah, I do. That's odd, huh? But when I get that feeling, something usually happens, like I break a nail." She giggled.

"I'm going to call Mom just to see how she's doing. It's been a couple of weeks since I've checked on her."

"Oooohhh! Bad, bad girl," she joked.

"I know, but I don't think she listens to me anyway. It's like I'm bothering her or wasting my time."

"At least she knows you're thinking about her when you call. I'm

349

sure your calling has some type of impact."

"To be honest, I don't think it does anymore."

"Why not?" Sheryl asked curiously.

"Mainly because she doesn't talk back," I said returning a light giggle. "She's clearly not happy where she is so we've asked her to live here."

"And?"

"And she won't. I don't know what else I can do. I've tried to do as much as I could but…" I picked up the phone and dialed her number. After the first ring, I hung up. "Forget it. I don't think she cares one way or the other if I call. It's only hurting me. And why? Apparently, she doesn't think about me," I said, still venting. I stared at the phone as if I was waiting for it to ring. "Maybe if I stop calling, she'll call me for a change. Just once, I'd love to answer the phone and hear my mother on the other end."

"This really bothers you, huh?" Sheryl got up and gave me a big hug.

"Yeah, well, it's hard to deal with. You'd think I did something to her. I just wish things were normal, that's all. I try to get on with my life but I'll always have a hole where she's concerned. I don't know what to do because I just miss her," I said, tearing up. "I can't live the rest of my life trying to fix something that evidently can't be fixed."

"Maybe you should call later and tell her how you feel," Sheryl suggested. She opened the refrigerator and took out the cranberry juice. "I can't sit here and let you get upset. Here we go… one hundred percent pure cranberry juice! This is what my little niece… or nephew wants," she said, lightly patting my bulging stomach. "Do you want me to pour some for Aaron?"

"Yes, I'd appreciate it." I returned to the sofa and laid my head back on the pillow to think.

"Remind me, shouldn't I give Aaron a *plastic* cup or glass?"

"Wow! And you want to be the Godmother?" I asked rubbing my belly. "I don't think so! You know better than to ask if he should have plastic or glass. He's four." I let out a big smile and stared at the phone, still thinking about Mom.

"Come on, girl, cheer up! I see my mother every day, and we don't talk." She giggled. "Trust me, maybe she'll change. My mother won't, but hey, maybe you'll have better luck."

"Luck has nothing to do with this situation. Trust me."

———————

A week later I laid across the bed tenderly rubbing my belly as I thought of the new life growing inside me and how differently I wanted my children raised from my own sadistic upbringing. I want them to be able to reflect on their lives with pleasant memories. They will know how much I love them, every single day. I want them to live without the suffering my brothers and I endured. I'll pray for peace to encompass their lives and for them to be free of physical abuse, emotional attacks, and bizarre intrusions from the hell we had. I'll continue to pray and maintain faith that it will be done. At that thought, my four-year-old son entered the room with a gorgeous smile, hiding his little hands behind his back.

"Close your eyes, Mommy," he said reminding me of Selvin.

I did.

"This is for you and for my baby brother."

When I opened my eyes, I saw two dirty rocks lying on my belly.

"What did I do to deserve these? They're beautiful. Aaron, sweetie, what if the baby is a girl, how would you feel about that?"

"That's okay because we'll give her back and get a brother."

He climbed on the bed and kissed my belly, then whispered, "Do you like them?"

"I love them," I said proudly.

"I know *you* do, Mommy, but I was asking my brother." He continued whispering to *his brother*.

"I brought you a surprise, so now you have to tell me if you're a boy or girl."

Rocks were like diamonds to Aaron. I'd have to remember to tell his wife one day.

"Can I talk to my baby for a while?" he asked while pressing his mouth against my stomach.

"Why don't you and I talk and let the baby sleep for now, okay?"

Just then, the phone rang.

When I answered it, Dad said, "Hello, honey." He cleared his throat, but his voice sounded strange. He was sad.

I sat up and asked, "Dad, what's wrong?"

"What are you doing?"

"I'm talking with my little son. Why?"

"Is Cole around?" he asked in an alarming voice.

"He's at work. Why? What's with the questions? Is something wrong?"

"Do you have anyone with you right now? Someone I can talk to for a moment?"

"Aaron, go to your room, baby," I said. "Dad, why would you want to talk to any of my friends? Don't beat around the bush. What's wrong?"

"I… I have some bad news. I hate to tell you over the phone, but I have to."

"What? What is it? Just say it," I said, becoming more concerned.

"Are you sitting down?"

"Yes! Now what is it?"

"It's your mom. She passed away."

CHAPTER SIXTEEN

**The Lord will guard your going out and your
coming in from this time forth and forever.**

Psalms 121:8
New American Standard

Shortly after the year Mom had the tumor removed, she collapsed in her mother's home. Danielle rushed Mom to the hospital, signed her in, and went to work. Mom was alone. She had a dissecting aortic aneurysm. The doctors carelessly injected another patient's medication into Mom, and she died. On the forms upon check-in, Mom's signature wasn't discernable because of her pain. The line to list family members once again read *none*. Mom would have turned fifty just three weeks later.

I wanted to believe my visits had a positive impact on Mom, even more so when she held her grandson, Aaron. She said it was like holding me. I knew those memories were there, but it wasn't safe for her to go back or reach out ever again. After each visit with Mom, sometimes I'd see tears sneak down her soft cheeks.

I helped prepare Mom for her funeral. I bought her a beautiful laced beige dress. At this point, a beautiful dress seemed meaningless. I wanted to find a piece of jewelry that I'd given her, but I was afraid to go into her room. I didn't want to encroach upon anything, in case *they* were still there. Her eldest sister Jeanie said there was something she wanted me to see, so I went up. The room was the same as it had always been. I was careful not to disturb anything as I made my way toward her bed, crying louder with each step. I wasn't crying because of fear; it was how she lived. This room became my mother's life. The demons were her life. Pain and suffering was her life. As I scanned the room, I asked myself, when was the last time she slept on her bed? What was the last thing she wore? What were her last words? What was her last thought?

Resting on the vanity table with the oval mirror above it was a tall stack of tinged envelopes wrapped with a red rubber band. I didn't want to touch them, but wondered why they were so neatly stacked when the room was messy and cluttered with junk. I read the address on top of the first letter. It was from 453. I moved that letter aside. The next one was from 453, so was the next. I kept going until I got to 907. My hands froze. Mom had every letter, and every picture that I had ever sent her. The letters were in order by the postmarked date.

The pictures that I sent inside the letters were still there. There were pictures of Selvin graduating high school, the birth of Aaron, Jimmy playing football in college, Stan in his Navy uniform, Colin making his illustrious muscular pose, Clark drinking a beer and several others. The photo that made me cry the hardest was a small color picture of Mom, with all of us, before…

Mom had the letters out, as if she read them often. The letters were the only organized things in her room. I thought about my statement to Sheryl… "*Apparently, she doesn't think about me,*" were my exact words. Mom *did* love me, and she *did* care about our lives. I was wrong! *I spent years being wrong about her love!* I dropped to the floor.

With Stan, Colin, Clark, and I having escaped his brutality, no longer did Dad have anyone to inflict it upon. Times had changed, and neither Jimmy nor Selvin would ever experience what we suffered through. Dad would remain Satan's pawn, who will ultimately answer to God. We all will.

After years of restless nights, unwanted memories, and pain, *I* couldn't manage to work it completely out of my system. For quite some time, I continued to fear what I could become, or what I was capable of emitting. Because of the abuse and terror that reigned in our house I thought I had an inferno ready to burn out of control inside of me. But God's love had extinguished the heat and energy that would allow the white flames to rage. God had removed my torment years ago, yet *I* preferred not to acknowledge it because I thought letting go would imply my mother's life was in vain.

Guardedly walking around my own emotion, I was careful not to arouse any connection to my recollections of *them.* I didn't want this in my son or daughter's generation. I didn't want this curse. I spent years consistently analyzing myself. If I revealed the slightest similarity to my father, I fought to change it. The notion of being anything like *Dad* sparked a wave of malice inside of me. The probability that I would turn out like him was great, due largely to the fact that abuse and hate was all I had ever known.

Deep in my subconscious was the learned, destructive behavior waiting to have life. *My father had a patent on hatred and rage! My mother had demons. We didn't want it... in our house!*

CHAPTER SEVENTEEN

Then Jesus was led up by the Spirit into the
wilderness to be tempted by the devil. Then
Jesus said to him, Go, Satan! For it is written,
You shall worship the Lord your God, and serve
him only.

Matthew 4:1, 10
New American Standard

The pastor's voice returned to my consciousness as I tried to focus on his words. I was supposed to speak, only there was nothing left for me to say to anyone, except God. I stared at the casket, continuously wiping my watering eyes. Although we all die, her death came as a shock. I conclude it was because she had survived so much. I had taken for granted that my Mom would always be here.

My mother *was* God's gift to me, to all of us and to future generations! She was a symbol of God's power and Satan's existence. The beautiful memories that Mom created with us were shrouded by darkness. There were only slight traces of good recollections in my life. As for my mother's life, I don't know how many slight traces she had, but I was determined never to submit to the fact of Mom's life being in vain. I opt to learn from it, which I have… I still am. My mother's life brought me closer to God, My true Father! We have no contract on life, and life has no time frame. It comes and goes as it pleases, leaving us full of emotions and questions either way.

My mother's life should not have ended this way. She died *twice* because of negligence. Satan didn't conquer Mom; we handed her to him. What remains are many unanswered questions, painful memories, and restless emotions. God shed his grace and mercy on me as a child. I didn't believe it then, because I didn't know what it meant or what it felt like until my own *near* surrender to Satan at the hands of my Dad. The signs of salvation were there, but I didn't see them out of my own confusion and fear. I spent more than two years in that room. I wasted time questioning my sanity when I should have been praying with faith.

I believe that the severe beatings rendered by Dad helped increase our mental strength in preparation for what was to come with Mom. Everything had a purpose. Had we not gained resilience from Dad's crazed episodes, Mom's demonic possession may have defeated us. Satan is temptation. *God is powerful!* I spent years in hell, but *He* protected me long ago and *He* is protecting my family and me, still. *God* delivered me from the horrific experience in our house. I was searching for peace by trying to answer the question, *why*. In doing so,

I held onto the dark memories with the taut grip of Satan.

The service concluded, and the church emptied. Mom's casket was taken to her gravesite where we said our final good-byes. I believe that I'd said mine a long, long time ago. I couldn't do it again. Besides, she was no longer here. They lowered the casket into the ground. The pastor said, "Ashes to ashes, and dust to dust…" I stared inside as my tears fell one last time. "Mommy, I'm sorry. I'm sorry that this was your life. I'm sorry I couldn't help you. I'm sorry for all the pain I've caused you. I'll always love you. I promise I'll never let your memory fade from my life or from this earth. I promise to tell your story. And Mom, I'm so sorry that I didn't believe that you loved me. I know you did! I know now…"

Mommy was gone…

———————

This memoir is my testimony that trust in *God* shall provide us with the strength to endure all things to come. There is a lesson in all tragedies. We may not understand why, but it is not for us to question, regardless of how painful it is. Many of us believe in *God*, yet we are not close to God. There is a big difference. Get closer to God and you will live the difference.

Unfortunately, we need to address Satan. The devil roams this earth searching for victims. He finds them everywhere, as this is his playground. We must *not* hide our problems but expose them so the help that is needed to resolve issues is provided. Today, opportunities are everywhere to receive treatment for any problem. Use the resources. Become a resource. Communicate how Satan is *preparing* to disrupt your life before you allow him to do so. Read the newspaper, talk to a neighbor, look at a family member or stranger and you will see evidence that signs of Satan's destruction are all around us. Seek deliverance from God and pass along his encouragement and the love he has for you.

As children and young adults, we didn't disclose the events that transpired in our house. We were afraid of condemnation from society. We cannot be saved if we don't ask to be saved. We cannot help others if we don't know the problem. I believe the tragedy of my mother's life should facilitate consciousness as to what exists on this earth. We have evil influences that surround us each waking day. Our challenge is to *resist* temptation. The key to resisting Satan is to be aware of Satan. The key to accepting God is to be aware of God. *Develop or strengthen your relationship with God as nothing or no one else can save you!*

After reading my memoir, if you cannot appreciate how powerful God is and recognize the extraordinary work he has done in my life, then Satan already has a hold on you! Satan's grasp on our lives is passed from one generation to the next and so forth. We, through God, have the means to remove ourselves from that cycle, as I have chosen to do here. God gave us free will. What we do with our life is our choice. I pray that my brothers, my children, and you do the same! Choose God... before Satan chooses you!

One generation shall praise thy works to another, and shall declare thy mighty acts.

Psalm 145:4
New American Standard

THE REALITY...

The March after Mom passed I had another amazing gift from God, a beautiful baby girl, Alyssa. She was a light for my dark heart. I was struggling with my past, but no one knew how much it consumed me. What kept the doors to our house open was that I now had two children and a house of my own...

Here's what happened... In my house!

AFTERWORD I

Due to the horrific childhood my Mom and uncles were subjected to, I would have never thought it possible for them to escape with their sanity. *Fortunately* for me, *my* mother, who lived in direct contact with the evil that plagued her family fought for hers.

This unique and chilling memoir was written to not only instill, but to inspire hope in those who require it, yet are too fearful to speak up. There are many of you out there that may be going through neglect, physical abuse, sexual abuse and psychological abuse. Among those, there are many other horrific circumstances that can devastate not only your *childhood*, but *adulthood*, as well.

If you were to look at the picture of my mother on the back of this book, I guarantee no one would ever fathom this to be *her* true story. It is purely unimaginable for her to have gone through the concealed torture that her childhood was saturated with. There are many of you out there that need help but are too afraid to seek it. This book was written as a testimony that you can't hold onto that unnecessary baggage or the memories that continuously haunt you. You must either look for refuge in *God*, or be willing to ask for help.

Whatever pain you may be enduring, please know that you are not alone. I pray that this memoir allows people everywhere to understand that although you may believe your experience is "one of a kind" there is always someone out there struggling through similar circumstances. As stated in the memoir, "tragedy is tragedy with the degree to one person no less than the value acquired in one's life." If your particular situation is unique, such as this one, do not hide behind a facade, or the *"perception"*, but allow the *"reality"* to surface so that the problem can be addressed and a solution can be sought after.

Given Mom's childhood, I don't think I'll ever understand how she was able to formulate her own parenting style when all she felt from Grandpa was hatred. My sister and I have experienced nothing but *true* love, something that she had no familiarity with during the entirety of her childhood. She was physically beaten, verbally abused, and neglected by the two people that were suppose to love and care for her, unconditionally. How my mother was able to mentally break away from the torture she endured for years will remain a mystery to me. Since my mother lived with my grandfather for 17 years, I should have been exposed to his abusive style of parenting. But, I wasn't.

If I had the ability to meet one person, other than *God* of course, it would be Grandma. I'd have an array of questions for her. Should I only be able to ask her about one aspect of her tragic life, I'd want to know why she let *them* inside her home and soul? Was it to get away from Grandpa? Or was it solely to protect her children? Either way, why didn't she choose a different path? If Mom hadn't established an early relationship with *God* while she was forced to live in that room with you, would she be possessed, too? I'd love Grandma to know that mom's *natural* beauty, quick and sarcastic, yet witty retorts were all qualities that she inherited from her.

If I hadn't heard the stories about Mom's childhood from her and my older uncles recollections, Grandpa would have deceived me, as well. As described in this memoir, he is one of the most charismatic and charming men that I have ever known. If I look through his façade, the hatred for Mom is still in his heart. His resentment for my Grandma was passed on to *my* Mom, and baby sister.

I remind Grandpa of his only child that hasn't acknowledged those recollections. Selvin, the youngest of my mom's brothers, has the strongest relationship with Grandpa, and with good reason. He doesn't have to forgive his father for anything. Nor did he ever have a spiteful brother or sister instill in him the reason he grew up without a Mom. Grandpa *always* tells me that I remind him of Selvin. He treats me similar to him and places me on the same pedestal. He doesn't know that I'm aware of what happened but I have always shown nothing but love and respect to him.

Mom raised us to respect Grandpa. She warned us about her childhood and demanded that we forgive him as she had. She reminds us that in the Bible it states, "Honor thy father and thy mother." Mom leads by example. How she continues to show love and respect to Grandpa after what he did to her can only be explained by her obedience to *God*.

I can only pray that this memoir gives hope and strong encouragement to those seeking it. I pray that it allows those whom have a weak or false relationship with *God,* to open their eyes and recognize how powerful *He* is. This memoir is a warning to beware of who you let enter your life, and to be conscious of those that are already in it. Satan is the master of deception...

Thank you for fighting to keep the generational curse away from our family. I love you mom!

Your Loving Son,
Aaron

For many deceivers have gone out into the world, those who do not acknowledge Jesus Christ as coming in the flesh. This is the deceiver and the antichrist.
John 1:7, New American Standard

AFTERWORD II

This story is an intense recollection of my mommy's life as a child. I believe that this story should be confessed to everyone. I am extremely proud of this because I am sure this is not the only family that had horrific tribulations behind closed doors. Families who have problems similar to our family should not keep it a secret because it can affect your future as you develop in life. This book is meant to help everyone understand what can happen if you don't address the issues and speak up. If there are problems, you need to immediately tell the proper authorities so you can protect yourself and family members from harm. Do not take matters into your own hands as my Grandmother did because that can produce more complicated problems.

I have forgiven my Grandfather for the affect he has had on our somewhat divided family. When we visited him, I was constantly treated differently than my older brother. My Grandfather was often critical of and unfriendly towards me. I believe this happened because I am a representation of my mother when she was young.

Although I ignore his comments when I am mistreated, my mommy always defends me. She always taught me to speak my mind, however, she never encouraged me to be disrespectful. I never spoke to him about his behavior towards me. For some reason, I always felt remorseful for him because every day of his life, he lives with knowing what he caused and that he will have consequences with God. I still don't believe that he was ever sorry for his actions.

The dreadful events that occurred during my mommy's childhood have personally affected our family in many ways. My mommy has relentlessly tried to be a better mother than she had in her life. However, she does not need to try so hard because she is always the mother that I hoped for. I believe we have the best relationship a mother and daughter could ever have.

With Love,
Alyssa